WHAT'S IN A NAME?

A few of the sacred privileges bestowed upon American citizens are the right to peacefully protest, question authority, and act to change the laws governing our society.

This book and the nom de guerre Spartacus Falanghina were created out of the necessity to change a system that's broken, unfair, and unjust. It represents an authentic grassroots movement to privatize alcohol. Utah's antiquated liquor laws were established and perpetuated by a government rife with religious zealots imposing their dogma on the entire state. It's time for a change!

So, why the pseudonym Spartacus Falanghina? Spartacus refers to an ancient Thracian slave who revolted and led an uprising against the imperious Roman government, much like the Utah legislature. Falanghina is the name of a native grape from Campania, Italy, that grows in tightly formed clusters overlapping each other as a sort of a barrier or shield. The word is derived from phalanx meaning "a group of people or things of a similar type forming a compact body," much like the army it will take to accomplish privatization.

And, the book isn't only for the citizens of Utah, but anybody wanting a good laugh and help change stifling liquor laws not representative of the modern era. If you're a forward-thinking citizen of the world, imbibing Utahans need your help. However, it won't be easy to wrestle control away from the state government; they won't give up without a fight. By purchasing the book, each person fuels the cause, funds the initiative, and also assumes the moniker Spartacus Falanghina.

LET'S DO THIS! BE YOUR OWN SPARTACUS!

MORMONS, MERLOT
& THE UTAH LIQUOR MONOPOLY

Stories, Rants, and Raves about
Selling Wine in Utah

By
Spartacus Falanghina

s F

Contributors:

Author
Spartacus Falanghina

Cover Design and Layout
Octavius Taurasi
a.k.a. Jef Serio
seriousCreative Group

First Edit
Meg Kinghorn
Kinghorn Literary Services
www.kinghornlitservices.com

Second Edit
Sutton Wemple
Freelance Writer / Editor

(Revised Edition January 2021)

U.S. Copyright©
Selling Wine in Zion
September 23, 2019
(Revised Edition January 2021)
SPARTAGHINA LLC

Dedication:

This book is dedicated to my fellow wine brokers and sales reps pounding the streets every day; restauranteurs who have spent inordinate amounts of money to appease and comply with ridiculous Utah liquor laws; owners, managers, and restaurant workers who need to explain the senseless laws to their guests on a regular basis; bartenders who have had to mix drinks in the "dark," and servers who have had to serve alcohol around the "Zion Curtain;" hospitality service staff that have been scoffed at or ridiculed; anyone who has felt taken advantage of due to Utah's anti-competitive alcohol prices, left wanting from lack of selection, or bootlegged alcohol across state lines; anyone who has felt oppressed or beat down due to the LDS Church's overbearing imperious presence or that state lawmakers and leaders are not representative of the people but rather select special interests; those outside of Utah who dislike our liquor laws, and finally, to my own sanity.

A portion of the profits from the sale of this book will be used to help fund initiatives to privatize alcohol in the state of Utah.

Author's note:

The stories contained in this book are based on the author's recollection of specific events. Names have been changed of some of the individuals and entities. Any similarity to actual people or real entities is purely coincidental. To aid in constructing the essentials of this book, any reference to emails and the content thereof is exactly that, a reference, a loosely based description without any actual content from the original. Many of the judgments conveyed within are purely the opinions of the author. Readers are encouraged to research and make their own assessments. Certain content is satirical to illustrate a point. Stories involving the UDABC are of public interest to establish the realities of alcohol control in Utah.

S F

CONTENTS

TO BEGIN	10
YOU DO WHAT?	15
INSERT CORKSCREW HERE	17
HOW DID WE GET HERE	22
CHANGING DIRECTION	31
THE BROKER LICENSE	44
UTAH DABC PRACTICES 2003 TO 2011	51
TASTING WITH THE STATE	64
NEW VINTAGES?	69
THE PENALTY?	71
DELISTING 101	74
MERCHANDISING	83
ILLOGICALITIES Part 1	90
BUYERS, ACCOUNTS, AND COMPETITION	99
WINO EVENTS	111
SUPPLIERS	126
PRESS, RATINGS, AND THE COST OF YOUR WINE	136
INNOVATION, TRENDS, BRANDS	148
Trend – AUSSIE WINES AND CRITTER BRANDS	154
THE REVIEW	156
ILLOGICALITIES Part 2	163
Trend – PINOT NOIR	171
THE ESKIMO	173
THE ANTI-SALES REP	194
Trend – NEW ZEALAND SAUVIGNON BLANC	208
THE DISEASE	209
Trend – WE'RE GOING GREEN BABY	223
THE UTAH WINEMAKER	225

CONTENTS

AND... IF YOU DRINK BORDEAUX, YOU ARE MY FRIEND   246

A NEW PLAYER IN TOWN   253

     Trend – MALBEC   260

     ILLOGICALITIES Part 3   263

THE ACQUISITION   269

     Trend – CARMENERE   276

A STAR GOES DARK   278

CHOPPING THE NOSE OFF TO SPITE THE FACE   282

THE TOWN HALL MEETING   286

THE ESKIMO RESURFACES   288

BECAUSE, IT'S WHAT MONOPOLIES DO Part 1   297

     Trend – MOSCATO   326

SOJOURNER TAKES OVER   328

THE NUMBERS GAME   333

     ILLOGICALITIES Part 4   344

     Trend – KEG WINES   347

CERTIFIED   349

     Trend – PROSECCO   356

THE SUPPLIER NEXT DOOR   358

     Trend – RED AND WHITE BLENDS   376

BECAUSE, IT'S WHAT MONOPOLIES DO Part 2   378

TRUTH IN MARKETING   400

     ILLOGICALITIES Part 5   404

     Trend – Rosé   416

UTAH – SEPARATION OF CHURCH AND STATE   417

     Trend – CANNED WINE   440

JUST ANOTHER JOB   443

References   452

TO BEGIN

I WAS TOLD THE LIQUOR INDUSTRY was created for "C" students by "C" students when I started this odyssey back in 2003, so I've always felt securely at home. But although comfortable, it's become necessary to step outside into the chilly air and take a stand to move forward. Though I have never written or published anything, my unique selection of experiences and interpretations accumulated over many years is enough to fill a book when it comes to the craziness of selling wine in one of the tightest alcohol control states in the nation. And, the simple fact that I actually finished writing a book is something I consider quite extraordinary for a mostly "C+" student with only a few years of college, acute dyslexia, OCD, and slight bouts of ADD.

I was raised LDS, or Mormon, in Murray, Utah, a suburb of Salt Lake City. And as interesting as it would be to write and possibly read a book about how I exorcised my personal demons as a Mormon selling wine, wrestling with religious pressures day to day, all the while drinking and dealing alcohol, sadly, this book is not about that, for I wrestled and slayed those demons in my youth.

Growing up, I wouldn't say that my immediate family

was fanatically religious, but I would say we bordered on being fervent churchgoers. When born into a religion, there's not much choice as to what is learned, formed into beliefs, and defended ardently for the rest of one's life. For a very long time, I didn't even know that other religions existed. Being raised Mormon wasn't all that bad, as a Christian religion, they do teach and instill important morals at a young age, which I believe are necessary to bring out the best in human beings. However, I grew tired of hearing the same thing over and over, the countless weekly meetings, tithing, and everything else required to be a *good* Latter-day Saint. Long before the smartphone, questions began to arise in my formative years with exposure to mass media, peer pressure and its associated experiences – which for me was around 13-14 years of age. I had several friends of other religious denominations and even some who were agnostic, and they seemed to be having a lot more fun with a lot less influence. So, I began to wonder if the LDS religion was really the one true religion as I had been taught, or for that matter, if one true religion actually existed.

My extended family, most of whom were also Mormon, practiced and went to church somewhat regularly, however some were "Jack Mormons." Though Jack Mormons may believe Latter-day Saint doctrine, they attend church infrequently, if at all, and for one reason or another shun various guiding principles set by the LDS religion. Jack Mormons may have one or more vices such as swearing, drinking, smoking, premarital or extramarital sex, or other nefarious conduct of some form, but they do not usually bring much attention to themselves; they may even attend a church meeting or two occasionally to atone for their sins. Mormons, just like everyone else in the world, have faults too, it's just that most Jack Mormons hide it better than others. I don't know, maybe they believe staying somewhat connected to the LDS church will help them get into heaven.

I officially became a Jack Mormon at the end of seventh grade when I tried my first taste of beer at a friend's house after school one hot spring day – a Coors Original Banquet beer. To this day, I can still recall the sound as the frosty can was opened, releasing a cool cloud of vapor, the smell of hops and barley, and the taste on that hot afternoon. Feeling confident, a few months later I tried hard alcohol, which like most youthful experiences, did not turn out well.

But growing up Mormon I was taught to abstain from alcohol, so what made me want to break the rules? Upon careful reflection, I guess if I could pinpoint the main factors, it would have to be pop culture. Most of my favorite movie and TV stars were shown consuming alcohol, and it looked intriguing. Hawkeye and Trapper John downing martinis on "M*A*S*H", Clint Eastwood and John Wayne drinking shots of whiskey in westerns, and of course James Bond with his martinis "shaken not stirred." I had no idea what *Bollinger* or *Dom Perignon* was, but if Bond drank it, so would I! Drinking alcohol looked fun, mysterious, and worldly – and I wanted more than anything to try it. Little did I know I would one day be selling it for a living.

As with others my age, high school wonderment turned into rebellion, rebellion turned into rejection, and in the progressive years thereafter, I formed my own religious deduction: To simply be a good and decent person without harming anyone, including oneself, is really the best way to live while not owning up to one set of beliefs. Because in the end, outside of this worldly existence - no one truthfully knows.

My first job entailed working as a line cook for several

years, then after turning 21, I bartended at a white tablecloth restaurant where I tried my first glass of wine, a sweet Riesling from Idaho. At the time, I was mostly a beer and occasional shot of hard alcohol kind of guy, but I became intrigued with the new liquid. For months I drank as much as I could get, which resulted in a few hangovers and headaches along the way due to the high amount of residual sugar. However, that changed one busy night while bartending.

I didn't have time to eat on this particular night, and I was fading. On a trip from the bar to the kitchen to replenish the ice supply, I grabbed a few bags of oyster crackers and some fresh mozzarella the cooks used to make fried cheese sticks, stuffing them in my apron. A few hours later after business had died down, I hit the wall, but then remembered the cheese and crackers. I sat down behind the bar on a milk crate out of view to eat. Tired and hungry, my mouth became dry from the crackers. Looking to my left, I spotted a bottle of Mondavi Napa Cabernet used as one of the glass pours. After glancing around to check for prying eyes, I lifted the bottle and tilted my head back, pouring Cabernet until it seeped from the corners of my mouth, running down my chin and onto my apron. The distinct smell, flavor, and mouthfeel characteristics of the wine combined with milkfat from the cheese and the yeasty cracker were immediately imprinted into my brain. Mesmerized at the taste, I held the bottle up to study the label. An epiphany, I thought. *If there is a true God, He indeed created grapes to be made into wine, and grain to be made into beer and alcohol, so it must be His intention that it's here for our enjoyment and meant to be consumed.* Besides, it would truly be a shame to get to Heaven only to learn God put these wonderful things on Earth for our enjoyment and we didn't take advantage.

As my fascination grew, I branched out with other wines

and began to hang out with my wine-drinking coworkers after our shifts, tasting, learning, and forming an appreciation. On our nights off, we went to dinner at other restaurants, eating, drinking, and over-indulging well into the wee hours, way past the time when anything good happens. (Which is what my dad always told me.)

After a few years of bartending, I was promoted to manager at the same restaurant and put in charge of the beer, liquor, and wine programs. I met with the local wine brokers of the time helping to further expand and develop my nascent enological education, then spent the next twelve years interacting with wine as a manager and wine buyer at several different fine dining establishments in Salt Lake City; cementing my affinity for all things wine.

While I did love the hospitality business, I knew I couldn't do it forever unless I owned a restaurant myself. I decided against that foray after reviewing P&L statements with some of the restaurant owners; it truly takes a large fortune to make a small fortune. Choosing to move on, I eventually found a career selling the very product I loved – still involved with the restaurant business, just on the other side, in the ridiculously mixed-up state of Utah, USA.

YOU DO WHAT?

OFTEN IN MIXED COMPANY, and for the purpose of mere conversation, the question is inevitably asked: "So, what do you do for a living?"

My usual response? "I sell wine in Utah." The answer often elicits quizzical expressions of disbelief, sometimes disdain (Mormons tend to look down on my profession), and even quite often a look of envy followed by a barrage of follow up questions...

"So... (long pause) How do you do that?"

"That must be as easy as selling pork in Tel Aviv..."

"You do WHAT?"

"So, when you say you sell wine in Utah, who do you sell it to? It must be out of state?"

"Oh really? Where are your vineyards located?"

"Must be like selling ice cubes in Alaska..."

"They drink wine in Utah?"

But my personal favorite came from an elderly German lady, a neighbor I met after moving into my new house, who knocked on the door offering a bag full of tomatoes from her garden. Wanting to reciprocate I said, "Do you drink wine?"

"Vye yesss, a leeettle rhed from time to time," she said.

"Well, I'm a wine rep; I sell wine to the state. Let me get you a few bottles. Hold on a minute." Upon returning, I handed her a bag with two bottles of red wine – leftover samples from an older vintage.

She raised her hand, forefinger pointing up, shook it side to side, then replied. "Oh, eet cood not be posseeble," and sighed.

"Oh, it's okay - please take them; I have plenty. I sell wine for a living and these are just some leftover samples." She looked at me questionably as I reiterated, "I sell wine... to the state of Utah. These are samples – the vintage just changed – please take them."

She paused, looked at me sideways while raising her right hand in the air, forefinger extended, shaking it back and forth. "Nein, I do not zsiink zo!" She then turned and walked back up the street to her home.

INSERT CORKSCREW HERE

I'M WORKING TONIGHT BUT NOT GETTING PAID, unless you count the gratis six-course meal with wine pairings chosen by moi. It's a Sunday evening or maybe Monday or Tuesday, usually a dead night, and although I'm no winemaker, I'll do. Sixteen years of selling wine and another twenty from a long restaurant career provide enough cachet to bring them in. And though just a lowly wine broker, it works. Sixty people, some begrudgingly, have prepaid $125 to bombard their senses and bodies, to indulge – and to hear me speak.

Waiting for the guests to arrive, I lubricate my courage with a beer, gin and tonic, or glass of wine, and check my tasting notes to develop my spiel while staring blankly out a restaurant window. But my mind wanders back to a checkered and often cloudy past, bathed in rose, gold, and crimson juice.

Most arrive in twos, but sometimes smallish groups or even a lonely soul shows up, their eyes telling the story - to appease another, hookup, party, enjoy some camaraderie, and maybe – just maybe, learn about food and wine. Once seated, the room quickly fills with boisterous conversation as they sip their first offering, usually a glass of bubbles or something light and white. Bread knife in hand, I forcefully rap the side of a bottle – the sound is atrociously deafening.

It's time.

Introductions aside, I explain simple protocol in hopes of enhancing their experience: "Check color first, cover the glass with a hand, then give it several swirls (always on a table-top to avoid stained clothes). When the liquid is thoroughly agitated and filled with intense aromas, deeply inhale for initial sensory impressions, and finally, taste."

"But wait!"

"Rather than just gulp, swish it around or inhale once again – but this time with liquid just inside the lips to induce obscene slurping sounds (however, don't asphyxiate please)." A hundred and twenty eyes stare as I demonstrate.

Throughout the evening stories are told to enhance the experience, stir conversation, and hopefully provide enough imprint for some to seek out one of the products when shopping in Utah's liquor stores. Many ask questions, while some have a-ha moments. The night wears on. Euphorically buzzed on my product, I do my best to calmly talk loud enough while walking around the room. But still I worry about missing a beat or stuttering and stammering (and I do, as my mind skips ahead but I catch myself just before the comedians catch on). They smirk and tell stories while I talk - forever the class clowns clinging to an endless need for attention. I shake it off, knowing that I know more than they do.

I'm a wine broker, damn it. I have a dream job, I tell myself laughing. Yet, after all these years, I've become bitter.

A job selling wine, a product many consider a hobby or a curiosity, can be one of the most stimulating, rewarding, and intriguing careers in the world. Since wine is forever evolving – through reinvented or modified techniques, hot trends, new varietals, and newly discovered terroir – so evolves the job. Jobs in the wine industry are highly sought because at the core level, one is decently compensated for, in its simplest description – drinking. Free wine, informing and educating others, exciting and diverse products that change and evolve, expense accounts, exotic food and travel to wine country around the world meeting interesting people in an industry that is basically recession proof – What's not to love?

However, as with most jobs, selling wine or alcohol has its own set of difficulties – difficulties that never go away and sometimes get worse. Along with an established highly competitive selection of products, a bevy of new items are introduced every year while the landscape of retail stores evolve, restaurants and hotels open and close, and the buyers that control the wines carried within these establishments come and go. Thus, it's a game of constant reinvention. And because this is a sales job, there are monthly, quarterly and annual goals (that are often impractical and unattainable). There's competition around every turn in life, but in the alcohol industry, the competition for shelf space, wine list placements, and delivering case volume goals has evolved into one of the most highly stressful sales jobs ever created.

Now, if the job entails selling wine in the state of Utah, that makes the job somewhat harder and often ludicrous. As a control state, the local government is tasked with the sale and distribution of all alcoholic beverages over 4% alcohol by volume. (Prior to November 2019, before changing to

5% abv). Because the state operates a monopoly without competition, they have implemented and erected barriers by limiting products they only want to sell at prices dictated by expensive set state taxes. And, as if selling alcohol in a monopoly isn't hard enough, the state legislature is predominately comprised of lawmakers belonging to The Church of Jesus Christ of Latter-day Saints. Since Mormons disdain alcohol, they control it in a way that only makes sense to them by enacting absurd laws (such as it being illegal for industry sales reps to sample and taste their products with anyone including restaurant buyers; restaurants must pay the same price as retail customers in their state-run liquor stores; and for a time restaurants were required to erect barriers on their bars so that minors could not view alcohol, just to name a few).

While there will be stories about wine and winemakers, I'll also include herein the realities of the LDS religion and its relation to controlling alcohol in Utah along with dealing with the Department of Alcoholic Beverage Control, ridiculous liquor laws, my job, and eventually how it all went wrong. Ultimately, I hope to outline how the state runs the business of selling alcohol in the most incompetent manner possible, while also illustrating they violate their own constitution and its citizens rights by operating an illegal monopoly – information I wish to pass along to you, the reader, in the spirit of enlightenment.

So, similar to the process of making wine, the beginning narrative necessitates some history and fact to comprehend and fully understand the state, its predominant religion, and just what selling wine entails. Therefore, some ground must be broken, vines planted, fruit grown, harvested, and crushed before the bottle is opened, allowing the contents to develop and unfold. I feel that it's important for me to tell these stories in somewhat chronological order so that the reader can assess and understand the evolution and immense challenges of the state and how disillusioning (and disappointing) it can be when Corporate America takes over. I'm sure I will anger, amuse, and outrage some people, which is why certain names have been changed. (I may even risk incriminating myself due to breaking various nonsensical laws such as sampling products, bootlegging, or other slightly scandalous activity considered illegal by Mormon lawmakers). I will note this: My record is absolutely spotless, so if I am to be prosecuted, then so must everyone else who has ever sampled alcohol illegally, had alcohol mailed to their home, or bootlegged into or out of the state.

HOW DID WE GET HERE?
Utah, Mormons, Prohibition and
the Local Government

LATTER-DAY SAINTS (LDS), commonly referred to as Mormons (in reference to *The Book of Mormon* that governs the organization), arrived in 1847 just after the Mexican-American War, three years ahead of what would become the Utah Territory in 1850. After several attempts to settle in other parts of the Mid-West, the Mormons left Nauvoo, Illinois, escaping persecution when founding prophet Joseph Smith was killed for preaching about utopian society, plural marriage, and a divine glorified afterlife. The utopian society in reference is a city or kingdom named Zion referred to throughout *The Book of Mormon, Doctrine and Covenants*, and other LDS religious publications. Zion is to be inhabited by people who have adhered to the practices, principles, and teachings of the Church – thus, deemed righteous enough to live in such an exalted place. To this day the members of the LDS Church ardently defend and practice their doctrine while zealously obeying their leader's every direction because of the belief that when they die, they will be admitted to a celestial kingdom, or perhaps even have their own kingdom in the afterlife.

Mormon Pioneers were led to the Utah Territory by Brigham Young, also one of the original founders and second president and prophet of the LDS Church. Though early settlement began in Salt Lake City, pioneers settled parts of Idaho, Nevada, Wyoming, and California. As the territory grew, Young assumed governorship, establishing the LDS Church as a lawful body. Distrust and anxiety grew between many U.S. citizens outside of the territory and the Mormons over theocracy, plural marriage, and other LDS teachings. A short war between the U.S. Army and Mormon militia ending in 1858 resulted in the establishment of a non-LDS governor to preside over Utah. However, even with a non-LDS governor, by sheer numbers alone the Church continued their dominance, maintaining significant strength within the government.

The early territory was much larger than the present-day state with borders stretching into what is now Nevada, Wyoming, and Colorado. After New Mexico and California applied for statehood, Mormon leaders began to petition the U.S. government for statehood under the name Deseret. While the state of Deseret would adhere to and be governed by the laws, rules, and regulations of the United States, underlying LDS theocratic principles would still be practiced. The U.S. government, however, would not grant them statehood due to the Mormon practice of polygamy, which was thought to be anti-American and an immoral way of living. In fact, Utah would not be considered for statehood until Mormons abandoned polygamy as a common practice within their religion.

In 1890, then-presiding church president Wilford Woodruff finally issued a public announcement and declaration stopping polygamy within the faith. Although he said it was a revelation from God that polygamy would cease within the LDS Church, coincidently, a short time later Utah was granted statehood. Several disenchanted factions within the Church split off so they could continue the practice of polygamy, which is still practiced to this day in parts of Utah and other areas within the United States. Anti-Mormonism subsided after the so-called revelation, and finally, in 1896, Utah was granted statehood.

Mormonism, considered a Christian religion, does have several eccentricities within its practices and teachings. Among them, members tithe 10% or more of their gross income, attend multiple church services and activities throughout the week to keep them on the straight and narrow, baptize the dead, and practice a health code called the "Word of Wisdom" strictly forbidding the use of tobacco, alcohol, coffee, and tea.

As with polygamy, the Word of Wisdom is said to have been enacted due to revelation, but other issues most likely contributed. During the early days of the religion, the home of founder Joseph Smith was used for meetings. When the house became filthy from the members' pipe and cigar smoke and chewing tobacco spit covering the floors, Smith issued the ultimatum. (Young 1869) Years later, in the new territory and ultimately state, many Latter-day Saints had difficulties adhering to the revelation as it is noted in history that numerous bars and breweries were operating in Utah, many even owned by LDS members. After several decades, the abuse of alcohol and smoking and chewing tobacco became intolerable, so the Mormon-dominant government declared the bars a nuisance to society, and the Church began to crack down on their members.

{ ❦ }

One of the more amusing facts about Utah is that it became the final vote needed to repeal prohibition. Church President Heber J. Grant did everything he could to halt the repeal of prohibition but failed at the last minute. During General Conference that year Grant stated, "I have never felt so humiliated in my life over anything as much as the state of Utah voting for the repeal of prohibition." Since prohibition coincided with LDS beliefs, the repeal was a tremendous blow. (Grant 1934)

When the 21st Amendment was ratified in 1933 ending prohibition, the federal government removed its jurisdiction over alcohol putting it into state and local government control. And, because LDS lawmakers have always comprised the majority within the state government, it is part of the reason the current liquor laws are archaic, ludicrous, and prohibitionist. Utah is known throughout the world as Ground Zero for the LDS religion, and in fact, no other state in the union has a population in which the majority belong to a single religion. However, as time has passed, the overall Mormon population ratio has declined to around 62% in 2018 and it was purported that 2016 was the first year since inception that did not see an increase in new membership. Due to badly gerrymandered voting districts, approximately 88% of the members of the state legislature are practicing Latter-day Saints. Though the state liquor laws have changed slightly over the years with population influx and modern thinking, it remains one of the most tightly controlled states in the union.

{ ❦ }

In Utah, as with other states, the state legislature makes the laws regarding alcohol. The Department of Alcoholic Beverage Control (UDABC, Utah DABC or simply DABC) is charged with overseeing, compliance, distribution and the sale of alcohol. The DABC is overseen by a commission of seven people appointed by the governor. The commission acts as a general policy making body; it makes rules and is responsible for issuing liquor licenses, banquet permits, etc., but also the suspension and revoking of such licenses and permits if laws and rules have been violated. Incidentally, the majority of people that over the years have made up the commission have been non-drinking Mormons. The only reason the modern-day liquor commission is not entirely comprised of Mormons is that in 2011 the imbibing public voiced their displeasure and concerns regarding a committee in charge of overseeing something they knew nothing about other than it's shunned within their religion. To avoid and appease the angry mob, the state legislature passed a bill stating that at least two people on the Liquor Commission must be "drinkers." Even though the liquor commission has some responsibility as far as overseeing the DABC, the LDS led state legislature is still the governing body imposing their morals on the Utah masses. The governor, which most of the time also happens to be LDS, usually acquiesces to the Mormon-dominant state legislature and the Church because Mormons compose the largest voting body within the state and... they have a lot of money.

From the Utah Department of Alcoholic Beverage Control's website, the following statement is made:

ORIGIN AND PURPOSE
The Department of Alcoholic Beverage Control has been in existence since 1935. In that year, the Utah State Legislature created the department by statute and charged it with the responsibility of conducting, licensing and regulating the sale of alcoholic beverages in a manner and at prices which reasonably satisfy the public demand and protect the public interest, including the rights of citizens who do not wish to be involved with alcoholic beverages. The legislature also mandated that the department be operated as a public business using sound management principles and practices. (Control 2019)

As I will demonstrate, The Department of Alcoholic Beverage Control directly contradicts the statement above by operating a multi-million-dollar business that is corrupt, inefficient, and incompetent due to a general non-caring attitude and severe mismanagement.

ARTICLE XII, SECTION 20 OF UTAH STATE CONSTITUTION READS:
"It is the policy of the state of Utah that a free market system shall govern trade and commerce in this state to promote the dispersion of economic and political power and the general welfare of all the people. Each

contract, combination in the form of trust or otherwise, or conspiracy in restraint of trade or commerce is prohibited. Except as otherwise provided by statute, it is also prohibited for any person to monopolize, attempt to monopolize, or combine or conspire with any other person or persons to monopolize any part of trade or commerce." *(Legislature, Utah Constitution - Utah Legislature 1851)*

Alcohol is, in fact, trade and commerce, and because of the way it is handled in Utah, it is under a conspiracy of restraint by the government. Therefore, the state and their Department of Alcoholic Beverage Control is a monopoly because they have no competition – the state makes all the money. This, in turn, violates the Utah Constitution and is a violation of non-LDS United States citizens' rights residing within the state.

Adult American citizens are granted the right to consume alcoholic beverages – any alcoholic beverage they want. While lawmakers can say they grant that right because they make alcohol available, they only carry products they want to carry at a price they want to sell it at, so in truth they violate a segment of the population's rights by blatantly ignoring United States antitrust laws and the Commerce Clause by erecting barriers against free enterprise. Utah's model of liquor control discriminates and violates competitive open market standards which is one of the pillars of capitalism in America.

Imbibing citizens of Utah do not have the same unhindered access to the same alcohol selection as open states such as Nevada, California, Arizona, Colorado, etc., and it's not cost competitive. Tens of thousands of cases of alcohol are illegally bootlegged across state lines every year by residents for several simple reasons: They despise Mormon control over a legal product that contradicts their value system, they cannot get the products they want readily, and pricing is not competitive. While it is true that after prohibition, Utah was given the right to govern alcohol by the federal government, I must believe that they did not envision at that time, the authoritarian model the state currently employs. By handing over the sale and distribution of a legal product that directly contradicts the doctrine of a religion dominating the state and its legislature, the federal government severely handicapped the rights of non-LDS inhabitants and enabled a monopoly to exist.

Furthermore, the word "monopoly" is used bluntly and flagrantly without rebuttal or denial by state lawmakers, the governor, the LDS Church, local and national newspapers, the public, and everyone else outside of Utah who knows anything about the state and its liquor laws. Yet, the State Constitution prohibits monopolies?

Even in this modern day, the LDS Church hierarchy continues to encourage its members to run for and maintain political office. While they will not admit why they encourage this, it is evident through many state liquor laws and other legislations, that it is solely to help maintain and enforce their beliefs in the state. There is not another religion or special interest group that blatantly forces their will on the entire state. The Church desperately wants to maintain their hold and control over liquor legislation for as long as possible because drinking alcoholic beverages, smoking marijuana and cigarettes, other drugs, and even caffeine can liberate a mind into thinking about other facets in life rather than staying on the straight and narrow path of their religion. By not attending church and the other weekly meetings, less is received in the way of tithing to power the LDS religious machine. Maintaining control of the delicate minds of their flock means money and wealth for the Church. The bottom line is the LDS Church, along with most other religions, are at their core businesses – without funding by the members, the business suffers.

"Religion is at its best when it makes us ask hard questions of ourselves. It is at its worst when it deludes us into thinking we have all the answers for everybody else." -
Archibald Macleish (MacLeish n.d.)

CHANGING DIRECTION

I WAS WORKING AS A GENERAL MANAGER during the summer of 2003 for a small restaurant group with a well-established semi-fine dining Italian concept and a newly opened French bistro in the suburbs of Salt Lake City when I had an "involuntary parting of ways" with my employer. The first morning back after a much-needed vacation, while sorting through the pile of accumulated mail, I came across a letter and bill from the company lawyer. The billing statement read: "For completion of paperwork in preparation for Spartacus Falanghina's termination." The inept lawyer inadvertently had sent the bill to my attention.

Completely shaken at first, my hands trembled as I read the statement once again. In total disbelief, my pulse and breath raced, eyes welled up and my stomach dropped. I was in shock. I loved my job and thought they felt the same after a seven-year stint with them, but apparently not. After several deeper breaths, shock and awe turned to rage and contempt. Leaving the office, I walked around the empty restaurant trying to clear my head. A local beer distributor dropping off kegs in the bar asked me a question I didn't even hear, his words a mishmash of barely audible syllables. Dazed, I looked right through him while scribbling something resembling my name on the invoice. Walking onto the patio, I stared across the street to Sugarhouse Park, becoming entranced with the joggers and dog walkers who somehow soothed my nerves before a truck down the block honked its horn, jolting me back to reality. My mind once again raced. *What should I do? Those assholes, how could they do this to me! Should I walk out or unlock the patio furniture and get it ready for lunch service?* Halfheartedly, I removed the locks and chains and began to unstack the rattan chairs. After placing chairs around the first table, I stopped. *Fuck this and fuck them!*

I wandered back to the office where I stared at the invoice a third time. Anger welled. I wrote in big black Sharpie across the bill: "I do not feel much like working today after finding this in the mail!" then faxed it to one of the owners. Slightly relieved, I sat quietly waiting for a reply, but deep down realized I should resume getting the restaurant somewhat ready for service. Part of me wanted to just walk out and leave and let them fail miserably with the busy lunch crowd now just a few hours away, but that wasn't me; my conscience knew better. Unenthusiastically, I made a feeble attempt to help. The hostess, servers, and busboys arriving for the pre-shift joked and laughed while exchanging pleasantries and stories from the week I was on vacation. I barely heard them, offering only a slight nod or fake laugh as acknowledgment so as not to completely ignore them.

After an hour or so had passed, I received a phone call from another manager stating he would be in shortly to relieve me of my duties. Arriving home later that day I made up my mind that I didn't want to work in restaurants any longer – twenty years of long hours had taken their toll. My back hurt, my feet were tired, I could no longer bear babysitting a staff of malefactors; it was time for a change. Once recovered, I would broaden my search, and only after exhausting every angle (and my savings account), my very last resort would be another restaurant job. Donning flipflops and swim trunks and armed with a small cooler of beer, I retreated to the pool of the condominium complex where I lived to spend the rest of the day wallowing in despair.

In 2003, the economy was good and the job market was hot. More and more people from California were selling their million-dollar properties, moving away from the hubbub of big city life in favor of the mountains of Utah. The state had experienced unprecedented growth from 1994 through 2002, and after hosting the Winter Olympics that year, showed no signs of slowing. Feeling as if there were plenty of opportunities to branch out into another field, I was excited about future prospects. After updating my resumé, I made numerous copies and began sending them out snail mail, email, and fax. I sent out at least eighty resumés during the first two months of my unemployment. However, I dismally received only three interviews. Though my forced vacation was partially enjoyable, I began to worry about finding another job, once in a while panic set in resulting in sleepless nights. I figured I had eight to ten months until unemployment benefits and my savings were exhausted, but until then, my search would continue.

Completely frustrated after the two months of job hunting, I decided that if I didn't have a new job or at least an offer by the end of August, I would go on a road trip to visit friends in Oregon and Washington, see the sights, relax, and play golf along the way; maybe even look for work outside of Utah. At the very least, I could drop off some resumés and write off most of the trip on my taxes.

August came and went - not a single job offer. The day before leaving, I received a phone call from a company based in Seattle regarding a position as a wine broker. The gentleman on the other end, Matt Tomlin, informed me that they were in the early stages of hiring a person for the Utah market and he was just interviewing by phone at this point; personal interviews would follow sometime that fall. Excitedly, I answered his questions, spending nearly an hour with him, covering many topics, including state laws, the local economy, and my wine knowledge, which at that point was very good, thanks to my former occupation. At the end of the interview, he said he would be in touch. However, not wanting to let a great opportunity pass, just before he hung up, I interrupted him to tell him about my upcoming trip. "Since I will be in Seattle in a few weeks, can I just swing in for an interview?" There was a very long pause. He was caught off guard. After a few deep breaths, he said, "Sure," and then gave me a date and time and the address. Even though it was the early stages of their hiring process, I had an interview, at least it was something. I was ecstatic; wine was a passion. My mind raced as selling wine would be a dream career. I had to get that job.

Other than wine, I have always been a bit of a car person, and at that point in time, I happened to have a one-year-old grey BMW 330. The car was flawless and fast, and I couldn't wait to get it on the country highways. I packed it full of golf clubs, snacks, a few bottles of wine, clothes (including a suit), and a 4-foot-wide massive, cheesy, gold plated chandelier that took up most of the back seat. The chandelier was given to me by a very dear old friend, Rick Peck, who, after hearing of my journey, asked me to deliver it to our mutual pal living in Klamath Falls, Oregon. Rick, carpenter and contractor by trade, always had something he had acquired from one of his jobs, that unbeknownst to us, we desperately needed. Apparently, the chandelier was the perfect size for our friend's stairway.

Slightly after noon, driving due west on I-80 from Salt Lake City just past Wendover, Nevada, I opened the car up, hitting well over 110mph. The landscape rushed by in a blur; my pulse spiked as nervous excitement gripped me. After twenty long years of toiling in restaurants, I finally felt free, as if the whole world were mine for the taking.

The first day I made it as far as Winnemucca, Nevada. While gassing up, I asked several locals about the two-lane state road heading north to the Oregon border. They all had the same response: "You don't want to get caught out there at night. You should probably stay here." Though I wanted to continue, the thought of spending the night in my car if something went awry got the best of me so I found a cheap motel.

The following morning, I drove north on the barren state road, that on a map looked like it could be the most desolate place in the United States. Just five miles out of town after picking up speed, *bam!* I was zapped by a state trooper and given a ticket for 20 miles over the speed limit. The trooper asked where I was going, then he told me, "If you wreck or get stuck out there, it would surely be a long time till someone found you." The ticket set me back $130, paid right on the spot with cash. Then like something out of a movie, glancing into my mirror while driving off, the trooper stood in front of his car smiling behind his mirrored aviators as he tucked the money into his front pocket. I hoped I wouldn't have to see another state trooper; it could get expensive. To this day, even though isolated, it is still one of the most spectacular drives I've ever taken. The land was mostly sagebrush, dried up streams, unique rock formations, small rivers and ravines, but occasionally I came upon an oasis with wild horses and other animals drinking water and grazing on the native grasses. Other cars, trucks, and bikers happened along infrequently, but for the most part, humans were almost non-existent.

Seven long hours later, I reached Klamath Falls, Oregon, to stay with my friend Michael Justin. Michael, even though quite a few years older than I, was a kindred spirit. With a head full of wavy white hair and matching prominent mustache, his disposition is akin to the father Tom Skerrit played in "A River Run's Through It," although more roguish than righteous. He and his wife lived in a large house with plenty of room as their kids were off on their own. I stayed for three nights whiling away the time with Michael, seeing the sights, playing golf at the numerous courses around the area, drinking copious amounts of wine, and stirring up a bit of trouble. We were kicked out of the local Foreign Legion bar for lying about being veterans – it was the last bar open in town – so we thought we would just give it a try. And I couldn't tell for sure what Michael's thoughts were on the chandelier, but at least it was finally out of my back seat.

After Klamath Falls, I drove west to the coast, then due north en route to Portland. Prime wine country exists in Oregon, particularly outside of Portland to the south and southwest, and I aimed to stop at a few wineries before checking into a hotel. Armed with a few old manager business cards from previous restaurant jobs, I knew I could get some free tastings just by showing a card and even quite possibly an "industry discount" on some wine. Luckily for me, it worked, and at day's end, I checked into a seedy motel just on the outskirts of Portland with three cases. I knew the wines would come in handy when I finally reached Kirkland, just outside of Seattle, to stay with yet another very good friend, Jef Serio. Jef had relocated with his family from Salt Lake City many years earlier to pursue greener pastures. We had met in our younger days when he was a waiter and I was a cook in a semi-fine dining restaurant in the suburbs of Salt Lake City. Even though five years separated us in age, we became fast friends. Blond and slightly balding with an athletic build from years of golf, running, and skiing, Jef is highly artistic, industrious, and witty with a dry sense of humor and an engaging laugh. Yet ever still serious, Jef was always up for a good time, and we have shared many.

Interstate 5 North between Portland and Seattle is quite pretty – the land is green and lush with vegetation, the trees and bushes all benefitting from the steady amount of rain. Three imposing volcanic mountains – St. Helens, Adams, and Rainier – stand guard peacefully over the verdant landscape, ever watchful but also willing to betray if Mother Earth decides to shift. I had never been to Washington State, but after passing a giant "Jesus Loves You" billboard, I knew it would be interesting. Tired but anxious after being on the road for almost ten days, I was ready to see Seattle, my friend, and his family.

That evening, I was welcomed by the family with a fabulous home-cooked meal and a few bottles of Washington wine. With the Serio home as my base camp, for the time being, I played more golf, explored the area, had my ass kicked at chess by Jef's son (several times), and lost hard-earned cash to his daughter after she won numerous bets that she wouldn't eat oysters, sushi, or caviar.

A little over a week had gone by when the day arrived for my interview at Alaska Distributors with Matt Tomlin. Just before one o'clock, Jef dropped me off at the front door wishing me good luck. Nervously, I went through the double doors into a room lined with glass-encased shelves holding numerous bottles representing the brands they sold in their region. After signing in at the reception desk and receiving a visitor tag, I waited until Matt arrived. Soon appearing, Matt was a rather large, slightly pear-shaped man over six feet tall with dark wavy hair and glasses that automatically tinted from the fluorescent lights. He smiled warmly and shook my hand before showing me into a small boardroom at the north end of the massive building within the corporate offices. Unbeknownst to me, two other men, William Geilston and Samuel Jacks would be involved with the interview process; each worked alongside Matt, overseeing different areas and divisions for Alaska Distributors and their sister brokerage company, Spirits West.

Seated at the conference table, the three men immediately launched into a somewhat broken interview, each spending time on subjects not addressed by the others. William's serious demeanor and Samuel's obvious extensive wine background were balanced out by Matt's gregarious nature. Caught off guard at first, I reeled and backpedaled, intimidated by their initial approach, until I began to speak confidently once I realized they knew nothing about Utah or Wyoming. We spoke at length about the state laws, rules, and regulations, competitive brokerages, what little I knew of Wyoming, the on-premise and off-premise account base (on-premise accounts are hotels, bars, and restaurants and off-premise accounts are state-owned liquor stores in Utah and retail stores in Wyoming), my previous work experience, and my wine and liquor knowledge. They answered some of my questions as well, the biggest being what products they represented.

They explained the reason they were hiring a person was due to a rather large contract they had landed with Diageo/Moët Hennessy USA for the Pacific Northwest states, which included Utah and Wyoming. Diageo, was one of the largest liquor/beer/wine companies in the world with brands such as *Crown Royal, Captain Morgan, Tanqueray, Baileys, BV, Sterling*, etc., and Moët Hennessy was a luxury brand company with brands such as *Veuve Clicquot, Dom Perignon, Domaine Chandon, Moët, Belvedere,* and *Hennessy.* Diageo also owned part of Moët, so wherever Diageo was represented, Moët was part of the deal, even though they operated independently. The Spirits West division already had two liquor reps based in Salt Lake City and one in Cheyenne, but part of the deal required them to hire someone to sell their wine brands. After two hours of nonstop Q & A, the interview was over. I thanked the men before Matt escorted me to the door, telling me they would be in touch in a few weeks. My head ached, and my eyes watered from the barrage of questions while I anxiously waited outside for Jef to pick me up. Excitedly, I reprised the highlights of the interview after stopping off at a bar for a toast and to settle my nerves.

After spending another week in the Seattle area with the Serios, it was time to go. I had been away for just over a month, and it had been the road trip of a lifetime. Driving the final leg into Salt Lake City, south from Idaho on I-15, I smiled all the way to the front door reflecting on my experiences. Once the car was unloaded, panic set in as I sat jobless in the living room sorting through a mountain of junk mail and bills. I desperately needed that job.

Several weeks went by when out of the blue, I received another call from Matt Tomlin. He explained that he and the other two gentlemen I had met with in Seattle would be in Salt Lake City to conduct interviews with other candidates, and they wanted me to come in for another meeting during the process.

It was getting close to the end of October when Matt and

company showed up in Salt Lake City; they had rented a large room at the Embassy Suites Hotel to conduct their interviews. My second meeting would be at five o'clock, presumably after they had spent the day with other candidates.

Matt met me at the front desk just before my appointment, ushering me up to the room. He told me to wait in the hallway as they were just finishing up with another applicant. Time slowly, agonizingly ticked by, and after thirty minutes, I began to wonder why I hadn't seen any other candidates coming or going. Another fifteen minutes passed when the door opened. Surely, I would see another candidate come out, I thought, but instead, Matt appeared. He thanked me for waiting and being patient while welcoming me into the room. I looked around for the other hopefuls to no avail. The three men stood grinning and chuckling in the center of the room with glasses of Champagne when William broke the ice. "Um… we really didn't interview any other candidates today; we like you and want you to come work with us. We just wanted you to sweat it out a little bit." Belly laughing, they congratulated and ribbed me about the look on my face, then each shook my hand.

Once the laughter had died down, Samuel stated, "Well, now that that is finished, let's go hit some bars and grab some food to celebrate!" And so, my career as a wine broker began with numerous drinks, bottles of wine, and a grand steak dinner.

Two weeks later I was back in Seattle to complete the orientation and the necessary paperwork for employment at Alaska Distributors, or ADCO, as it was referred to. They put me up at the Washington Athletic Club (The WAC), a sort of private hotel downtown with restaurants, bars, meeting space, and several floors of sleeping rooms. The owners of ADCO were members, so I could stay there while in town; all bills including incidentals were sent to the company after checking out. I knew one thing for sure: For however long this lasted, I was going to enjoy it!

ADCO was founded in 1934 and distributed spirits, wine, beer, and non-alcoholic beverages in Alaska, Washington, and Oregon. In the outer states of Idaho, Montana, Wyoming, and Utah, they created a sister company called Spirits West that acted as a brokerage. The difference between a distributorship and brokerage is that in open states, or states that have privatized liquor, beer, and or wine, the distributor owns the warehouses, offices, and trucks, and purchases the products for resale to private entities such as restaurants, grocery chains, retail shops, etc. Conversely, in a brokerage state such as Utah, a company may own an office or even have a company car, but it doesn't own or touch any of the products, so it's more information-based. Distributorships make a higher margin on the products they sell, but they also have quite a bit of overhead and infrastructure that can reduce profitability. Brokerages make smaller commissions on each case sold within their region but with minimal costs of doing business. Commissions on products can either be percentage or dollar-figure based. Percentages on liquor tend to be higher due to volume and the cost of making the goods, whereas wine commissions are smaller because of the time it takes and the higher production costs.

After showing up the first day at ADCO, I anxiously walked behind Matt as he showed me around the offices and warehouses, introducing me to many people at the immense facility. Matt, never one without words, bounced around from subject to subject as he explained the inner workings of the business. The first day was rather uneventful as I spent the majority of the time at Human Resources and in the breakroom reading the company material and the 401(k) and health benefit programs.

The next day was spent in company meetings from 9 am until noon covering topics I knew nothing about but didn't care. I was just happy to have a job. For lunch, Matt took me to Wild Ginger, a well-known Seattle Thai Restaurant to meet Hubert Trimbach from Trimbach Winery, and two gentlemen that I would learn were my counterparts for Washington and Idaho, Rod Hansen and Robert Smith. The four of us made up the entire wine division of Spirits West. Mr. Trimbach was in town for three days, so the restaurant and ADCO, along with Diageo (the Trimbach wine importer for the U.S.), kicked off his visit with a wine pairing luncheon. I couldn't believe it, it was my second day on the job and I met a very prominent winemaker. I learned after lunch that two Trimbach dinners were also planned that week, one that night at Oceanaire, and the following night at the Marriott Waterfront Hotel. Lucky for me, I was able to attend both.

After three days of meetings, information overload, introductions, and eating and drinking at magnificent wine events with Hubert Trimbach, Friday arrived with a hangover. Somehow, I made it through the morning meetings. I learned from that point on that I would report quarterly to Seattle for Spirits West division meetings. Realizing I could spend more time in such an incredible city, and from time to time even stay the weekends with my friends, the Serios, I felt like Br'er Rabbit from the famous Walt Disney story "Song of the South." "Please, please don't throw me in the briar patch!" (Harris 1881)

Once the final meeting had adjourned that afternoon, I stood in the company lobby waiting for a ride to the airport. Just as the cab pulled up, Matt appeared. "Spartacus," he said, "thanks for coming to the meetings. I know they didn't particularly correspond to how business is done in your two states, but I wanted you to get the culture."

"That's okay, I learned a lot this week," I replied.

"Great, great," Matt said as he grabbed my suitcase to walk with me to the cab. "Look...Spartacus... Our company doesn't know anything about the way Utah and Wyoming work, and in fact... We don't care. That is why we have you. We want you to learn the business and report back. Got it?"

"Uh... yes," I replied.

"We'll try our best to help you along the way, but there won't be anyone to train you, so you must take the initiative. Due to the big contracts we have in our region, we had to have someone in your market selling wine in both states – and that's you, got it?"

"Yes," I said again firmly before he continued.

"We know they are not big states, and in fact, your position may lose money, but we've budgeted for the losses. That said, I want you to do the best you can, and above all, have fun. Let me know if you need anything and I'll call or email from time to time."

Stunned, I shook his hand and thanked him.

Settling into the cab, I was still trying to comprehend what he just said – Not only had I landed a dream job, but they didn't care if I lost money. I laughed the whole way to the airport.

THE BROKER LICENSE

THE FOLLOWING WEEKS WERE A BIT SLOW after my return. I had never had a sales job before or worked on my own without some direction, let alone from my home. This much I did know: Almost everyone needs a ritual – whether it be work, exercise, religion, or something; without regular processes, something could fall through the cracks. Since there would be no formal training, it was literally up to me to create my job duties and work habits. I needed a designated space away from any form of distraction, or my mind would wander, so I set up a small desk off to the far corner of my loft in my condo. Once my office space was set up and organized, the most important piece to the puzzle came – obtaining a Utah state broker license.

I stopped by the Department of Alcoholic Beverage Control (DABC) to pick up an application and the information for what is called a "Local Industry Representative License." Although now employed, I could not technically work unless the DABC granted me a license. The DABC offices and warehouse are located just southwest of downtown Salt Lake City, maybe five miles outside the city center in a large architecturally boring, single level, vanilla, monolithic building. As with many other state governments, Utah is notorious for a variety of unremarkable government buildings. Maybe they're cheaper to make and maintain – I don't know – boring buildings for boring work?

Two massive warehouses sit to the rear of the main office building that store alcoholic products before they are shipped out to their state-owned stores. One warehouse is a horizontal building for staging, loading, and deliveries, and the other is a tall vertical building. The vertical warehouse is quite remarkable in that one person can operate a machine that moves a pallet of product (a typical pallet is 56 cases; however, it can be more or even less), assign it a code, then relocate it in a space on one of the fifteen floors where it will reside until they need it – kind of like a hotel for liquor, beer, and wine. When the product is needed, a code is punched in corresponding to a pallet of product, then the computer locates the product and delivers the pallet to a conveyor belt where it is moved into the horizontal warehouse in under 30 seconds. The product can then be broken out into cases off the pallet, loaded into trucks, and delivered to the state stores.

In the main offices, just inside the front doors of the foyer, is a bulky U-shaped receptionist desk. Directly behind the receptionist desk sits a large rectangular meeting room resembling a courtroom; they hold monthly Liquor Commission meetings and other formalities that I am not privy. To the west side of the reception is the Compliance Division; everything regarding licensing, state laws, rules, and regulations; several people including their director, deputy director, on-staff lawyer, and compliance officers reside in this wing. The other side of the building is the Purchasing Department, including billing, receiving, and administration, but most notably, two buyers and their support staff that handle all day-to-day minutiae pertaining to buying, warehousing, and selling alcohol.

After obtaining an application from one of the compliance officers, I was informed it needed to be turned in with the required background checks, fingerprints, and the mandatory fees by the end of the following week so it could be put on the November Liquor Commission meeting docket. If I didn't get the information to him by then, it would have to wait until December, thus delaying my ability to actually work. Since this was all new language to me, I asked a few questions for clarification then went on a quest to obtain all the required documentation. The compliance officer acted as my own personal "license life coach" to walk me along the path of successfully obtaining my permit to act as a broker. And though I did call him a few times, obtaining a Manufacturing Representative License is a lot easier than all the other liquor licenses they distribute. I guess the DABC figures a broker must have suppliers or products to sell, therefore be able to make enough commissions to live, so they do not really care how many licenses they distribute (and compared to restaurants and bars, a broker's license is relatively cheap, too). The only thing the DABC really cares about is if the applicant does not have any DUIs or felonies on their record – and of course, work within the laws and rules set forth.

After compiling all the necessary information, I submitted it along with the required fees and appointment letters from each supplier I would be representing, then waited patiently until the monthly Liquor Commission meeting, usually held on the third Thursday of every month. My compliance coach explained, "You will have to get up in front of the audience and the Liquor Commission briefly. After introductions, they will simply ask you a few questions about suppliers or laws. Just answer them the best you can, and the process will be over. You will have a liquor license at the end of the meeting."

It sounded easy enough.

Slowly the weeks went by until finally the time arrived. Dressed in a tie and sports coat, I anxiously pulled into the DABC parking lot along with other hopefuls vying for a restaurant liquor license, banquet permit, or God forbid, to defend themselves for breaking state laws or other infractions. I had never been to a monthly DABC Commission meeting but what I found out is this: It can be a bit of a circus. The lengthy boardroom is set up like a courtroom. The members that make up the DABC Liquor Commission and several members of the purchasing and compliance committee sit in huge leather chairs behind a long wall-to-wall desk topped with microphones at each seat. The rest of the room is set lecture-style with rows of uncomfortable plastic chairs and a podium facing the Commission. The room reeks of bureaucratic mediocrity and the typical bullshit that comes from the bad decisions of an alcohol-biased Liquor Commission tasked with levying fines, interpreting state laws, implementing them, and granting and suspending liquor licenses.

I was given an official *Proposed Agenda*; the meeting that day was mostly full. I read through the pages patiently waiting for my turn at the podium while a series of topics were discussed and voted on, including restaurants or hotels with liquor violations, fines, suspensions, liquor license transfers, forfeitures, etc. Finally, several hours later, the meeting moved into the granting of liquor licenses. One by one, each of the prospective licensees was given a chance to voice their reasons for a liquor license, which was either granted, held up, or denied for one reason or another.

At around the fifth application, an unfortunate incident happened with one hopeful restauranteur's liquor license review:

A soft-spoken gentleman from a foreign land stepped to the podium wishing to obtain a full-service liquor license for his family-run restaurant. He had filled out the paperwork accurately, obtained all necessary background checks, insurances, and local permits; even paid the fees. Once settled at the podium microphone, one of the seven people on the Liquor Commission said, "Sir, thank you for attending. You are applying for a full-service liquor license, correct?"

"Yes, sir," the tall thin man stated in a very mild manner.

"Could you tell me why you would like to obtain a liquor license?" the Commissioner asked.

There was a long pause as the man gathered his thoughts to form this sentence, "Yes, sir. We applied for a liquor license because it would help get more people through our doors to dine – It would help us show how great our food is and become more successful."

After a long pause, the Commissioner asked, "Sir, you have been in business for a few years already, is that correct? And, the business has been relatively successful since you have been opened?"

"Yes, sir. We have had some success; it's a family business."

Now, at this point, I have to assume the Commissioner was Mormon because of his follow-up statement. "I see. But certainly, if you've been in business already for a few years, you do not need a liquor license? If your food and service are that good, you shouldn't need to sell alcohol to help your business be successful. Correct?"

Silence hung in the air like a thick dark cloud. I had worked in the restaurant business for almost 20 years and never heard of such an asinine question. The audacity of this dumbass Commissioner questioning and belittling the man in front of the large crowd about his obviously good intentions to keep his family-run business afloat was completely unacceptable.

After what seemed like ten minutes but was probably more like thirty seconds, the man replied. "Well, sir, that may be true...but you see...there are about four to six other restaurants within a few miles of ours, and they all have a liquor license of some sort – I just think it would make us more competitive."

The Commissioner stared over his readers at the man for a moment before stating, "I see, thank you for coming. We will take it into consideration."

The gentlemen didn't get his liquor license that day, but I heard he did a few months later after answering the questions differently. Absolute absurdity.

Finally, it was my turn. I waited nervously in my chair, fidgeting uncomfortably. The Commissioner leading the agenda said into the microphone for all to hear, "Now we have one application up for a Local Industry Representative license. Spartacus Falanghina, please stand and take the podium." After taking my place, he asked, "Mr. Falanghina, do you know and understand the state laws and rules regarding alcohol?" What was left of the audience that stuck it out to the bitter end watched and listened intently.

"Yes," I replied.

"What company will you be representing, and do you have suppliers already lined up?" the Commissioner asked.

"The company is called Spirits West; it's a division of Alaska Distributors based out of Seattle. I have several suppliers already in place," I stated nervously, my voice cracking, hoping I said everything correctly.

Again, another uncomfortable silence passed while he flipped through various papers in front of him, until he replied, "Very, well. Thank you, and good luck to you."

After taking my seat, the Commissioner questioning me, quietly stood, then announced, "Thank you all for attending - meeting adjourned."

The Commission and the rest of the department heads retreated to another meeting room across a hallway and shut the door. I wasn't sure what to do at this point, so I loitered in the lobby. I asked the receptionist if she knew what happened next. "They meet for a short time, could take ten minutes, could take an hour depending on the issues. If they grant any liquor licenses, they will be distributed immediately."

"Thank you," I said, sitting down in one of the waiting room chairs.

Not more than a few minutes later, the compliance officer who had helped with the paperwork appeared from the room and walked directly up to me, handing me a piece of paper. The top read – "Temporary Industry Representative License."

"Congratulations," he said as he shook my hand. "Good luck, and call me if you have any questions in the future."

UTAH DABC PRACTICES
2003 to 2011

IN THE BEGINNING, I really didn't know what my responsibilities were in relation to "working or dealing with" the DABC, but I knew it was a priority to find out. I made an appointment with DABC buyer Dennis Crossland, the person in charge of all "General Listed" products, and Cliff Bradford, the fine wine buyer in charge of all the "Limited Listed" products. I didn't know Dennis, but I'd met Cliff approximately fifteen years earlier when he ran one of the liquor stores located next to a restaurant I'd managed. Cliff had moved up the ladder as the DABC restructured over the years into a position that allowed him great latitude on purchasing fine wine, specialty alcohol, and beer. Cliff possessed an excellent palate and unsurpassed knowledge of the trade; at the time, he was probably one of the most highly regarded wine professionals in the industry, or at least in the west. Dennis, on the other hand, was a good old boy with a dry wit and an ability to look at all sides of any situation. He did not jump to conclusions, and more often than not, tried to look for fair resolutions.

After being greeted by the receptionist at the DABC, I was shown into one of the offices within the purchasing division. Cliff was sitting behind his rather bulky desk, reviewing a paper from one of the many stacks dotting the surface. There was a computer with two monitors and rows of filing cabinets spanning the wall behind him; a small round table sat just to the side of his desk with two office chairs covered in cheap burgundy upholstery. The office had the usual personal effects, but his were wine oriented. An empty three-liter dummy bottle of Perrier Jouët sat atop his filing cabinets along with an old wooden French wine box, now the resting place for a few potted plants. Maps of various wine regions were prominently placed on the walls where pictures normally resided. Stacks of wine publications such as *Wine Spectator, Wine & Spirits, The Wine Advocate* were scattered in various nesting places around the room. Cliff, a slightly overweight man of medium height with wispy light brown hair and astute eyes bearing crow's feet that hid years of wisdom, rose from his desk with a wry smile as he held out his hand. "Come on in, Spartacus. Have a seat; great to see you."

"Good to see you too," I replied.

"Hold on just one minute while I grab Dennis."

Nervous and slightly intimidated, I sat impatiently trying to remember all the questions scribbled down on a notebook stuffed into my shiny new black pleather messenger bag. Instead of retrieving it, I decided at the last minute to just talk and go with it rather than risk looking like an amateur. This was it – It was time to make a good impression; these two men had the power to make or break me. They were the deciders – I'd even go so far as to say, executioners, since they had the final say on if a product would be sold in the state liquor stores. If they didn't like me or my company, or if I did something wrong, the supplier's products I represented could be discontinued and new product presentations thrown in the trash. Without products for sale on the state liquor store shelves, commissions would dry up and so would my job.

"Spartacus, this is Dennis Crossland," Cliff said upon reentering the room with his colleague.

I stood and anxiously extended my hand to acknowledge Dennis, my voice cracking from my dry mouth. "Hello, Mr. Crossland, I'm Spartacus Falanghina. I just started with Spirits West as their new man in charge of the wine business in Utah."

"Call me Dennis," he stated, as we shook hands then took our seats. Dennis, middle-aged and balding with a few extra pounds, was informally dressed in jeans, checked flannel shirt and round eyeglasses. He sat at a separate small table off to the side, leaning back into the chair, reclining in comfort as we spoke. His casual nature put me slightly at ease.

"It's been quite some time since we've seen each other, Spartacus," Cliff stated.

"Yes," I replied, staring straight ahead at Cliff while Dennis studied me from the side. "I think the last time we talked was at the Salt Lake Magazine Award Ceremony when Tuscany Restaurant won Best Wine List. Thanks again for voting for Tuscany."

"Well," he said, "I didn't think there was another restaurant in Salt Lake City with as much depth and range on their wine list at the time. It appears you have a new calling... Please tell us about it."

Temporarily tripping over myself, I stuttered and

stammered before explaining the story of my falling out with the owners of Tuscany and L'Avenue, elaborating on the fact that I decided to get out of the restaurant business and focus on wine. Being completely honest with both men, I added that this was a new position for me, and no one was there to train me, so if they could help with any information, it would be greatly appreciated.

"What suppliers will you be representing?" Cliff asked.

"Diageo, Moët Hennessy, Pernod Ricard, Shaw Ross, and Firesteed," I stated sheepishly. "It's a smallish book but manageable, and there are some great wines within their portfolios."

"Diageo is not that small," Cliff retorted, "and their Bordeaux and Burgundy offerings are of particular interest to me, along with Trimbach from Alsace. I would suggest you ask them for updated information and pricing so we can get an order together. The state stores are somewhat depleted of Bordeaux, so that should be the first priority, in my opinion."

Cliff paused for a moment before glancing at Dennis. "I think Dennis would agree… These suppliers and brands have not had any representation in Utah for quite some time – sales have suffered, and many of them may be in jeopardy of being delisted if sales don't turn around."

"No problem," I said, realizing the notebook in my bag was now necessary. I struggled with the clips before wrestling it from the new bag. *Dammit,* I thought to myself while the two men watched. *Why did I have to buy a new messenger bag? It wasn't even real leather- there were already cracks in the corners. I should have splurged and gotten the nicer one; then I wouldn't be having this problem – What a dumbass.* Finally, I pulled the notebook and a pen from the bag, placing them on my leg (now used as a desk).

"Dennis, what should Spartacus be aware of on your side of things?" Cliff said as he grinned.

"Let me print off the supplier information worksheets so we can go over them," Dennis said, chuckling as he rose to leave the office.

Cliff and I made small talk about the past restaurants I had worked at and how they were doing as I jotted down notes while we waited.

Dennis returned a moment later to explain the ways of working regarding General Listed products. As he spoke, I did my best to keep up with him, but my handwriting turned into barely legible scribbles that proved to be nearly worthless later. I was given several pages of paper showing the state-listed products they carried from each of my suppliers, a packet outlining the necessary forms for presenting new products for a General Listing, and information regarding trading out products that were underperforming, delisting and closing-out procedures.

The meeting lasted about an hour – long enough for me to fumble all over myself while exhausting all questions. Once finished, face flushed, my mind raced, trying to think of anything else before leaving. After shaking hands, they escorted me to the exit. However, we stopped briefly at the cubicles just outside of their offices so they could introduce their administrative assistants and briefly explain each of their duties.

Dennis' second-in-command was an older lady named Betty Hansen. She cut purchase orders, reviewed new products with Dennis, and monitored daily inventory. Betty was, at the time, a stout single mom with wavy long gray hair; sometimes curt and to the point, she was strictly by the book – as dangerous as a rattlesnake one moment and as nice and reserved as a doe the next. She wielded considerable authority as I would later find out – One false step, and she could jump to conclusions threatening to delist or discontinue products or some other loss of business such as cutting down one of the upcoming sale months. Dennis was the only one who could step in and analyze the situation and offer a remedy.

Danny Mann and Marien Liddle worked under Cliff's direction in the fine wine department. Danny, although a seasoned employee, had retained his youthful glow; he was smart and witty, and he was Cliff's right-hand man. Danny had worked for the DABC since his early twenties, sort of a wunderkind, and Cliff depended on him greatly. He knew everything about the computer system they used for ordering and inventory, the warehouse, the state stores, and anything else needing attention.

Among other duties, Marien was mainly in charge of processing all incoming samples so they could be reviewed as either a General Listing or a Limited Listing. When samples arrived, she logged them in, labeled them with codes, bottle price, supplier, and broker name, then placed them in a small locked room designated for sampling on a shelf assigned by broker. Marien, a tall, middle-aged dirty blonde, was sociable and light-hearted; she loved a good anecdote or a humorous joke. It was common after entering the purchasing department to overhear her whispering stories tucked away in her cubicle hunched over her phone.

Before leaving, Danny showed me how to order Limited Listed fine wines and how to submit new wines for Cliff to review. Just as I had opened the door to exit the purchasing department, Cliff reiterated that he needed Bordeaux pricing ASAP from Diageo to replenish the depleted shelves in the state stores. He added, "Please ask Danny or try to get ahold of me if you need anything; we'll do our best to help with your transition."

Now official, I could start "brokering" wine – but what did that really mean?

A liquor or wine broker (or what the state calls a Local Industry Representative) works in a similar way as a real estate professional. We don't actually own the products we represent, but we (or in my case, my company) get paid a predetermined commission on every case that is sold to the state from each corporation, importer, winery, distillery, or brewery we represent.

It is the broker's job to filter, compile, and consolidate all new item information from the suppliers, then present it to the DABC. Suppliers rely on brokers to act on their behalf to maintain and grow their presence and sales within the state – In the end, all three benefit. When issues arise, the DABC works through the broker to find a resolution rather than dealing with the thousands of suppliers across the world directly. One of the most significant components is to work with restaurants, bars, hotels, and events, to showcase their products so an account can make a sound decision as to what product to carry.

A broker's relationship with the DABC is most definitely one of "love/hate." They most certainly love to have us complete and present paperwork, help in the state stores as unpaid merchandisers, and wave any red flags if problems arise. And when those red flags or problems arise, they want them fixed immediately - not tomorrow, not next week – but now. Brokers, in turn, despise the DABC a bit because when we need something, they take their own sweet time getting back to us (quite often not at all). From time to time, they even make new protocols but don't even bother to tell the brokers, so it's a constant game of trying to figure out what the hell's going on. But, since there is no direct competition, that's what monopolies do!

I think the folks at the DABC resent the brokers a little as well. (Maybe it could have something to do with the fact that they have to work in a drab, tasteless building with shitty lighting and use inferior office equipment eight hours a day - day in day out, all the while looking over their shoulder because the public and licensees despise their actions?) The DABC takes most of the abuse on behalf of the state legislature – They are on the frontlines working within an unfair system where there is little chance for advancement or incentive to do a good job. Another reason could also be the freedoms brokers enjoy: working somewhat flexible schedules, lavish expense accounts, the products we represent and often taste free of charge, the money we make, and the many fringe benefits of which they are not allowed to partake. Or, maybe even a combination of all?

The state is the buyer and the retailer. Wholesale pricing simply is not available – they buy it, then sell it. Everyone in the state pays the same price for alcohol. A customer walking into a state store pays the exact same price as the restaurants and bars. The only break restaurants get is not paying sales tax at the cash register. They collect sales tax and remit it to the state when they resale the product on their premises.

State taxes on alcohol – After the DABC purchases an alcoholic product such as wine, they mark it up roughly 88% to come up with a retail price. So, if they pay $100 for a 12-pack of wine, after mark-up, the same case costs

$187.68. Then, to top it all off, there is another 6.85% sales tax added on at the cash register – two state taxes without any competition – a good old-fashioned mob shakedown.

The state offers a reduced mark-up on products produced by small wineries or manufacturers by taxing their products at approximately 64% mark-up rather than 88%. Production must be less than 40,000 barrels of beer, 20,000 gallons of wine, or 30,000 gallons of spirituous liquor annually. An application must be filled out, then verified through TTB reports filed with the federal government. What this essentially does for the small producer is help their products maintain a competitive stance against the large powerhouse brands, which is actually quite rational.

The state could give a tax break allowing restauranteurs to pay a lower wholesale price, but they're just too damn greedy, and it would be downright immoral in their eyes. It seems the Mormon-led state lawmakers are worried that a licensee trying to operate a business for a profit may actually turn a profit, in part from selling alcohol.

And what could possibly happen if a licensee bought booze or wine at a lower price making their business more profitable? *Oh, heavens to Murgatroyd,* it's hard for anyone to fathom; it could cause the heavens to open and strike down the legislators who let this happen. But, let's explore that possibility: Said business that operates on already thin margins could turn a larger profit ultimately resulting in the entity literally staying in business. It could also mean higher profits to help pay higher wages, incentives, and even offer insurance to the employees of said business, which ultimately could lead to happiness. For the love of God, Pete, and Moses... that is just plain crazy thinking! However, lawmakers could be at risk because it would be considered promoting alcohol consumption and against public safety in their eyes. The simple reality is this: It's hard enough to run a restaurant or bar for profit, and because of Utah's state taxes, it's even more difficult because alcohol margins are considerably less.

As one can imagine from the tax mark-up, the state profits quite handsomely from the sale of alcoholic beverages. From the annual report for the fiscal year ending June 30, 2019, the state collected just over $479 million dollars in sales, a 5.43% increase from the previous year, and reaped in a healthy profit of over $175 million dollars plus over $26 million additional in sales tax. The profit goes into what is called the General Fund, operated by the state government. It is used to support various programs, including public schools and their lunch programs, roads, highways, alcohol abuse programs, public access areas, state parks, and so on.

When dealing with the DABC, be nice, and above all, be patient. Maintaining composure at all times is a must when dealing with the Purchasing Division of the Department of Alcoholic Beverage Control. Patience is truly a virtue in this arena. The DABC does not move particularly fast; they don't have to – Again, because they're a monopoly with no competition. One false step, one backhanded comment, or failure to fix a problem can result in purchase orders taking a longer time to get processed or presentations and samples on new products getting lost or rejected, or even products being delisted. So, working as a "Local Industry Representative Licensee" or "Broker" is a constant waltz on eggshells – pissing off the buyers in the Purchasing Department or getting caught doing something construed as illegal by the Compliance Department could disrupt business or lead to license revocation and fines.

Manage state listed products – When a product is chosen by the DABC to be carried in their state stores, it's called obtaining a "State Listing" or "Listing." The broker's duty is to look after sales, and in some cases, help with inventory of said products so that decent profitability is maintained. If a product is not profitable and they decide to stop selling it, then it becomes a "Delisting" or a "Delisted Product," and they get rid of it to make room for another product.

The DABC has two main designations for State Listed products: General and Limited.

A **General Listed** item is a product that is sold in mass volume, like most liquors and wines such as *Smirnoff Vodka, Knob Creek Bourbon, Barefoot, Ménage a Trois, Mondavi Private Selection,* and so on. A General Listed item will be in almost all state liquor stores. General Listed items can be put on sale five months per fiscal year by the supplier through what is called a SPA, or Supplier Purchase Allowance. The supplier decides which months they want to put their products on sale by offering a case cost discount to the state, which they pass onto the public in full-dollar increments. For instance, for a product that is $12.99 on the shelf, it is reduced in price by two, three, or four or more dollars during a full month.

A General Listed product is most certainly a high-volume mover, especially in a sale month, so the state buys and inventories a considerable number of these products, often tens of thousands of cases, depending on the brand. Once a General Listing is obtained, the purchasing department manages the warehouse inventory. The DABC requires that the product always be available to them. If at any time a General Listed product is not available, sales suffer, or a supplier fails to ship it in a timely manner, the product may be delisted.

A **Limited Listing** is a product that the DABC buys in small quantities; usually, products that are unique or of a higher price, and may not sell to more than a select segment of the population. These products are usually smaller production wines or liquors that may get very good press or ratings and may be collector products and very expensive. Limited Listings are not put on sale unless they are closed out or delisted for a lack of interest. Limited Listings have an everyday low-price year-round. It's up to the brokers to manage the inventory on Limited Listings. If a Limited Listing starts to sell very well, then it can possibly be moved over to a General Listing status.

A **Special Order** is an order from a licensee such as a restaurant or hotel that may want something completely different than what the state inventories and sells in their state stores. Private citizens can also ask the DABC to find and purchase a product for them, as long as it goes through their system and is taxed accordingly. The caveat here is that the product must be purchased in full-case increments, and the state reserves the right to take one-third of the product if it's something that they want to put in their stores for the general public to buy. An example of this would be something like a highly sought-after small production wine or liquor only made in small batches each year – for instance, *Scarecrow Cabernet* or *Pappy Van Winkle* bourbon.

So, here is the thing about special orders – the state will issue a PO to buy a case or ten cases or more for just about anyone who requests something that is not state listed. If it's a large amount or a high-end item, well then, a deposit to guarantee pick up may be required – they do not want to get stuck with anything. So, one would think it would behoove the DABC to issue purchase orders quickly and expedite this service as best as they could. Why? Because it is what is called an in and out. A full case comes in, then it's bought at full retail, resulting in pure profit to the bottom line – no inventory, and it's guaranteed that the full case will be bought, not just a bottle here and there.

The Special-Order business, in fact, has always been looked at as a pain in the ass by the DABC purchasing department, and therefore expediting orders has always taken a back seat. Instant pure profit without inventory should be a priority, but because they are a monopoly, the DABC bastardizes the system. Purchase Orders often take weeks or months for the one person at the special-order desk to issue, then another four-to-eight weeks for delivery. Yes, that's right, even in the modern age of 2019, the DABC employs one person to punch in special orders for the entire state. Asinine. In fact, I'm quite sure the general lack of interest from the DABC to expedite this type of order has caused a loss in sales and revenue for the state resulting in pissed-off accounts and citizens.

TASTING WITH THE STATE

THE BIGGEST HURDLE TO SELLING ALCOHOL in Utah is getting the DABC to list a product and put it in their stores. Since there are two buyers, one for General Listings and one for Limited Listings, there are two protocols. General Listed products required multiple pages of information and samples, reviewed in private by the purchasing department, which can often take several months. Limited Listings, on the other hand, required the brokers to simply submit pricing and samples every few months, then conduct a tasting prior to the buyer (Cliff Bradford) tasting the wines. If Cliff liked a wine, or it had a great rating, the trigger was pulled immediately, so I preferred to use the Limited Listing route. If a wine designated as a Limited Listing sold well enough, then it could be moved over to a General Listing by just submitting current sales data and a price quote.

Tackling both protocols, first I submitted several products for General Listing, knowing it could take months before they were reviewed. Then after discussing priorities with my suppliers, settled on about twenty wines to submit for review for Limited Listing status. On an Excel spreadsheet, I listed the wines, vintage, pricing, supplier, and other details, then faxed it to the DABC. The next morning, I received a fax back with Cliff's approval on which wines he would like to review. Not everything made the grade; about a fourth of the products had been crossed off. I emailed the suppliers directing them to send two bottles of each wine – the protocol just in case one was corked or tainted in some way. Then I waited for a tasting date.

Several weeks later, Danny Mann, Cliff's assistant, called to inform me it was time to review wines at the DABC for Limited Listing. Many of the competitive brokers had also submitted wines, so the process would take a few days. I was given a morning time, mid-week at the DABC offices.

After checking in with Danny and Marien Liddle, they escorted me to the sample room on the other side of the building. Once inside, they showed me a shelf labeled with masking tape; printed in black Sharpie was my name and company name. The shelf held all the samples I had requested – fifteen different wines, two bottles each for a total of thirty bottles. We loaded one bottle of each wine into one of two small shopping carts that appeared to have been purchased or confiscated from an old corner store or market that had gone out of business. Once filled, Danny opened a second door within the sample room that led to a smaller room housing a tiny kitchenette complete with counter, cabinets full of wine glasses, wine buckets, other miscellaneous items, sink, dishwasher, and a refrigerator. A small table sat against one wall with a few chairs, and in the far corner, sat a metal cart holding some sort of mechanical device I had never seen before.

Once the wines from the shopping cart were unloaded onto the small table, Danny stated, "You have one hour. Will that give you enough time?"

"I guess, it's only fifteen wines," I replied in a less

than confident tone.

Danny, pointing to the top kitchen cabinets said, "Great. All the wine glasses are up there, openers are in the drawers, and buckets for spitting are in the corner. Please put the dirty glasses in the dishwasher and clean up after yourself when you are finished. Any questions?"

"Well, yeah," I said quizzically. "What's the procedure? I've never done this before."

"Oh, yes, I forgot. Do you have some paper and a pen or pencil?"

"Yes."

"You need to open the wines, taste them in any order, then write down your assessment, as legibly as possible please. Double-check that the price and vintage, and all other information is correct. If you find any flawed wines, let us know so we can retrieve the second sample from the other room – Got it?"

"Uh, yes, I think. So, no one else is tasting with me?"

"No, it's just you."

"How do they make a decision on what wines will be brought in?"

"There are two other brokers scheduled to do the same thing later today. At the end of the day, Cliff, myself, and usually a few qualified employees from the downtown wine store meet to taste through the wines to come to a final decision."

"Okay, I get it. Do I have to taste the white wines and sparkling wines at room temperature, or should I chill them?"

"There won't be time to get them chilled, just taste them

as they are and write down your impressions."

"How will I know if any wines are chosen?"

"Either tomorrow morning or the day after, we will fax all the results to you. You'll need to search through the tasting notes for your wines. Out to the side in the column, Cliff will write a simple 'no,' 'yes' or 'deal.' Then you'll need to fill out a new worksheet including codes, case weight, price, and any other pertinent information, and fax it back to us so a purchase order can be generated."

Brief silence ensued while I wrapped my head around the protocol, finally asking, "If it says 'deal,' next to the wine, then what?"

"It means that Cliff may consider buying it if your supplier will make a better deal on the price; it's negotiable."

"Oh, okay. I think I got it. Anything else?"

Danny then turned to point to the machine on the metal rack in the corner. "The most important part. You must take a breathalyzer test before you can leave."

"What? No way – really?" I said, grinning in disbelief, "What happens if I'm over the limit?"

"Then you have three choices – either stay here until it wears off, have someone pick you up, or call a cab."

I snickered skeptically. "How does it work?"

"When you're finished, come grab either Marien or me and we'll walk you through it." I watched Danny turn and walk off.

The door to the sample room was closed and locked, but a second door to the main hallway remained open. Other than the kitchenette, a couple of pictures on the wall, and accompanying accouterments, the room was cold and stark. I grabbed a wine key from the drawer, then opened every bottle on the table to begin a rapid-fire tasting.

I swirled, sniffed, sipped, and spit each wine, one after the other, while writing down my perceptions. Relying on first observations, color depth, body, and smell, I worked my way through the allotted hour. Once finished, I cleaned up the table, rinsed the glasses and spit bucket, re-corked all the wines, and left my tasting notes on the table to be perused and mocked by the DABC staff later that day.

I notified Marien that I was finished, and after plugging in the machine, she handed me a sterile mouthpiece to place on a long tube. I was instructed to blow into the device for as long as I could. Once finished, a piece of paper was loaded into a slot, and the results were printed. An alcohol level of .01 registered, and I was cleared to leave. I was told a copy of the printout would be kept in a file with my name, which I am guessing, could still be there to this day.

The very next morning at eight o'clock, my fax machine began to print the results – around forty pages. I scanned each page eagerly looking for my wines. Seven wines were approved for purchase, one of which said, "deal." Later that afternoon, I met with Danny to learn how to fill out worksheets for new submissions. I notified all my suppliers of the new successes then the whole process started over.

About two months later, after I had finished tasting the wines at the DABC a second time, a thought or rather a question came to me that I had never considered – *What happened to all the unopened samples?* Brokers submitted two bottles of every wine each time just in case one bottle was corked or flawed. However, corked and flawed bottles were few and far between, which left a lot of free fine wine sitting in the sample room. After I finished conducting the breathalyzer test, I posed the question to Danny Mann as he helped me straighten up the room. "I have a question regarding the unopened samples left over after the tastings. What happens to them?"

Danny sighed. "We come up with a value for each wine. The staff here at the DABC is given an opportunity to buy them to take home. If we still have bottles left, then we set them out for sale on a table at the front of the wine store downtown."

"Oh, okay... So what do they usually cost?"

"Anywhere from $2 - $10 per bottle. Again, depending on what it is."

"I see. Well, that could be a really good deal, especially on the higher-end wines?"

"Yes, sometimes there are a few nuggets that are offered for sale."

"Okay, thank you." I stated while gathering my things before departing.

I guess it made some sense, but it was still kind of shitty; jokes had been circulating for years betting the folks in the purchasing department sure had nice wine cellars.

{ }

NEW VINTAGES?

Though Limited Listings were somewhat easy to obtain, there were two big caveats or problems: If a vintage had changed and or the price jumped from the previous year, fine wine buyer Cliff Bradford required the wine to be re-tasted to ensure it was still the same quality as in prior vintages. With fine wine, the quality can vary from year to year depending on growing conditions, winemaking changes, and other factors.

This new wrinkle I could understand, but it also exposed a few problems. For instance, there could be a wine on the shelf, such as a $20 bottle of Chardonnay selling very well. However, if after verifying all info with the supplier before obtaining a new purchase order, I found that the vintage had moved from 2002 to 2003, then upon this new information, it was my job to cross out the vintage, handwrite in the new vintage, double-check pricing, case weight, and other pertinent information, then fax it to the DABC. Once the fax order was reviewed, it was not uncommon to immediately receive a fax back that simply said, "re-taste" or "send sample," meaning the wine would not be ordered again until it had been re-tasted and the new vintage approved.

Therein was the problem – if a sample for a new vintage needed to be sent, reviewed, and approved prior to a new purchase order being generated, there could be a risk of running out of stock on the state store shelves. This meant that several restaurants, many of which could be on my account sales route, whom I convinced to carry the wine, along with the public, may be shit out of luck if the sample did not arrive in a timely manner, missing the monthly tasting. All the arduous work be damned, and I would lose face with the accounts that carried the wine because it would be out of stock until approved by the buyer. An account could place a special order circumventing the tasting, but this also required a long period of time before the product could be delivered and available. Even if the account wanted to try and special order the wine to get around the protocol, the special order could be held up by Cliff Bradford himself because he knew he was going to re-taste the new vintage and did not want to create a new code. Most often, accounts had to replace the wine with another the state had in inventory. The reality: vintage changes turned out to be a giant pain in the ass.

{ }

THE PENALTY?

Just as I was starting to get comfortable with the DABC processes, new problems arose.

One morning while working on my second cup of coffee, the fax machine spit out several pages from the DABC. Two of the pages were old purchase orders that had been generated for products I had asked them to reorder about a month prior. On the first PO, one item had the vintage crossed out by hand – written next to the vintage was, "Wrong vintage – we received 04." Next to the case price it said "$- 6.45 per case," then a new lower price was handwritten next to the crossed-out grand total. The second PO for a different product had the same writing. "Wrong vintage – we asked for 2004 but received 2002." However, this one said, "Send back!"

Talk about a rude awakening! I immediately called the DABC to talk to Cliff Bradford about the problems, to which he explained, "We're very vintage specific when it comes to Limited Listings. We publish the prices and vintages in our price books, so we want them to be correct when they are shipped. Fine wines change from year to year, so that is why we want the vintage that was approved."

"But the first fax says -$6.45 next to the case

price, then a new total price is written. What does that mean?"

"If a vintage is sent in other than what we ask for, then we impose a penalty to keep the product. Due to set state tax percentages, -$6.45 equals a dollar off on the shelf price to the consumer, so when the next price change happens, the shelf price will go down a dollar. We are such a small state; sometimes, suppliers will send in whatever vintage they want. When we ask for a certain vintage, then that is what we want because it's been tasted and approved for its specific quality."

"So...what do I tell the supplier?"

"You don't have to tell them anything, but it would probably benefit you to do so."

"Why is that?"

"Well, because we will just short pay the invoice -$6.45 per case. Once the supplier gets the check from the state, they will probably call you to ask why it was short paid."

"Are there any other options?" I asked.

"Well, you can have the supplier pick up the product at their cost, but we will need to know ASAP if that's what they want to do – Keep in mind that they may lose the listing with the state if they pick it up."

"That could get expensive, especially if it were hundreds of cases. What happens on the next order for this product? Can it be ordered at the old price?"

"Yes, if the vintage stays the same, you can raise the price on the next order, but future vintages must be tasted and approved."

"Okay, what about the PO that simply says send back?"

"With that, we asked for a specific vintage – the new fresh vintage. The supplier sent an older vintage; we do not want to go backward. They probably found some old cases lying around in a warehouse somewhere and want to pawn them off on us, but we won't accept them, so please have them pick the cases up at their cost."

"Okay, no problem. I can understand the second PO, but my suppliers will not be happy about being paid less than what is on the first PO because a newer vintage was sent than what was asked – prices generally go up, not down."

"Like I said, they can have the cases picked up at their expense, but it could cost them the listing and sales in Utah."

I paused briefly while I thought out the conversation points. "Okay, I'll send out some emails and make some calls to let them know of the problems. Thank you for the time, Cliff."

It was unfathomable that the DABC fine wine buyer would just alter a purchase order, essentially assessing a self-imposed penalty that the other party didn't know about until after the product had shipped or been paid. While the bottom of the purchase orders said, "YOU MUST ADVISE US OF ANY PRICE OR VINTAGE CHANGES BEFORE SHIPPING," in fine print, it said nothing about a monetary penalty. I thought a PO with a set price that was delivered was a binding contract. There had to have been some sort of law that prevented this sort of thing, but the DABC, as I would find out, made the rules, and if you were a supplier, then you played by them or someone else would.

{ }

DELISTING 101

Though new and still on a learning curve, I was cruising along, feeling great about my new job, bragging it up a little among friends and acquaintances. I finally felt like I had a career path. The first year was trial by fire dealing with the DABC, but I learned to keep my mouth shut, ask a lot of questions, and do whatever possible to improve our supplier's business. When I had met with Cliff and Dennis, I thought I'd asked all the necessary questions; however, there was one extremely important question I forgot to ask: *How do I put General Listed products on sale?*

One afternoon, a letter arrived from Dennis Crossland informing me nine wines from my small base of suppliers would be reviewed for Delisting six months later at the annual Delisting Review meeting held each fall. This was a big deal. I panicked. Immediately, I called my boss to inform him of the letter. The wonderful thing about my boss Matt was that he knew he didn't have all the answers, but he always gave great advice as to how to solve a problem – even if it took him an hour to explain.

"This happens all the time," he said. "Just like distributors, control states don't want any dead weight, so products are cut after they've had their run. Then it's basically just about managing the decline until the product is discontinued."

"So, I'm not going to get fired?" I quizzed in a hopeful tone.

"No! Don't take this stuff personal; all you can do is your best. Just touch base with the DABC to learn how you file a SPA (sale) on an item and how long the SPA runs. Then get with the suppliers to implement a calendar highlighting which periods they want to put the products on sale. Either you or the supplier will have to file the paperwork with the DABC to get the sale implemented."

"Great, thank you," I replied, relieved that I was spared from unemployment.

The following day I met with Dennis to find out how to file a SPA. As it turned out, it was actually pretty easy; it was just one area that I was not aware I had any control. Supplier conference calls followed, with all agreeing to support the maximum discount periods allowed per year. The only problem? SPA paperwork had to be turned in almost seventy days in advance of when the actual sale took place. With only six months to show an increase in sales, it didn't give me a lot of time before the fall meeting. I did, however, manage to get a few SPAs implemented, so at least it showed steps toward turning sales around.

For the next several months, I went about other business, trying not to think about the looming meeting. Later that fall, I entered the DABC building for my first Delisting meeting. I had no idea what to expect or how it would go down. The meeting was held in the same conference room where I was granted my broker license, in much the same manner. Upon entering, agendas were given out by the receptionist. Staggered throughout the small audience were most of the other brokers, my competition – some I recognized, some I'd never met. The staff from the purchasing department, along with the DABC director and deputy director, sat behind the long wall to wall desk. I cordially said hello to a few of the brokers before taking a seat in the middle of the room. Most sat quietly reviewing their products up for delisting; an overwhelming feeling of hopelessness permeated the air.

While waiting for the meeting to start, I read through the agenda containing an outline referencing the rules regarding profitability in relation to maintaining a General Listing. The last page was a list of products grouped by broker to be reviewed for delisting that day.

Dennis Crossland started the meeting by welcoming everyone and explaining the morning's proceedings. Luckily, the wines I represented were about halfway down the page, giving me time to watch and learn how the other brokers handled themselves.

Dennis stated, "First item up for review today is Lancers White."

Each person from the purchasing department began flipping through a pile of papers in front of them. The room was completely silent while the information was examined and scrutinized, then Dennis spoke again. "Is the broker here today?"

"Yes," said a gentleman sitting on the other side of the room lifting his arm, waving it halfheartedly.

"Okay," Dennis said while taking a deep breath. "Lancers White is down 280 cases from this time last year. Do you have any explanation as to the decline?"

The broker stated in an awkwardly light tone, "Well, this is a mature brand, but I think there is still some life left in this product."

"Do you have any SPAs in place on this product?" Dennis replied.

"Yes, we have run SPAs," said the broker.

"How many SPAs have you run in the past year?"

"Three were run, all of which were two dollars off the shelf price."

Dennis looked at his papers one more time. "With a product that is primarily sold in the stores, rather than on wine lists, it seems to me you would want to run the maximum amount of SPAs available. But you've only run three in the past year. Why?"

"That's all the supplier would budget for this product."

"Well, obviously, that's not working, as shown by its negative profitability over the past year."

Cliff Bradford looked up from his papers, raising his hand slightly. "Dennis, may I?"

"Sure, go ahead, Cliff."

"This product has been state-listed in Utah for over twenty years. Its heyday is over, the low case sales show a loss of interest by consumers, and the product is not even profitable enough for the supplier to run the maximum amount of SPAs. I vote to delist."

There was a short silence as Dennis looked around the room. "Okay, I have a vote to delist. Do I have a second?"

Betty Hansen, Dennis's assistant, raised her hand to second the motion but was beaten by the DABC director. "I second," he said in a firm tone.

"Sustained," Dennis said as he banged a gavel softly on the counter, signaling the outcome.

And just like that, a wine that had been listed in Utah for over twenty years was delisted due to a decline in popularity relating to profitability.

"Next product up for review, Chateau Souverain Merlot," Dennis stated. "John, you're the broker for this wine also - correct?"

"Yes, I am."

"This product is down 178 cases versus this time last year, and just below the profitability level we would like to see for us to retain the product. What's going on?"

"We've run 4 SPAs in the past year – two SPAs that were two dollars off and two SPAs that were three dollars off. We've also been working hard to get this wine on as many wine lists as possible to help boost sales."

Brief silence again filled the room while the committee shuffled their papers. "Is there anything else you can do to get this product going again?" said Dennis.

Betty Hansen sat quietly reviewing her notes at the far side of the long desk. Breaking the silence, she raised her hand then spoke without being called on. "Dennis, if I may? We've had nothing but trouble with this supplier. Over the last year, many of the orders have been late, and some orders have even arrived short cases from what was requested on the original PO. We do have a rule with General Listed products." Betty paused, shaking her head slightly all the while looking at the broker, head tilted to one side with a concerned maternal look, "If a General Listed product is not shipped by the date on the PO or is out of stock in the warehouse, it could be an automatic delist."

The panel all looked up from their papers to concede the rule while Dennis peered over his metal rim glasses at the broker.

The broker looked at a ledger in front of him before responding in a shaky soft tone, "Yes, I understand, and I do apologize. I'll make sure that the company understands the rules regarding General Listed products." He paused briefly before adding, "I think I can get the supplier to post one more three-dollar SPA per year and possibly look at reducing the shelf price permanently by a dollar to a frontline price of $10.99."

Cliff Bradford looked up again from his paperwork. "Chateau Souverain is one of California's first wineries that still has a decent following. I suggest we keep it for another six months, then review it again."

Dennis sighed. "I second, but keep in mind that sales need to be going in the right direction for us to retain this product after six months. If sales do not show positive movement, it will be an automatic delisting with no argument. Agreed?"

The broker looked up from his papers. "Agreed." His turn at defending his products from being discontinued lasted another 45 minutes. Concessions were made, but in the end, the carnage was done; they delisted over half of the products up for review that day under his brokerage.

About two hours and three wounded broker souls later, they finally arrived at the products I represented. After reviewing the set of products, Dennis sat back in his chair, peering over his glasses. "Mr. Falanghina, it looks as though you were able to increase sales slightly on five of the nine wines under your brokerage, so they were taken off the list for today's meeting. However, that still leaves four wines not performing to expectations. Let's talk about them as a collective for just a moment before we go through them one by one. How long have you been a broker now?"

Other than the flutter of a few shuffling papers, complete silence fell across the room as most of the Delisting Committee took a moment to look in my direction, while my peers and competition all stared at me, waiting for my reply. I shifted slightly then replied as confident as possible. "Just over a year."

"What took you so long to run SPAs on these products? You understand that a SPA can help boost sales tremendously."

"Um…I guess I was not aware that was part of my duties," I stammered. Several of the other brokers snickered and scoffed at my amateur mistake. "I do now, though. The letter informing me of the delisting meeting got my attention, but like I said, I really didn't think that was one of my duties. I guess I thought the suppliers were supposed to handle that piece of the business."

"We don't care where the SPA paperwork comes from; you can submit it, or your supplier can; we just expect you to pay attention to the profitability threshold on General Listed products. Is that clear?"

Feeling as though my father had just chastised me in front of the other brokers now acting like covetous siblings, I replied guiltily. "Yes, I now understand the process. Thanks for not making me go first today so I could see how the meeting progressed. I'll make sure to pay more attention."

One by one, each of the four products I brokered was reviewed as a formality. Betty stressed her concerns, even two times voting to delist. In the end, they said they would review the sales of each wine in six months to make a final decision. As a rookie and my first time at the meeting, I think the Delisting Committee took pity, but also because they knew the products up for review were still viable to the state. The wines just didn't have any attention for quite some time due to the lack of a broker.

The meeting lasted just past the lunch hour before adjourning. Some of the other brokers stopped to say hello and offer supportive comments on the way out of the building. However, I knew they were faking it – we were now competitors on a small playing field – each vying for domination.

Driving home, I couldn't help thinking about Betty Hansen's contribution to the meeting. She rarely offered anything positive, chastising most of the brokers for performance or other issues. In fact, she must have voted to delist over half of the products up for review. If Dennis hadn't been there to steer the meeting, the massacre could have been a lot worse. There were no grey areas with Betty except her hair, which by the way, I actually liked because she owned it; with her, it was going to be strictly by the book. After the delist meeting, I made a concerted effort to boost sales on the wines up for review the following spring.

Six months quickly passed after the Delisting meeting, and the four products that had escaped the ax were now up for sales and profitability review. This time there would be no formal meeting with all the other brokers. A product's retainment or delisting would be decided alone by the purchasing committee with no argument. However, before they could have their meeting, I decided proactively to call Dennis Crossland to find out the status. Dennis informed me that sales for two of the wines had increased, so they were taken off the delisting probationary period, but the other two wines would most likely be discontinued for underperformance.

I asked him if there was anything else I could do to save

the products from being delisted? He informed me that he would consider a trade if I could get the paperwork and a sample to him in time. "Don't you mean two trades since there are two wines up for delist?" I said.

"No," he stated matter-of-factly, "we don't trade one for one, but we will let you trade one new product for two old. It's not completely fair, but it allows us to consider other products that've been presented recently for new listings."

I thought for a moment before replying. "I suppose it's not all bad news; I'll discuss it with my suppliers. But what if one of the products is from one supplier and the other product is from another supplier?"

"Then you'll need to make a judgment call as to who will get the trade. But I'll caution you to consult with both, so we don't have problems arise in a few months because one or the other was not informed."

I knew both suppliers would want one of their wines to be the trade because suppliers, in general, are just plain greedy. It would have to be my call. Going against his advice, I told just one supplier that their product had been delisted, then allowed the other supplier to present the new wine for the trade out. It did work. I employed this method several times during the ensuing years; it really was the only way.

These were the basic workable standard practices and ways of doing business with the DABC up until 2011, when a new person would take over Dennis Crossland's job in the General Listing arena. Even though it was already a bizarre way of doing business, the whole Utah alcohol control system would turn into a giant shit show.

S F

MERCHANDISING

AT THE TIME OF THIS WRITING, the state owns and operates 47 liquor stores, meaning they often own the land along with any buildings or long-term leases and all the infrastructure to support the business. The state also employs hundreds of employees as store clerks, warehouse workers, and store managers. In metro Salt Lake City and surrounding suburbs, the liquor stores are predominantly very large to accommodate the diverse number of state-listed items. State stores in rural areas tend to carry a limited number of products due to their smaller size. And approximately twelve of the liquor stores are really only large enough to carry every state-listed liquor, wine, and beer. Two of the 47 stores act as smaller warehouses rather than retail stores serving only restaurant and hotel licensees in the Salt Lake City and Park City surrounding area.

Because wine is sold only in state liquor stores, there are no worries about servicing several grocery store chains, convenience stores, or big box stores like Sam's Club or Costco. However, the public must drive several miles out of their way to buy a bottle of wine for dinner rather than just grabbing it from the wine aisle in a grocery store while they're shopping - like most other civilized states in the union.

Even restauranteurs and bars are affected as they often have to drive miles to buy and pick up products or pay a fee to a service to deliver the product, adding costs to the final mark-up.

The stores themselves are unpretentious basic models with a large sign somewhere out front that simply says, "State Liquor Store," usually in big red letters. Since the state legislature doesn't want to promote alcohol in any way, they keep the stores simple and non-descript; it fits their puritanical thinking.

Inside, the stores are clean and well-kept, set up in a traditional model – checkout stands in the front, shelves full of liquor and beer around the perimeter, and racks formed into aisles for wine; the store's inventory is located behind the liquor shelves. As a deterrent, they do not refrigerate anything because they believe consumers may open a container right after walking out of the store. With products, it's all business – basic black and white price tags – color tags are only put up when a product is put on sale for a month or delisted. The stores do not allow signage or gift racks from suppliers to showcase products. Color case wrap and floor stack signs are not allowed either because they want the playing field to be level with all products. Brokers can put up what is called a shelf-talker with a review of the product, but it must be a certain size and in black and white – nothing allowed that would falsely sway the consumer's eye and decision. Also, stores do not sell anything other than alcohol – so, no wine openers, gifts, gadgets, snacks, or mixers of any kind.

The stores are very limited in space, so the buyers at the DABC want to fill the shelves with the best products they can get in all categories. Trends dictate how big a particular section may be within a state store. For instance, from the

90s to just after the millennium, the Australian section was quite large because of public demand - the juice in the bottle compared to price outweighed all the other categories. A short time after the millennium, sales started to drop off, so the Australian section shrank in favor of Pinot Noir, Malbec, and Spanish categories. As a broker, presenting everything within reason is necessary because the DABC may just take something out of the blue. If a product is highly sought after or allocated because of small production or the product received an excellent rating from a national publication, then chances are they will find room even if they must get rid of another product.

Many of the liquor store managers are something of an enigma. They start out as humble employees. After demonstrating loyalty and enough skill set to get promoted, they graduate from an hourly employee to a salaried position with benefits and a possible retirement package; most develop enormous egos and attitudes. I guess with all that time invested, some of them feel like the store is their own personal kingdom to oversee and rule with an iron fist. God forbid you do something wrong when in the empire of a ruler with a chip on their shoulder, for it could mean banishment from their realm until they retire, get fired, or worse – move to another store.

The store managers I've encountered over the years have ranged from evil to extremely nice, receptive to domineering, and some with the plain attitude of, "just staying until I can retire." I've been chastised, reprimanded, and lectured by said rulers for several petty offenses, including putting up shelf-talkers, not putting up shelf-talkers, and even moving a few bottles from a lower level to eye level to better catch the customer's eye.

The store employees, on the other hand, are almost always mistreated, underpaid, and uninsured, which often fosters a non-caring attitude resulting in a lack of product knowledge and how fast and efficient they can do their job. The ones who do care usually don't last very long.

With the state making such a healthy profit, one would think they would invest more in their employees, the stores, and overall way of doing business to increase profit. However, they don't want to over-deliver because the LDS-influenced government really hates the fact that it profits from the sale of alcoholic beverages.

The DABC allows brokers to help merchandise products in their stores. The two big reasons: we are bound by our licenses to act accordingly when in the state stores, and they don't have to pay us, so it's free labor as far as they're concerned. Aside from making shelf-talkers and dusting and straightening shelves, we're allowed to build displays for products that are on sale and help replenish empty racks and shelves.

Regularly, when helping in the stores, customers would mistake me for an actual store employee. Sometimes I told them I was a sales rep, but most times I didn't. I just stopped what I was doing and offered to help guide them in the right direction – which often meant steering them to buy one of my products rather than that of a competitor.

Because wine and liquor are not sold on national holidays and Sundays, one of the busiest days of the year in the state liquor stores is the day before Thanksgiving. I usually dedicated part of that Wednesday helping at state store # 15 in the Cottonwood Heights area of Salt Lake Valley. Around noon I'd show up with pizzas and sandwiches for the staff and even some swag – (the stuff we sales reps give away at accounts – t-shirts, hats, wine openers, and other tchotchkes). My competitors would usually be there in full force also, all with one common goal – to help get our products out to the sales floor if they ran out.

One particular year while carrying out a case of wine to restock one of my products, a very nice lady in her mid-fifties stopped me. "Excuse me, do you work here?

"Uh, well, not technically, but I'm a wine rep, so maybe I can answer a question?"

"Oh, great. I'm hosting Thanksgiving tomorrow for friends and extended family, so I need three nice bottles of red wine to go with my turkey."

"Well, how about Pinot Noir?"

"Uh, sure, I guess. I don't know much about Pinot Noir."

Glancing up, I noticed one of my competitors listening to my spiel from across the other aisle. "It's lighter than most other reds from the United States, so it won't overpower the flavors of the meal."

"Sounds interesting. Where are they located?"

"Just over here," I said as I led her to the Pinot Noir section. "How much do you want to spend?"

"Well, not too much, but not too little either."

I pointed to several low to mid-priced Pinot Noirs while my competitor watched intently. "You could go with any one of these wines, but if you really want something that sends a message, then spend a few dollars more and go with this," I said, picking up a well-made $35 bottle.

"Hmm, what message will I be sending?"

Sensing an opportunity and wanting to have some fun, I replied, "This wine possesses subtle power, yet it's sultry and sexy with a firm backside and nice legs."

She looked at me trying to comprehend what was just said, then her eyes grew big. "Oh my God, then this is the perfect wine! I just lost fifteen pounds, and my ex-husband will be there with his new wife, and so will my new boyfriend!"

We both laughed as I helped her get three bottles from the rack. "Maybe I should get some white wine also – What do you recommend?" she said.

"Let me show you…right this way," I replied, leading her to the white wine section while glancing across the other aisle to see my competitor laughing hysterically and giving me the thumbs-up.

After I finished helping her, it was back to stocking shelves until the next customer tapped me on the shoulder.

"Excuse me," said an older man of about seventy. "You got any Blue Nun?"

"Uh, sure, right over here." I showed the man to a shelf on the lower level tucked back into a corner of the store.

"Well, how in the hell is anyone supposed to find it there?" he asked, his voice slightly raised.

"Um, I guess because it's a… specialty item?" I replied quizzically.

"You're damn right it is, son! They've been making this stuff for decades. Hell, probably even centuries. It's a hell of a lot better than any of this other expensive swill out here in the main aisles!"

"Uh, yes, I've heard it's pretty good," I said, trying not to break into laughter.

"Do yourself a favor..." he said, staring at me holding a bottle in each hand, "buy a bottle of this, or maybe two, get your best gal, then make an evening of it!"

I couldn't take it any longer, and as I busted out laughing, he started laughing with me.

Bumping me in the arm with his right fist wrapped tightly around the bottle, he said, "Just make sure to wear a condom; that was my only downfall. Now I've been with her for over fifty years."

We were both rolling with laughter at this point. People from other parts of the store began to point and stare; some even started laughing with us.

I thanked him, then patted him on the back, wishing him a happy Thanksgiving as he turned to get into the checkout line. I barely made it into the backroom before I roared once again. As the store manager tried to calm me down, I shared the story - it was too good not to.

A few hours of working in a state store is a tiring, humbling, and a rewarding experience, but the people met along the way make it all worthwhile.

ILLOGICALITIES:
Various Past Utah Liquor Laws – Part 1

THERE HAVE BEEN MANY CHANGES with the Utah liquor laws over the years – many of the laws still in effect are downright goofy, illogical, and unwarranted. If the LDS Church and its lawmakers had their way, they would totally ban alcohol within Utah borders. However, rather than keep their precious little purified maws off and privatize, alcohol is regulated in a way that makes sense only to Mormons. And what could possibly go wrong with LDS lawmakers' control over a business that contradicts their religious values – a mishmash of nonsensible ludicrous laws? Some present-day laws, such as those regarding the various liquor licenses issued by the state, need such explanation that the general public is constantly dumbfounded as to what they can and can't do. Spread throughout is topical information and anecdotes of some past and present-day liquor laws up through 2019.

Enjoy.

 Buying liquor from the state was the earliest form of "profiling".

I am too young to remember such nonsense, but I have it on good authority that if a person wanted to buy a bottle of wine or alcohol, they had to have their own sort of personal liquor license. The license was issued to the individual in the form of a 3"x 5" index card, and on the back of the card, there were several lines where words could be written. The person holding the liquor license would go to the local liquor store (which long ago were few and far between), present the card through a window to a state employee standing behind a walled or curtained off area where alcohol was kept (out of sight, of course), then tell the employee what they wanted to buy from a very limited selection of products. The employee would take the card, close the curtain or door to the window, then reappear with the product. The product and license were returned through the opening (after payment, of course), and recorded on the back of the liquor license card was the product, date, and price. This had to be one of the earliest forms of profiling I can imagine, probably to keep track of what and how often one was consuming.

 Restaurants were required to have liquor lockers.

I also have it on good account, well before I was of age to imbibe, that when a person went to a restaurant or a bar, they could rent or be given their own personal "liquor locker" in which to keep their preferred libation. The locker would hold the product for the consumer until they arrived for dinner or just to have a drink. The customer opened and poured the liquor into a "set-up" consisting of juice or another mixer or just straight up, then returned the bottle to the liquor locker before leaving for the evening. If liquor lockers existed during these modern times, I would need about sixty lockers around the state with enough bottles to fill them. I'm guessing the person in the business of making liquor lockers for restaurants in the old days probably had a healthy bank account and was possibly LDS too?

After liquor lockers disappeared, it was still legal to take a 750ml bottle of liquor into a restaurant and pour your own cocktails.

During high school, I worked at an Italian restaurant. Partway through my junior year, I was given more duties, so I could help close up, count the day's proceeds, and make the bank deposit before heading home for the night – somewhat assistant managerial, I guess. One night while counting the money, I found a stack of credit cards and driver's licenses wrapped in an elastic band in the office safe, tucked neatly to the rear, that people had left behind. After thumbing through them, I found a driver's license with a picture that not only resembled me but also my very build and birthdate and would put me at about 24 years of age. After careful thought, a few nights later, while again counting the money with my coworker, I took the license while he wasn't looking. The next day at school, I produced the license during lunch to the oohs and ahhs of my close friends. I remember feeling like a superhero while they congratulated and high-fived me, then proceeded to hatch a plan for me to buy us all beer that coming weekend.

After a few months of buying beer for my pals, my confidence was at an all-time high. One night at work, I told one of the senior managers about my new fake ID, leaving out the fact that I stole it from the safe, of course. He congratulated me then began to explain a few things about the liquor laws of the time. As it turned out, not only did certain restaurants sell mini-bottles as their way of distributing a strict portion, but they also let a person take their own 750ml bottle or pint of liquor into a restaurant as well. The restaurant just provided the "set-up" or side to mix the cocktail so a person could pour their own drink at the table. Upon hearing this, a new game plan was hatched.

I knew that a local Mexican restaurant had an all-you-can-eat taco/margarita bar every Friday night for a set fee, and they had a liquor license. So, I went to a liquor store and purchased a bottle of tequila. That night, one of my friends and I proceeded to the restaurant to take advantage of as many tacos as we could put down and get stinking drunk in the process. Upon approval of our IDs (my friend had one as well) by the server, I slapped the 750ml bottle on the table and ordered two pitchers of frozen margaritas – about three hours later, we were both rip-roaring drunk and full. We hung out in the parking lot for the rest of the night to let our buzz subside before going home. Thus, began a new ritual with several of my friends until we graduated from high school.

 Utah: Mini-bottle capital of the United States?

Because people were getting smashed due to the ability to take their own bottle of booze into a restaurant, the state legislature decided to ban the practice, making the mini-bottle the exclusive size for restaurant use. And for a period of time, Utah became known as the mini-bottle capital of the United States.

After turning 21 and spending many years as a line cook, I began bartending. Bartending during the mini-bottle years was less than glamorous - basic cocktails, blended drinks, beer, and wine, but no real mixing to speak of – a little boring. Behind the bar and even on the back bar were huge cabinets of drawers, each filled with a variety of one alcohol, or several, depending on sales. For instance, one drawer housed a mixed variety of different vodkas, and each vodka was sectioned-off within the drawer to delineate the brands. There were drawers for gin, bourbon, cordials, etc. The mini-bottle was given as a side to a set-up, or whatever it was being mixed with – rocks, cola, juice, blended Piña Colada, and so on. The cocktail server gave both the mini-bottle and the set up to the guest, then the guest would pour the bottle into the drink at their discretion.

A couple of things about the mini-bottle: at just under 2 ounces of liquor, they were a stronger portion size than what is in current use in the year 2019. Utah law dictates that drinks are made according to volume – which at that time meant that an 8-ounce cocktail could not contain more than 2 ounces of alcohol. A mini-bottle holds 1.7 ounces of liquor; if a drink required many different liquors, such as a Long Island Iced Tea, a "flavoring" was free-poured from a standard-size bottle into the set-up to enhance the drink – for example, adding a splash of rum or gin to complete the Long Island Iced Tea if the primary liquor was a mini-bottle of vodka. Depending on the volume of the cocktail, the set-up would equal the number of mini-bottles and or "flavorings" a guest could be given to be put into the drink.

As anyone knows, there are loopholes to everything in life, and it's a person's intrinsic manner to beat a system if they can. That being said, the owners of the restaurant took full advantage. They had invented a drink called the Toucan consisting of 6 ounces each of mango, pineapple, orange, and cranberry juices, and a hint of Orgeat syrup poured into a massive snifter resembling a fishbowl. When a person ordered this cocktail, they had their choice of three mini-bottles – usually vodka, tequila, and rum or any combination thereof.

Since the drink contained 24 ounces of mixer and the three mini-bottles totaled 5.1 ounces of liquor, it left room to free-pour almost a whole ounce of additional alcohol into the set-up – so we floated 151 rum on top then lit it on fire – Why not? Aside from maybe a Long Island Iced Tea, the Toucan was not only the largest cocktail I'd ever seen but also the strongest, with six full ounces of liquor. As it turned out, this was the preferred cocktail by all the employees at the end of a hard shift. One or two Toucans, could set up an evening for revelry and debauchery – after three Toucans just making it home was an accomplishment.

{ the classic mini }

Mini-bottles were around for twenty or so years until the lawmakers stated they had a problem with the portion size, as it contradicted "federal recommendations." Using the recommendation as a scapegoat to lower the amount of alcohol in a drink, the legislature discontinued the mini-bottle altogether in favor of a mechanical system that poured only one full ounce of liquor, thus stifling a decent cocktail.

Doing away with the mini-bottles simplified the back bars at several establishments by eliminating the massive drawers and cabinets needed to hold enough product to get through a busy shift. However, the legislature always seems to come up with the most simple-minded gimmickry and chicanery whenever a major change is involved to appease their LDS beliefs. As if it weren't bad enough that during the mini-bottle years, they forced all establishments to spend piles of money building elaborate cabinetry to house the mini-bottles, they now required licensees to install intricate metered systems and/or use individual metered "clickers" so any alcohol poured did not exceed one ounce.

The metered systems themselves could be chosen from a small list of approved products and could only be bought through an approved list of vendors – and, I'm guessing they were probably Mormon too. The vendors, to this day, continue to make piles of money on the dispensing systems as they are still used in Utah and even in many other states around the country as a way to help profitability. The cost of a system can exceed thousands of dollars depending on the model and how many different liquors are used with each system, and where it is located in the restaurant. The first dispensing systems often required a restaurant to install hundreds of yards of tubing strung under floors or through walls and ceilings from the bar to a locked room somewhere on the premises housing the booze. Bottles were hung upside down or inserted upside down into a nipple draining the alcohol into the tubes running to the bar. The tubing alone housed several hundred, if not thousands, of dollars of booze at any given time. Each time a button was pushed on a gun behind the bar, a little counter tallied and registered the drink that later had to be reconciled against what was rung at the register.

As time went on, newer systems simplified the process using a plastic nipple with a metal ring on the end. Each bottle of booze behind the bar had a nipple inserted into the top, secured with special tape, that ensures it can't be pulled off and free poured. The bottle is inserted through a magnetic hoop with a cord running to a meter recording each pour every time the bottle is turned upside down. The number of rings or the size of the metal rings on each nipple corresponds to a specific counter on a meter tracking each variety or cost of liquor. All in the name of control.

The individual metered clickers, on the other hand, were, and continue to be, their own special form of madness, often costing licensees hundreds of dollars per year. Individual clickers are used when an account cannot use either system mentioned above for various reasons: the establishment may be very small or perhaps a country club needs to pour alcohol off a beverage cart. Clickers may also be used in banquet settings in a hotel or used in instances where liqueurs with high amounts of sugar simply do not work well with nipple or gun systems. The clickers have a handle, that when squeezed, registers a drink poured by a meter on top of the clicker tallying the totals. When squeezing the clicker, the bottle must be turned upside down to allow the alcohol to drain into a chamber within the clicker. When the handle is released, the alcohol then flows out of a hole on either side of the clicker into the glass. These devices must have a special piece of tape wrapped around the base to secure it to the bottle in order to prevent free-pouring. Clickers are notorious for breaking down due to the amount of residual sugar in certain liqueurs gumming them up. Depending on the size of the establishment, it's not uncommon to have to buy one or more clickers per month to replace broken units, creating additional expenses that cut into the bottom line.

BUYERS, ACCOUNTS, AND COMPETITION

SINCE THE STATE HANDLES MOST OF THE WORK selling products in their stores, the focus for a guy like me has always been selling to on-premise accounts, or rather, developing relationships by working with restaurants, bars, and hotels.

My first boss told me I should build an account base of around 80-100 accounts in and around Salt Lake City, Park City, and the resort areas. The account base should be divided into three main categories (I later learned that this was an old Gallo approach) – "A Accounts" were considered fine dining or white table-cloth accounts – "B Accounts" were semi-fine dining – "C Accounts" were most chain restaurants, family dining, and bars. A simple enough formula, and it worked.

In my view, there are four types of wine buyers. All of them are equally important, and each has their own eccentricities, and some buyers are even a combination of one or more types, but the one common denominator and single-most important goal: building a relationship.

"**The Professional**" – This small demographic of wine buyers are consummate experts, often holding one or many accreditations. Choosing wines they will sell according to their cuisine and theme is a must for this bunch, but they will venture into the unknown, tapping into obscure categories to excite and titillate their regular customers. A Pro knows they must have a broad array of wine that will suit and satisfy the ever-changing tastes of their clientele, regardless if they personally like the wine or not. The Pro is at the forefront when it comes to information; they generally have more experience, have tasted more wines, and have been exposed to several wine regions, often traveling on their own dime if necessary, to further expand their wine knowledge. Tasting with a Pro can be intimidating and daunting. Some Pros are straight-out arrogant jerks, but luckily, they are a select narcissistic few. Most, in my opinion, are just people trying to maintain a high level of professionalism to set them apart from the rest. Do not try to teach the Pro, for if you do, you risk getting shut down, scoffed at, or even worse, not invited back. It's okay to cover brand info and winery heritage, but never second-guess their senses, and above all, never speculate about something if you don't know the correct answer. You may as well sign your own death warrant. It is better to engage, ruminate, and absorb while tasting and talking with a Pro. Who knows, you may even learn something, and even better, sell something.

"**The Claimant**" – This person will say they know "a lot" about wine; in fact, they may even have a wine certification of some sort. And yes, maybe they do know quite a bit about wine, to some degree – but they make their decisions based upon personal tastes. "If I don't like it, it won't be on my wine list," is a phrase commonly associated with this person. A wine list that is too heavy in one category or region without diversity is a dead giveaway that a Claimant is at work.

A classic example is when the new *Waldorf Astoria* opened in Park City. Because Park City is a ski destination, they brought in some hot-shot sommelier from San Francisco, and even though he should have been considered a Pro, his ego thrust him into the Claimant position. Mr. Cali's palate leaned toward Alsatian wines; he was the consummate expert on Alsace, and he let you know it! So, low and behold, Mr. Cali loaded the wine list up with a selection of the most beautiful Alsatian wines he could get his hands on. What Mr. Cali failed to understand is, Park City first and foremost attracts many from the West Coast, so most sales were predominantly California, Oregon, and Washington wines. After two seasons, he was finished, limping back to California complaining that no one understood him or his vision. It would take the Waldorf three to four years to sell through their Alsatian inventory.

"The Enthusiast" – This group loves it all: wine, beer, and alcohol; not committing to any special area. They like what they like but are willing to explore and learn, and they know their boundaries, so they ask for help due to their limitations. And, if they happen to catch a little buzz along the way, all the better. This group is easy to work with, and many will let you rewrite their wine list alongside them, as long as they can keep some of their personal favorites. They are not dupes by any means but simply enjoy the process and the attention. Enthusiasts are passionate about sipping, smelling, and learning as much as you can offer, and they are fun to hang out with outside of work. Enthusiasts may even have inclinations in obtaining a wine certification someday. A little love goes a long way with this group. Wine keys, shirts, event invitations, wine tours, or an afternoon of golf will secure a long friendship that will prove the test of time, even when they move on to manage another account, which happens quite often.

"**The Indifferent**" – The Indifferent knows nothing about wine, liquor, or beer. They may not even personally imbibe but know they need alcohol to satisfy a percentage of their customers. This type of person often relies on friends, family, distant associates, and even customers to help them make decisions about their wine list. To them, having to serve wine is a necessity in order to gain traction into their restaurant, for they may lose out to the competitor down the street. When a broker shows up to call on this type of account, they are often met with distrust and uncertainty. Although untrue, the Indifferent believes just another bum has shown up to offer their services but will later find out it comes with a fee. It may take several calls or trips to finally break through to the Indifferent, but once invited in, you are part of their home and family, often forever. If a competitive broker ever happens to darken their doorstep, they're sent packing. Once the Indifferent has you, be sure to stop in, dine, and even help when asked, or you could be rejected for another.

The owner of one of my accounts, a Thai gentleman by the name of Prasert is a perfect illustration of the Indifferent. We met while he was working for yet another Indifferent before he went off on his own to open Prasert's Royal House of Thai. Prasert and his wife happened to be Mormon, most likely baptized by the missionaries that periodically invade his country hunting for gullible converts to ante up a 10% tithe. Prior to Prasert's grand opening, he enlisted me to help build a small wine list for his tiny restaurant and train his mostly Thai-Mormon wait staff about wine (talk about difficult). However, what I didn't know after numerous visits and a few complimentary meals, was that I was now entrusted with helping Prasert obtain his liquor license. And even though it was time-consuming, I had experience with that sort of thing from my prior profession, so I said: "Sure, no problem, I can certainly help get all the paperwork in order."

Somewhat painfully, as it took a few weeks, we finished the paperwork just before the deadline. Prasert submitted everything, paid his fees, and appeared in front of the licensing committee to voice the reasons as to why he needed a liquor license. The next day, Prasert triumphantly called to let me know he got his liquor license. He had a very good first year; business was brisk, and he even sold a decent amount of wine. The following year around the same time, Prasert called to tell me he now needed to renew his liquor license. I remember laughing to myself, realizing this was now my responsibility. I guess the words "wine broker" meant anything involving liquor would fall onto my plate from that time forward. I ended up compiling all the paperwork and info for many years to come until Prasert sold his business, relieving me of my duties.

As with all other sales jobs, building reliable relationships will make a wine-selling career easier. Having accounts return emails, text messages, and phone calls because they genuinely like you and your products is a necessity because there will be times when favors are called in, such as obtaining placements because goals are excessive or some ass-hat brand manager, owner, winemaker – whatever, from one of the big wineries is coming to town for a family vacation; they want to dine, and most importantly, they want to drink their own products. Even though their wines may be plonk and the accounts may not want to carry a product, a good relationship can help ensure the placements magically appear, even for just one night. If by chance a few more strings need to be pulled, such as offering to help reprint and stuff wine lists, or God forbid, buy the product back – which happens regularly in this industry – they know you are as good as your word.

Occasionally a relationship can turn into a "relation-shit," and that can take years to correct once soured. For instance, I received a call on short notice from one of my big suppliers to let me know that a brand manager for one of their very large Italian wineries would be in Park City to ski during the holidays. At the time, only one of the wineries' products was carried in the state, and it just happened to be a mandated Olive Garden wine – in fact, it had been a staple at Olive Garden for years. With little time to spare, I called several buyers in Park City to pitch them about bringing in the wine. To say it was extremely hard is an enormous understatement. The buyers at most of the accounts in hoity-toity Park City did not want to put an Olive Garden wine on their wine list. Finally, a good friend who was the sommelier at Stein Erikson Lodge consented to put the wine not only on her list but at their sister Italian restaurant as well. And luckily, I was able to get one other account on Main Street in Park City to also commit. Hopeful it was sufficient, I relayed the info to the brand manager who was coming to Park City, but it wasn't enough. I was immediately chastised and lectured that his fine wines should be in every account in Park City. To which I replied as nicely as possible, "Take it or leave it, considering the time frame and only one product to work with, it's all I got, but please make sure to say hello to the buyers when you dine in the accounts." Which after calming down, he said he would.

His vacation came and went, but on the first day of his return to work, I received an email reprimanding me because his wine was not at any of the restaurants I recommended. Dumbfounded, I called my restaurant contacts, who stated they indeed had added the wine to their list, confirming it with photos via their smartphones. The accounts also said they had not sold a single bottle, which told me that Mr. Ass-hat brand manager never went into those accounts. Furious, I emailed him the pictures of the wine lists along with a note of disgust that he did not follow through. I never heard from him again - ever. Three relationships soured by one dumb ass; however, after a bit of time, the buyer at Stein Erikson did forgive me.

FROM TIME TO TIME IT IS NECESSARY TO PLAY TRAVEL AGENT.

As a broker, it's necessary to field requests for winery visits on a regular basis from managers and owners of our many accounts. It's part of the job; one of the undeclared duties of being a wine broker. And as much as we want to help, it's really a pain in the ass to schedule wine tastings and even overnight stays for other people. Quite often, hours upon hours are spent lining up appointments only to have them change their mind, not show up, or even cancel the trip at the last minute. I can only imagine what a real travel agent goes through every day. But we really want to help, and we do so because it strengthens relationships and could mean more placements on a wine list despite the fact that it's a massive, time-consuming life-sucking agony.

Wanting to get set up in wine country somewhere could mean an overnight stay and tasting, several nights at many different wineries, or just private tours and tastings. Before the 2007 financial meltdown, overnight stays were prevalent, granted to just about any industry member; an overnight stay could certainly help sway a buyer into carrying more products from a winery. After 2007 however, many companies and wineries did away with overnight stays as a permanent cut-back to help profitability. Some still offer this service though it's become very limited, often reserved for big wigs only. When I was in the restaurant business, I took the opportunities to visit wine country every chance I could.

It's one thing when we brokers plan our own tastings and tours, but completely another when planning for an account. Usually, an account will have several brokers trying to set them up with tours and tastings and even overnight stays – each broker trying to outdo the other. Moving, canceling, and strategizing several appointments is just a downright pain in the ass – the hardest part, however, is making sure that the account actually shows up.

Keeping appointments in wine country is of utmost importance, but sometimes it's just plain difficult. Often, accounts will ask for more appointments than they can physically make it to in one day, or they will wander into a winery because they had an hour to kill, then find themselves speeding to try to make a set appointment. Several desperate, frantic phone calls and text messages later, they finally reach their destination – late. I know; I've been there - on numerous cattle calls and puke busses, speeding around frantically – casting blame on directions or traffic, trying to get to as many accounts as possible. Touring around wine country is time-consuming, so usually a morning tour/tasting then lunch and an afternoon tour/tasting will suffice; that way, appointments are kept, and they are most likely on time. It is better to take it slow and enjoy the full experience rather than run around like a jittery rabbit.

Here are a few other points to consider:

Overextending is not acceptable at any time. This happens fairly often – we make an appointment for a private tour and tasting that includes several high-end wines, but magically, the account somehow shows up with four or six people instead of just the two they originally booked. This is a big fucking no! It doesn't matter if old friends just turned up or new acquaintances have been forged at lunch or in another tasting room, and everyone has fallen in love – do not do this! Wineries are very busy, usually requiring 1-3 months' notice, depending on if it's international or not. Stick to the plan, Stan!

Sometimes an account may get drunk and belligerent at a tasting, in which case overindulgence could result in banishment. Very important message here: It's called a tasting, not a drinking! This type of behavior warrants phone calls to suppliers, brokers, and even the local police. It is a sure-fire way to get 86'd from our priority list and a winery.

And, while this really doesn't happen that often, sometimes an account will make contact to say they just happen to be in wine country somewhere, then ask, "What can you do for me?" or, "Are there any wineries that you want me to see?" Usually, with enough time to go through the proper channels, it would mean yes, but since there was complete failure to notify – No goddamn way!

I recall an account calling me from France one day. "Hey, Spartacus. I'm in Bordeaux. Can you line up any appointments for me?" I politely declined, but my mind said, *Hell no – go jump in a lake, bitch! Foreign wineries usually require a 60-day notice – get a clue!*

And lastly, wineries offer a very good discount on almost everything in a tasting room, so for God's sake, buy something - anything! If lucky enough to have a complimentary tasting and/or tour, or if really lucky, perhaps wrangle a stay in a winery guest house - pony up dammit. Look, if the wines are absolute swill, buy something else, even if it's just a fridge magnet – but spend some money. If the trinket purchased somehow abhorrently is reminiscent of their non-palatable wines - give it away for hell's sake.

"WHAT HAVE YOU DONE FOR ME LATELY?"

We are all guilty in this life, maybe some more than others to varying degrees, but we plain often forget things as our memories fall victim to our hectic daily life. Gratefulness is pushed aside from past victories, experiences, dinners and drinks, rounds of golf, tickets to a big game or skiing, the time it takes to set appointments in wine country – or when someone just plain went out of their way for us. We don't mean to forget; it just seems we move through life very fast, day to day, pushing our experiences past us as if trudging through a jungle of grasses and vines. Sure, we say "thanks," but we forget.

I have noticed this phenomenon over the years, and I'm guilty of it myself, giving in to selfish frivolities that I really don't mean to infer. That's why I recognize it for what it is: subjective self-centeredness. Most of the time, it isn't meant as thanklessness by the perpetrator, but rather felt by the unassuming victim. It happens in all facets of life, day to day, an innocuous crime committed at various levels.

Since we do not physically touch the products we sell as brokers, our business is largely a service. We offer our expertise on our products to help make decisions, help construct wine lists and train wait staff, constantly present new items, and act as a go-between with accounts and suppliers. From time to time, we are able to go above and beyond with the accounts with which we have built our reliable relationships. Sometimes we give freely, but often we are asked, and when we are asked, we generally work hard to make sure that whatever is requested is given. So, it's easy to become offended when an account asks, is accommodated, then simply forgets, pushing us aside in favor of a competitor that is willing to step up next.

On the flip side, it's very unnerving when we brokers make a significant goal or obtain a new listing for a supplier, only to find out it wasn't enough; and with suppliers, it's never enough. Each year before the confetti has been cleaned up and the Champagne has lost its fizz, new programs, products, and goals for the following year are jammed down our throats without a second thought as to whether it's possible or not.

We take it hard, this "What have you done for me lately" attitude, and are left feeling as if we were the dregs from the spit bucket left in favor of the flashy new label or a 100-point rating. Perceived loyalty is often betrayed. But, we understand. We cannot possibly satisfy everyone's needs all the time. And there's competition; lots of competition, but please - just don't forget.

{ }

THE COMPETITION

I won't spend a lot of time on this topic. While I may allude to my competition in parts of this book, it's merely as a reference rather than a focal point.

There's competition in almost every facet of life, especially in America; it's what helps make this country great. Without competition, any entity can have total control leading to limitations, lack of diversity, stagnation, and an imbalance of power, often resulting in price gauging and corruption. Utah's model of alcohol control is a classic example.

The broker world is small in Utah and Wyoming. When I started in 2003, there were around ten brokers in Utah doing 98% of the business - some were small one-person entities, some were two to six-person brokerages, and the largest brokerage employed approximately twelve salespeople encompassing both their liquor and wine-selling divisions along with administrative positions.

Since building relationships with accounts was the primary focus, I never really had the time to worry about what the other brokers or their sales reps were doing; I just kept my head down concentrating on the business I could control. I knew the limitations of my portfolio and my time constraints. If I didn't have a product that fit a category or niche an account was looking for, I simply acknowledged the shortcoming and moved on to another category or topic. It's very difficult to be everything for everybody with a small portfolio.

A couple of more important tidbits I learned in the beginning: never bad-mouth another broker because they may be on your team at some point, or worse... be your boss one day. And never bad-mouth a competitive brand because you may have to represent it, sell it, and even drink it.

WINO EVENTS

WINE-RELATED EVENTS CAN BE FUN, entertaining, and informative. If you enjoy wine, the chances are good that at some point in your imbibing life, you may have been to a winemaker dinner, a food & wine festival, charity event, or even stumbled upon an afternoon tasting at your local wine shop or market (where legal, of course).

An experience of this sort can reintroduce you to an old friend in the way of a wine you may have not had in years, or lead to an "a-ha moment" discovering a new varietal, region, or style, or even uncovering a winemaking factoid that when enthusiastically recited in future discussions shows how well-versed you've become as a budding oenophile. Wine events are a place to be social, relax, let go and let the good times roll. However, be careful, as one step across the line can lead to extreme embarrassment. Slurred speech, stumbling around drunk, soiling yourself, or passing out is a sure way to get your picture splashed across the internet or target you as the brunt of jokes around the office cooler or your own neighborhood.

Furthermore, stating untrue tidbits or answering questions incorrectly may essentially back you into a corner for a browbeating by someone possessing more wine knowledge under their pinky fingernail than you will have in a lifetime. Yes, a little knowledge can go a long way as you ease along the path of discovery, so stay with what you know and above all, do not embellish or improvise. As my father always told me: *It doesn't matter how great you think you are, there's always someone out there that's richer, stronger, faster, and smarter - so stay humble.*

As oppressed as Utah is in all thing's alcohol, it surprises many people that we too have wine events; it's just that there are a lot more hoops to jump through to adhere to public safety laws, liquor laws, and local rules. Sure, permits and such are required in other states, but hosting a wine event in Utah is a lot like building a minimum-security prison that can be broken down and resurrected the same time the following year.

The Park City Food and Wine Festival, for example, is run by an out-of-state entity that starts the process of licensing, permits, and contracts many months before an event can come to fruition. A lot is spent in the way of money, advertising, and time. God forbid a liquor license application gets hung up, or worse, rejected by the Mormon-majority-led liquor commission. Liquor licenses, banquet licenses, and license extensions all must be completed before an event opens its doors for its short lifespan. In Utah, specific areas must be cordoned off admitting only ticketed or invited guests, 21 years or older, of course. Festival-goers are not allowed to take alcohol out of these zones, and often everyone must wear a wrist-band to prove age and payment, usually administered by a volunteer so tightly that blood supply is cut off resulting in hands becoming the very shade of purple in the glass. At some events, only a prescribed number of drinks are allowed, while others can resemble a mosh pit of drunken fools throwing back booze rather than elbows.

Since there is no such thing as free alcohol in Utah, anything donated must be handled per the set state laws, meaning the event or account must purchase said wine, liquor, or beer at the state retail price, then the broker or supplier may issue a check to reimburse the incurred expenses. As one can imagine, paying retail for donated products can get very expensive, but as I have learned, there is a cost of doing business in every state; it just so happens that in Utah, it amounts to exacting a "pound of flesh." (Shakespeare 1596) Does this happen by the book all the time? Yes, for the most part, but if in a pinch, no one is really going to find out if a broker drops off the cases at a private event unless it's monitored by the DABC; something that's physically impossible because they don't have enough manpower to police every event or infraction in the state.

Aside from the festivals and such, there are no shortages of charity events looking for alcohol donations to offset their costs; there is no better way to loosen up their guests, pry open their wallets, and increase overall profitability, than free alcohol. I know this firsthand because I have woken up with buyer's remorse on more than one occasion accompanied by the requisite hangover. But alas, I tell myself, "It's for charity, grow a pair." The most amusing phrase after the heat of the bidding war is over is when the auctioneer closes with, "Congratulations, the winner is...." Or, "You had the highest bid – Congratulations, you've won..." As Americans, are we so competitive that outbidding someone is considered winning? I guess, in some cases.

Charities come crawling out of the woodwork every year working their spiel and offering enticements as an ideal opportunity to showcase wines to their well-heeled guests.

"It's bound to increase your sales," they say. But after the last bottle is poured or shot is thrown back, the now broke guests usually depart too buzzed to remember a label or a name. And while there are many charity events that deserve attention, regrettably, it's impossible to donate to them all, so picking and choosing the right ones through the course of a year is imperative. After all, almost any opportunity to get people to taste a product may help sales.

The first charity event or fundraiser I took part in was with the *Reparatory Dance Theater* of Salt Lake City, a fundraiser called Charrette, which they told me was a loose French term for "impromptu." Since I was still new and learning the ropes, I simply bought the product, then dropped it off. To reciprocate, the nice folks at RDT gave me four tickets in return for four cases of wine. Once I arrived with a date and some friends, we mingled with the crowd drinking the wines I had donated. While walking around, I ran into the compliance officer who had helped me with my broker's license. After handshakes and pleasantries, he said, "Do you represent the wines being poured tonight?"

"Why yes," I said, proud of the fact that my wines were being showcased.

"Did they buy the product, or did you?"

Not thinking that anything was out of line, I stated, "Well, I did of course!"

"Hmm, do you know that what you did was illegal?"

"Uh, no. I had no idea."

After a brief pause and look of concern, he said, "Please stop by my office first thing Monday."

"Shit, am I in trouble?"

"Well, just stop by my office please."

Oh great, I thought to myself, how am I going to get out of this? I couldn't enjoy the show and I was a mess for the rest of the weekend. All I could think of was that I could be fined (or even worse, have my license suspended) because I broke a law that I should have known.

The following Monday, I arrived at the DABC offices for my meeting. After being buzzed through the main door, I knocked on the door jamb and poked my head around the corner into the gentlemen's office.

"Oh, come in Spartacus," he said. "Great show Saturday night. It looked like everyone was enjoying the wines."

"Yes, it was a fine event, but I guess I did something wrong?"

"Yes, you did." He went on to further explain the proper protocol for donating alcoholic beverages.

"So, am I in trouble?"

"Oh... I think since you're so new, you deserve a break, so consider this a warning. In the future, please just check with me or any of the other compliance officers beforehand. Deal?" he said while holding out his hand, which I gladly shook. He then gave me a small packet of papers. "This should explain the ins and outs of donations and a few other points that need consideration."

"Oh, thank God," I said. "And thanks for the warning, it won't happen again."

Driving away, I felt relieved I was given a break. I expected the worse but received a hall pass. Two lessons learned: handle donations correctly, and if you're in a time crunch or just lazy that day, at least don't tell anyone.

Each year usually starts with a bang as Park City hosts the Sundance Film Festival during the last two weeks of January. This event is its own special pile of bullshit, in part because it's a mostly private "who you know" type of event that grants access to the dinners, parties, and after-hours clubs. It's a time that Utah and Park City bask in the international spotlight. Fans, movie stars, directors, producers, and their minions descend on Park City to support independent films and jockey to sell a well-made low-budget movie for a large sum. Along with the A-listers, there are numerous wine, beer, and liquor companies donating tens of thousands of dollars' worth of products, hoping that a celebrity will be photographed with their brand. A photo of this sort is usually worth millions of impressions often resulting in higher sales. Club owners from Las Vegas, L.A., and New York set up shop renting out art galleries, hotel suites, and any space they can convert into private pop-up lounges for performances by some of the world's top country, rap, rock, and pop groups. Amateur singers, songwriters, and performers of all genres vie for their big break.

As is common with any major event, there is a dark side: bootlegging, broken laws, DUIs, and fighting often equaling time in the Summit County Jail. And aside from a few unsavory individuals, it's generally a good time. Fans and locals try their best to get movie tickets or seats in busy restaurants just to get a glimpse or perhaps rub elbows with the rich and famous. For two solid weeks, it's a daily shit show of delusion parading up and down Main Street, Park City, USA.

The infuriating part of the festival is that even though it

takes place at the same time each year, almost every company waits until the last minute to try to get their product into the state. A state that cares very little, if at all, about promoting alcohol. What many suppliers don't understand is: all alcoholic beverages above 4% alcohol by volume (5% after November 2019) must go through the DABC, so it is accounted for and taxed properly. If a product is not carried and warehoused by the DABC, then it needs to be special ordered through the special-order desk, a one-person show. Over time, the demand for special orders has soared to new heights due to the dramatic growth of the state, so purchase orders often take weeks before they are generated. Once the purchase order is generated, it can then take several more weeks to months before the product arrives. It's very rare to get an email or phone call prior to mid-December from a supplier about a possible sponsorship of a party or event at Sundance. Due to the start of the ski season and the holidays, the DABC is overwhelmed trying to keep up with ordering and expediting the existing state-listed products in their warehouse, so they have little time to deal with the special orders for the festival. Suppliers tend to overlook this process, which often requires their product be delivered via UPS or FedEx, costing them exorbitant shipping charges to ensure it's at the events on time. And these charges, dear reader, usually get passed on to you in the form of higher prices. Yes, Utah enjoys the notoriety and money that the Sundance Film Festival brings but it's a dreadfully painful experience.

Following closely behind the Sundance Film Festival is the Red, White, and Snow Event hosted each year by the

National Ability Center, again, in fabulous Park City. The National Ability Center (or NAC) is truly a great charity because they help people with disabilities excel in all facets of life, especially outdoor and recreational activities.

Each year the NAC hosts winemakers, winery owners, and chefs over a long weekend filled with skiing, snowboarding, and wining and dining. Sadly, I only participated in this event a handful of times; I think in part because my main competitor wanted the lion's share of exposure for themselves. But I can't blame them really, there are only a limited number of events to showcase high-end products in Utah.

One NAC event in particular, stands out from the rest. I was asked by the sommelier from Stein Erikson Lodge if I could donate and talk about several wines paired with food donated by the property for a wealthy local socialite hosting a few dozen of her friends. All proceeds from the dinner would go to the NAC. Since Stein Erikson Lodge is one of the best wine-selling accounts in Utah, I said, "Absolutely, I'll be there!"

On the day of the big event, a Friday night, dressed in a white French-cuff shirt and dinner jacket, I gathered the wines and my tasting notes to make the short journey from Salt Lake City to Park City with my date. As I approached the top of Parley's Summit on I-80, the mountain pass leading to Park City, a loud noise began emanating from my SUV. Upon pulling over to inspect the car, I found that one of my rear tires had blown. Perfect timing – the event was forty-five minutes from starting. At least it was now March, so there was still enough light to see what I was doing, however as it was the tail end of winter, the air cooled significantly with the setting sun. Thirty minutes later, which is record time for me to change a tire, I limped into Park City with my pants soiled, French cuffs ruined, and hands that were frozen to the bone.

I apologized profusely upon arrival at Stein Erikson Lodge but was told that none of the guests had arrived, which seemed strange. Not to worry, the sommelier stated, she is a good customer – they should be along soon. While waiting in the banquet room I made small talk with the staff and the chef, who happened to stop in to see if the event had started. After thirty minutes passed, I began to get impatient. Several calls to the host of the party and the NAC went unanswered. After an hour, the dinner was called off. Disappointed and bewildered, I offered the staff a few bottles of wine as a consolation for not making any money that evening. Deciding to make the most of it, my date and I sat down for an enjoyable dinner before heading back to Salt Lake City.

The next morning, I received a call from the hostess of the party – she was completely mortified. Somehow, she had confused her dates thinking the dinner was Saturday night instead of Friday night. "It's okay," I said, trying to console her. "I've done similar things in the past."

"Thank you, but no, you don't understand," she sobbed. "Most of my guests are from out of town – they're flying in today specifically for this event. I feel like such an ass!"

She offered to pay for my time and the wines, but I declined. I consoled her again, then hung up. I found out later that week that she was so horrified, she actually paid Stein Erikson Lodge and tipped the servers for a dinner she didn't have, plus she made a large donation to the NAC. As it would appear, sometimes money can buy you class.

{ }

One of my least favorite events each year is the Park City Food and Wine Festival, for many reasons. Since it's run by an out-of-state outfit, the profits do not stay in Utah. We brokers donate tens of thousands of dollars in product and our time pouring wine at several events over a three-day weekend. But the folks who run the festival have a hard time reciprocating, often doling out a very limited amount of event tickets that brokers can give away to accounts or family and friends. It's very frustrating when an account buyer asks for tickets, but we have to turn them down.

When I first started as a wine broker in 2003, I enjoyed pouring wine at the event, partly because of the interesting people I encountered. Also, an actual wine buyer may be attending, so it was another way to get them to sample the products. Whenever I poured at the event, it was a sure bet that I had a few bottles of really expensive, great wine behind the table, so if a buyer did happen by, I could lure them in with a taste. However, it's important to note that when pouring an expensive bottle, do so stealthily because if the public catches on, there will be a bum rush.

After several years behind the table pouring wines, I began to loathe the events, mostly because of the many moronic people that seem to show up year in and year out. Dealing with the attendees is its own distinct form of punishment. Don't get me wrong, most are generally well behaved, nevertheless, there is a segment of people that probably should be required to take etiquette lessons before entering such a setting:

"The Know It All" – These individuals are usually very well off and well-traveled. They possess a decent amount of wine knowledge, mostly highlights for conversation

purposes to show off their worldliness, but they're jaded. When pouring them a dose of wine and reciting a quick story about the product, they usually interrupt because they must impress with long-winded anecdotes of their favorite wines, wineries, winemakers, etc. Typical questions from the Know It All include: "Have you ever tried XYZ wine?" If your reply is no, they often remark in pity, "You really should. I know the winemaker personally." Or, one of my personal favorites, "I have a friend of a friend of a friend that owns BFD winery, they gave me a few bottles - it's wonderful. You should call them to see about representing their products." I know they're only trying to make small talk or to help by somehow doing me a favor, but honestly, I have enough business already. Trust me, I'm a professional. Chances are, if I haven't heard of the winery, then it most likely may not be worth my time and effort.

"The Drunk" – These individuals can be spotted a mile away. Staggering, slurring words, forgetting sentences, shirt laden with wine and food stains, or even having purple teeth are a dead giveaway. These individuals are there for the party, not to learn or discover anything. Wine festivals aren't cheap; they feel that since they paid a fee, they're entitled to as much alcohol as they can pour down their pie hole before last call. When poured a taste, which is usually around an ounce, they scoff, asking for more or even sometimes saying, "Filler up!" while holding the stem of the wine glass in their fist so firm they may pulverize it back into sand. At the end of an event, they are often seen frantically running table to table, begging for one last glass before the wines are pulled. Pitiable and pathetic.

"The BBD Girls (Bigger, Better Deal Girls)" – Women only in this group. "Fuck me" heels, strappy sandals or cowboy boots, halter tops, tight jeans, Daisy Dukes, and

see-through blouses topped with a cowboy hat and aviator shades are the preferred uniforms. Roving in packs, usually taking selfies or sending texts, they bat their eyes, purse their perfectly dressed lips, flick their hair, and even sometimes offer an innuendo to try and coax a larger pour. These good-time gals are social butterflies always looking, hunting, and scavenging for the bigger or better deal, and it certainly is not you, dear wine broker. Self-assured and aloof, they barely listen when told about the wine they're drinking, often asking over and over, "What was it you poured me?" The slightest movement from across the room or plaza can capture their interest before they can upload their selfies, snap a picture of the label or scan the QR code.

"The Granola" – The scent usually arrives first, most often their own musky body odor, but sometimes disguised with patchouli making it extremely difficult for others to discern if the aroma in their glass is pleasant or offensive. "Do you have anything organic?" they ask. Though I do have organic wines in my portfolio, I have failed to bring any on this particular day. Quickly I scan the bottles, searching my mind for anything that may work. When I tell them I only have a few that are sustainable and one over here that's bio-dynamic, they smirk and reply in horror, "If it's not organic, it's not going in my body!" Though incredulous, I briefly think to myself: *Maybe, just maybe they're right. What with all the additives and flavorings put into wine these days – who the hell knows what'll happen to us? Maybe a three-headed purple wine monster will pop out of us one day in search of chemically-laden grape juice.*

"The Indecisive" – Hemming and hawing, they approach the table, bending over to look at every label, blocking the rest of the crowd, for no one knows what they'll do next. "Whatcha got?" they ask, swaying back and forth or twirling their wine glass. *Did you not just read every fucking label, you imbecilic turd?* I think to myself as I take a big breath. Okay, I will inform them. I will help them decide. I'll help them explore and expand their horizons - it's my duty as a wine broker. "What do you like?" I ask. The worst answer often follows: "Something sweet." And the other dreaded response, "I don't know..." Argh! After further stimulating conversation, taking my best shot, I offer them a wine I think may work. (Keep in mind other people are waiting for their turn at this point, and the line is building.) Describing the wine in simple details, offering little tidbits they can understand, I wait as they sip, watching for any indication of success – a smile, a raised brow, more swaying back and forth, or even lifting their glass for more. But sadly, rejection often follows as they pour the wine into the dump bucket and walk away – another "ungrapeful" customer.

There is also a plethora of other individuals encountered at wine festivals that display some characteristics from the aforementioned factions or even fall into their own categories with their own quirks. I abhor the individual that lifts their glass to stop me from pouring too much wine, not for their responsible approach, but the actual act of lifting the glass and pushing the wine bottle up is insolent – they should just say how much they want before it's poured. And, then there are the folks who wear the wine lanyards around their necks (usually made of leather, the lanyard holds the glass of wine against their chest so they can use their phone, talk, and eat) multi-tasking at a low level, for one false step is a sure way to spill wine all over everything. I'm sure the creators of the wine lanyard have made a pretty penny from the invention, but it serves no real purpose other than to make these poor souls appear to be doofuses.

Then there are the over-stimulated. These hormonally

elevated deviants cannot wait to get home for the foreplay to start. Inhibitions lifted by their wine buzz, they grope, kiss, and are sometimes caught fornicating under a blanket on the grass, behind a curtain, or in one of the bathrooms.

Yes, to get through the Park City Food and Wine Festival is a huge achievement. In my opinion, some sort of commendation aside from an "atta-boy" should be granted the victors, for it's truly a futile exercise in patience.

I have been fortunate, and even somewhat unfortunate, to have attended literally dozens upon dozens of winemaker dinners. I get propositioned countless times during the year by restaurants looking for some action; a ringer to bring in the customers. Some dinners are excellent with a considerable amount of time, effort, and thought behind the pairings, while others are ghastly excuses, usually on the culinary end as the chef forces the pairings out with no time to spare. In these cases, thank God for the wine, which is really its own food group, if need be.

Some dinners are drunk-fests, while others don't pour enough product. And sometimes the courses are so small, a stop at Micky D's is required on the way home. These miserly accounts fail to understand that a wine dinner should mostly be a loss leader for getting customers through the door; it's a time to showcase the food, service, and atmosphere to faithful regulars and unfamiliar guests, thus hopefully securing future visits in the process. Don't get me wrong, making a small profit is good, and it should never cost more money than taken in, but let the other days bring home the bacon; buckle up, put on a show, and wow them!

Overall, winemakers are fascinating people. The best ones know when to interrupt each course; they are animated and tell clear, concise stories and anecdotes to enhance the sometimes-dry parts of the winemaking process. Hearing about terroir, oak aging, concrete tanks, soil and how it influences the winemaking process is great, but when the speech drifts into phenolics and chemical compounds, it can lose a crowd rapidly.

When I conduct said dinners, I never think to impersonate a winemaker, for they have experience and knowledge second to none. I usually put my own spin on such a gathering, giving just enough information to hopefully transcend the drunkenness, resulting in future sales when the attendees foggily reflect while searching their wine stores shelves.

Oh…, and lastly, when attending wino events, please try to remember to drink some water or coffee (or something other than alcohol), preferably one glass of water for every glass of wine. And if you cannot or do not remember, at the very least, please don't drive.

SUPPLIERS

SUPPLIERS COME IN MANY FORMS: small independent wineries, breweries, or distilleries to those of the large independent variety; small import companies to massive ones; small conglomerates with a modest selection of brands to behemoths with substantial selections often even owning some or all of the brands they represent, import, market, and sell within the United States. Regardless of the size of the operation, there are a few things that most suppliers have in common:

1) *They all think their brands are the best, and they deserve the most attention.*
2) *They are long on promises in an effort to sell cases of their product, but often fall short on delivery.*
3) *All are extremely demanding.*

The greed factor rises exponentially in relation to the size of the entity. Not necessarily so much with the small independent wineries, importers, breweries, and distilleries because they're just trying to survive while attempting to gain (or maintain) a foothold in a highly saturated market.

But eventually, it can even happen to them. Some gain that foothold, building themselves into a well-known brand then selling out their marketing rights (or even ownership) to a major corporation, and so, the greed factor escalates. Why is this? Well, the bigger the company, the greater the need to produce sales to sustain infrastructure, growth, and distribute profits to their owners and/or shareholders. Often the mantras for most major companies become, "We deserve the most market share because of who we are," and, "Our brands sell, so by selling more of our brands, your profits will soar," or, "We're outpacing our competition on every forefront, so justifiably we require more of your attention." However, as the avaricious need to produce sales increases, many companies often forget; they lose focus, even bastardize the very thing that allowed them to ascend to their current position – frequently quality is traded for gluttony, then sales begin to suffer.

Many suppliers have a driver brand or multiple that they sell mass amounts of, thus allowing them to also have niche brands or more expensive brands so they can access a broader account base. For instance, Banfi had *Riunite*, which after years of big profits, allowed them to buy Castello Banfi in Tuscany and produce higher-end wines. Gallo has a bevy of drivers such as *Barefoot, Redwood Creek, Turning Leaf, Andre, Tisdale,* and more; the profits allowing them to create more brands and swallow up other wineries to bolster their ever-growing empire to include *William Hill, J, Talbot,* and others. Deutsch has *Yellow Tail*, Kendall Jackson its *VR* line of wines, Shaw Ross has *Blue Nun*, Palm Bay has *Cavit* and *Roscato*, MHUSA has Champagne and sparkling wine along with liquor, and so on and so on.

{ }

THE TERRITORY

Depending on the size and chintziness of a supplier, they will give their unlucky new sales reps Utah and Wyoming as part of a territory included with larger states within the same geographic region such as Arizona, New Mexico, Colorado, Idaho, and Montana, or even Oregon and Washington. No one really wants Utah or Wyoming in their territory; they're a pain in the ass with too many rules and regulations, so it's usually just handed to them to deal with – It's the equivalent of being sent to time-out or being put on KP duty in the military. It's one thing if you're tasked with selling soda pop and diapers in Utah – something Mormons can't do without – and entirely another if your job is selling a sinful product.

The common thread among most supplier representatives is that they are never around for very long. It's a transient business, often moving up or lateral, or to a new supplier in another market, forever looking for the bigger, better deal. Supplier reps are really gung-ho in the beginning; they want to show their new bosses they can make a difference even in the tough markets of Utah and Wyoming. Market visits, conference calls, bi-monthly and quarterly business reviews are all the norm. But usually, after several months, far too often, the restrictions of dealing with both control states turn them off, so they tend to just do the bare minimum until they fade away. Only when business starts to seriously suffer will a supplier rep resurface; most of the time, it is too late.

{ 🍾 }

MARKET VISITS

Supplier representatives often want to pay a "market visit" to their territory to help with their brands and promote sales so they can make their goals and ultimately their bonus – and more importantly, keep their jobs. A market visit usually entails meeting with the state buyers, a visit to several state liquor stores to survey the shelf set-up and competition, staff meetings, and meeting with several restaurants. A market visit might also include a review outlining current business to-date in relation to goals, or a review of the results from the previous year and outlining new goals and priorities. Sometimes they may even host a wine dinner.

Before the arrival of any supplier, it is imperative to "stage" or dress up the market by making sure their retail products are displayed properly within the specific area of competition; the products are dusted off, faced, and have shelf-talkers highlighting press or ratings. It's also very important to make sure that a few restaurants have one or many of their brands on the wine list for purchase. Sounds pretty simple, but dealing with the state store managers, limited product supply, and getting several restaurants to carry certain wines is a pretty tough job. If any of these areas are not up to the standards of said supplier, criticism is sure to follow.

Meeting with the buyers at the DABC is mostly just an exercise in futility because they usually will not promise or commit to anything, and they are not allowed to accept any "gifts" as they work for the state government. During a meeting with the buyers, suppliers will often ask, "What are you looking for?" The single most common answer from the state buyers: "Nothing. (Long pause) ... What do you got?"

The buyers know they sit in the catbird seat since they're a monopoly without competition. They know that if a supplier cannot give them what they want, they can simply find an alternative product from someone willing to work with them. Most will brag about the next hot craze, a brand that's "on fire" or that their juice "over-delivers for the price." They like to talk about the latest press on their brands, the success of their company, or about the millions of cases they have sold of a particular product. They are looking for some type of opening or an inclination that sparks the buyer's interest, hopefully creating a sale. The buyers, however, usually just listen patiently without making a commitment to anything. They want to decide on their own behind closed doors, reviewing the product info, pricing, supplier performance, and overall fit to the store shelves before making a decision.

Supplier or market visits can be many things: constructive, informative, effective, ineffective, controversial, aggravating, productive, offensive, defensive, loose, driven, social, meet and greet, party down, friendly, and even adversarial – or any combination thereof. I've witnessed them all. And when the end of the market visit finally arrives, no matter the outcome, the anxieties subside, accompanied with a big sigh of relief as the supplier reps fly out of town.

However, it's not over by any means. Once the supplier leaves the market, it's almost a sure thing that they'll send a "recap" of their visit, copying all bosses and supervisors involved. The recap sends a message to their superiors that they've been out in the market doing their jobs, making placements, working the broker's butt off, and demanding more from them. (Job justification.) The recap is usually in bullet-point format, including a number of particular "deficiencies" or "opportunities" for the broker to work on. A good supplier may even follow up a few months after the recap to find out if any of the bullet points had been corrected or achieved. In truth, most suppliers only send the recap then let the follow-up go by the wayside.

Example of the recap market visit from a supplier:

Good morning,
As you know, your market has been a priority for our company for 2017. The sales year-to-date have not been indicative of the time, energy, and money put forth to build our business. I want complete devotion on how we grow depletions and on-premise distribution. It is a big ask - I get it. I want you and your team to let me know what it will take to get the job done. I understand that we need to be aggressive and creative in how we build our presence. Please let me know what market support you need to make these numbers. I have listed some of my thoughts below on some of the accounts we need to be in. I need to know if these suggestions can be accomplished ASAP.

Montage Hotel - We only had one wine on the entire list. I didn't see any spirits either. We need at least one BTG (by the glass) and four bottles of vital high-end items. The wine list is enormous - there are many opportunities here; please present everything within reason and do not take no for an answer.

Waldorf Astoria – Yes, it's a national account, but you need to be creative in showcasing "limited time/seasonal offerings." Anything that could get a foot through the door and open up opportunities for the property to separate itself from the other extravagant hotels in the market.

Downstairs - Pouring our White Zinfandel, but that's it! Nice to have the placement, but assuming we are not selling much because it's a bar? The place was very busy. We need three wines by the glass at minimum and all our liquors.

Silver – Seems like they don't like us? WTF? You need to get involved! Need 45% of BTG in four months, then solid progress all year. Why is this so difficult?

The Brew Pub - I know it's primarily a beer account, but it's a perfect low-hanging fruit candidate – make it happen!

SUPPLIER SPEAK

Just like any other business, people who sell alcohol use a plethora of acronyms, verses, and slang that are thrown around as often as monkeys fling their own poop. When I first started selling wine, I watched, listened, and paid attention. As time went by, I began to pick up on certain terms and phraseology, some of which make sense and some that are just plain abused out of a lack of other words or terms to support conversations. Terms such as: game-changer, grow your business, market share, dealer loader, aligned with priorities, carve out some time, low-hanging fruit, PODS (or points of distribution), VAP (or Value-Added Package), market blitz, and CHEERS just to name a few that dominate each day's email chains and phone calls. The first time I used "push-back" or "brand is on fire" or "the wine over-delivers," I felt like I belonged; that I was somehow now qualified to employ all the terms and phrases I was hearing from other industry members. (And, I did use them because it's part of the lingual requirements to work in this field. However, as time progressed, I found that I was just another monkey.)

CHASING THE CASE

Most suppliers have a team they employ and refer to as their National Account Teams. National Accounts are chains such as notable restaurants like Outback Steakhouse, Applebees, Olive Garden, California Pizza Kitchen, PF Chang's, Hilton Hotels, Kimpton Hotels, etc., and grocery stores, liquor stores, ballpark concessions, airport outlets, sports arenas, and so on. A National Account Team's sole job is to pitch products they represent to the chains, often making deals on pricing that coincide with the amount purchased or even coming up with a private label that may reflect the name of said operation. This can be a very big deal to a supplier because it can equate to thousands or tens of thousands of cases in volume. Chains want to have the exact same menu at every location, so their loyal customers are assured that wherever they are, they can get the same service, food, and drink to which they are accustomed.

Now, National Accounts are all well and good, and I'm sure their recipe may work for many people, but not this hombre. You see, when I visit another town, I want to try the local flavor: different foods, local beers, wines, and ciders. I mean really, why even leave the goddamn house if you plan on eating and drinking the same crap you consume day in and day out?

The biggest problems that the National Account Teams

face is ensuring adequate supply and pricing (which can vary by state) and making sure that 100% of all the units within the chain comply. Because of this, National Accounts are somewhat of a conundrum for Utah and Wyoming because each state cannot carry every single wine, liquor, or beer that is required on the many mandated product lists; they simply do not have the warehouse space.

The products that National Accounts will carry during a year can either be mandatory or in some cases, optional placements. Most of the time, when I tell a National Account sales rep a product is not carried by either state, their response is something like this: "Well then, this placement should help get the item listed with the state so the account can readily have access – right?" After explaining that neither Utah nor Wyoming gives two shits about National Account placements and they will not just bring in a product to support a National Account program, they're dumbfounded; it's hard for them to believe they can't get their way – I would even go as far as calling some of them National Account Nazis! These folks will email, call, and text until the product is on a purchase order for an account. Then they will call, email, and text until the product arrives and the account has actually made the purchase. I have to hand it to them – they're very good at follow-up, but they're as annoying as a case of poison ivy or a pesky ingrown toenail.

Due to pricing and availability problems in Utah and Wyoming, National Accounts are given some autonomy to massage or augment their wine, liquor, and beer lists. Even though a National Account can place a special order with the liquor division in either state to legally obtain products and comply with the rest of the country, they must order in full cases; a process that can sometimes take up to 4 – 8 weeks for the product to be delivered. That said, if a restaurant has a wine on their list that's a special order and they run out, they run the risk of having to tell every patron that they are out of said product, which makes them look inadequate. Likewise, a grocery chain could have a similar problem with an empty shelf while waiting for a special order to arrive. And because National Account placements are negotiated each year, it's very possible for an account to be stuck with leftover bottles of something they had to buy full cases of via special order the year prior (which if the product is expensive, can be a big problem; thus the reason for autonomy).

In the end, all suppliers are guilty. They just want to dominate; each supplier wants total control and the utmost attention. They constantly look for opportunities to make a sale and steal market share from their competitors. The wine, liquor, and beer business is highly cutthroat and competitive due to the recurring disposable needs of the public. As time evolves, so do supplier initiatives in order to counter and create trends and innovation so they can remain at the forefront to the end consumer. Suppliers prey upon the weaknesses of their competitors in efforts to capitalize and gain momentum and market share, ultimately hoping to ascend to a higher rung on the ladder and dominate the industry.

PRESS, RATINGS, AND THE COST OF YOUR WINE

"WHY DOES A CERTAIN WINE COST MORE THAN ANOTHER?" and "Why are some wines so expensive?" are questions I've often been asked by people wanting to know why one bottle could cost seven dollars yet another of the same grape hundreds or thousands. Their next questions are usually, "Is it really that good?" and "Can you really tell a difference?"

The reasons are simple: Supply and demand, along with whatever the market will bear. And, as far as taste? Yes, you can tell a difference. A commercial mass-production wine costing $9.99 can be made every day of the year, bottled fresh, then shipped to market, employing a specific recipe for unsuspecting consumers. Smaller production wines are produced from the most premium vineyard sites on the planet, where terroir and micro-climates, along with the art of crafting and making the wine (frequently aged in expensive oak barrels) contribute to the final cost. Plus, it just plain takes longer to make great, highly rated sought-after wines – often several years.

A lot of overhead costs come into play when producing

a wine – even low-end mass-produced wine: packaging, importing fees, shipping charges, salaries, incentives, samples, marketing & promotion, expense accounts; profits for the winery, distributor, and retailer; even gas for the owner's Lear jet and maintenance on their Ferraris. Ultimately, all of this is passed onto the lucky consumer. Which begs the question: Could a $30 bottle of wine actually be worth less than $12 after all the layers of greed, shipping, taxes, marketing, and everything else are stripped off? You betcha.

A high rating from a respected international publication will help drive demand and prices – And the supplier, importer or retailer know it. Ratings and accolades are bestowed upon wines by folks of a seeming nobility unlike any other in the wine world. (Hopefully, it's their palate on display rather than their agenda.) Publications such as Wine Spectator, Wine Enthusiast, Wine Advocate, California Wine Connoisseur, and many others all judge wines; some include spirits or beers, and even cigars. It's their duty to their subscribers, whether industry professional or end consumer, to provide a fair rating and description with unbiased, unprejudiced, or preconceived notions so that a sound decision can be made by the customer.

But are all the publications really unbiased? Some lure us in with full-page full-color glossy ads of wine country, barrel rooms, scantily clad women with a glass of wine, fancy cars, vines, soil, chateaus, and culinary delights. These magazines impress the reader with a lifestyle; they make wine sexy, leaving the reader yearning, wanting, desiring. Though I cannot say for sure, I've heard that spending a pile of money with a few of the aforementioned publications will help guarantee a decent rating (whether that's true or not is entirely up for speculation, for they will never admit to such depravities). Most of these publications are fine, and they do a reasonable job engaging the consumer. In fact, I happen to enjoy them for the stories about wineries, winemakers, techniques, and regions. But the no-frills publications are the ones I look closely at; they pull no punches, for they rely on subscriptions rather than ads to pay their bills. It's fairly easy to deduce – just order a copy of California Wine Connoisseur, find a well-known California wine, then compare the rating with Wine Enthusiast or Wine Spectator. My bet is that there's a marked difference. If you're a winemaker submitting wines to California Wine Connoisseur, you better have thick skin, a sense of humor, and be damn sure your best effort is in that bottle because anything subpar will be detected, followed by a serious vocabulist shellacking.

An example of how ratings boost prices would be the story of *Chateau St Jean Cinq Cepages*. The 1995 vintage scored 93 points with Wine Spectator at an average retail price of $24. The extremely good rating for such a low-priced wine increased interest and sales for the wine exponentially. The next vintage scored 88 points, but due to demand for the previous vintage, the price had already moved up slightly. Sales may have softened a bit with the next vintage's rating, but the bar had been set, so the price was not going down. The 1997 vintage received a 96-point rating from Wine Spectator in the November 2000 issue with a quoted average retail cost of $50. Thirteen thousand twelve-pack cases were produced, and if memory serves me right, it was also named *"Wine of the Year"* by the same publication, further driving up demand and the price. The average retail price doubled in just two vintages with just a few excellent ratings. Again, the pricing bar had been set, and there's only one way to go from there – up. The average price in 2018 ranged from $70 to $100, depending on the retailer. Good juice with high ratings drives demand, and depending on supply, the winery or supplier will raise prices to not only make more money but slow demand, so they don't run out (that is, until they figure out a way to produce more of the same wine – which, consequently, doesn't lower prices).

Ratings are often used as bargaining chips when a high score on a wine comes out in one of the many venerable publications. A distributor in an open state may say, "If you buy four cases of Bar Mat Pinot Grigio or eight cases of Toad Sweat Sauvignon Blanc, I'll get you a case of *Leonetti* – the 96-point wine," Or, "If you want some *Leonetti* you'll have to order a significant amount of Ass-juice Shiraz." However, this type of bargaining doesn't really go over very well with the buyers at the DABC; with no competition, they hold all the cards, so they simply take a stand by asserting something like, "Well, if you don't get me any *Leonetti* for the Utah shelves, you can tell that company that we aren't going to do business with them in the future on any of their wines." (Usually, after that statement, the DABC buyers get what they want.)

During my restaurant days as a wine buyer and manager, I visited California wine country on numerous occasions. Back then, and prior to the 2007 economic collapse, wineries rolled out the red carpet with complimentary room and board, food, and bottles upon bottles of courtesy wine. On one such visit during the summer of 1999, I witnessed something that changed my understanding and perception of the wine industry.

I was staying at Sutter Home Winery for a few nights. Sutter Home is not the most upscale winery due to their inexpensive line built around a very popular wine they helped create (White Zinfandel), but they are very hospitable. Sutter Home, however, is located smack dab in the middle of the most expensive wine region in America – Napa Valley, situated on old Highway 29. They have a majestic manor house and several rooms to accommodate guests that either pay to stay or are comp'd rooms for carrying their products. Sutter Home also employs several chefs to cook complimentary breakfast and lunch for their guests each day. When one stays at a winery, and it's comp'd, as with Sutter Home, it is essential to take the tour, taste the wines, and even buy some (they're hosting after all).

On this particular stay, after finishing breakfast, my guests and I waited patiently in the main foyer of the manor house with a few others to take the tour and taste wines. The hostess, a lovely woman, appeared with a tray of glasses half-full of Sauvignon Blanc. When everyone had a glass, she proceeded to give us a tour of the old house while explaining the heritage of Sutter Home Winery. Once finished with the tour, we climbed into a van and drove a short distance north of the manor house to what we were told would be the winery. After turning onto a side street, the van took another quick right turn into a driveway where we came to a stop in front of a large gate. After the gate opened, we were driven into a compound, housing what appeared to be more like a factory than a winery.

Standing in the hot sun, we were given another glass of white wine, then shown into the facility, which was indeed a winery, but with a massive factory feel – complete with crush pad, sorting line, bottling facility, and stainless-steel tanks larger than the bus we rode in on. The host showed us around, explaining each process until we ultimately ended up on the walkway above the lower level bustling with people. A bottling line was in full swing where workers filled every station on the line, each job a vital component to the end task. Empty bottles were loaded onto the line, cleaned, then filled with pinkish liquid (their very popular White Zinfandel), corked and labeled, then put into boxes to be shipped around the world. I watched blank-faced, amused at the precision with which the people and equipment worked. High above the busy bottling floor on one of the walls, a whiteboard had the numbers "91,431" written on it in red marker. I raised my hand and yelled loudly so I could be heard over the noise. "What does that number signify?"

"That's the current record for bottles filled, labeled, and packed into boxes in one day!"

We all looked at each other in shock. Exiting the factory (and the incessant clinking of bottles), still dumbfounded, we walked back to the van in a silence broken only by birds chirping and the distant sound of farm equipment. "How often do they bottle White Zinfandel?" I asked.

The host paused. "Well, that depends on what's needed – they bottle on demand. I really couldn't tell you, but I do know they bottle White Zinfandel every month of the year to satisfy demand."

"How is that possible when grapes are only harvested once per year?" I replied.

"Well, they're able to obtain a vast amount of juice each year from around the state, allowing them to freeze it in the tanks I showed you. When they need to produce and bottle wine, they simply bring the juice up in temperature, take it through fermentation, then bottle it."

Bewildered, because I'd never witnessed anything on that level before, I took my seat in the van to contemplate her answer and the scale of production. After we made our way out of the gate, I turned to look back at the facility. It was only then that I noticed the whole winery/factory was completely surrounded by very tall pine trees, no doubt planted to help muffle the sound and shield the repugnant exterior in the heart of one of the most beautiful valleys in the world.

This illustrates how a product is made efficiently and inexpensively, satisfying demand on an extremely large scale with a low cost per bottle to the consumer while still making a profit for the company. We did visit other wineries on this trip, both big and small, but none of them compared to the scale of Sutter Home. It was after this trip that I realized the difference in supply and demand. Or did I?

The following summer I found myself back in Napa Valley, this time at Phelps Winery eating a vineyard lunch with two close friends and a winery host. The host had brought six bottles of the latest releases for us to taste while we dined at a picnic table in the vineyard on the western exposure of the winery. As we sipped, the host spoke about the history of Joseph Phelps and about how each wine was produced. (The lunch was exquisite; there is no better way to taste than in the vineyard.)

After lunch, we tasted through the wines once again (which were, by the way, the lower to mid-tier priced offerings from Phelps), and the host returned with the marketing director. In his right hand, he held a current vintage of their finest wine, *Phelps Insignia,* and in his left, a bottle of their dessert wine called *Eisrebe.*

The marketing director poured a liberal amount of Insignia into each of our glasses (the 1997 vintage scored 100 points from famous wine critic Robert Parker). The price in the summer of 2000 with no discounts was $75 per bottle – considered pricey at the time but not out of reach by many. The director began to explain the unique qualities of Insignia, paying special attention to the select vineyards they used to make the blend along with the oak and aging process and the growing season that year. (He also added that they made 20,000 cases, causing me to do a double-take as I thought back to my Sutter Home visit where I'd witnessed such mass-scale production just a few short miles away for a cheap wine costing no more than $7 at the time.)

"How do you make such incredible wine on that massive of a scale and demand a premium price?" I marveled.

"Well, we haven't always made that much Insignia; we grew into it. Plus, we have some of the very best vineyards in Napa that comprise the Insignia blend and a massive winery that's able to ferment and age all the wine. Also, we possess a proven pedigree along with a loyal following that allows us to just about sell out every year, so we must be doing something right!"

I thought for a minute about the differences of Sutter Home and Phelps while the others talked and I savored my glass of Insignia before asking, "Do you anticipate a good 1998 and 1999 vintage?"

"Yes," he said, "but if I were you, I'd buy some of the 1997 vintage today while we have it; it's not often you get to taste and buy a 100-point wine. The price will go up to $125 per bottle with the next vintage."

"Wow, a $50 jump from one vintage to the next? How do you justify that when you make so much wine?"

"Well, as I said, the amount we make each year varies. A few years ago, we made less than 15,000 cases. The climatic conditions were related to what our vineyards were able to yield during that growing season. The 1997 vintage is the most we've ever produced, and as I said before, we have a pedigree of solid press and ratings." He paused for a moment while we contemplated his response before adding, "Plus, have you ever heard of the smaller boutique wineries like Colgin or Araujo?"

"Yes," I replied.

"Well, we figure that we're every bit as good. Insignia gets similar ratings and press, so if they can get the high prices that they demand, then we should command higher prices as well." With that, he stood and straightened his perfect tie as he gazed off into the vineyards for a brief moment. Before walking off, he said, "It was a pleasure to meet all of you; thanks for visiting Phelps. I do hope you'll buy some 100-point wine and some of the others. Have a safe trip back to Utah."

We thanked him and our host, and indeed, on our way out, we all bought some wine, including a few bottles of the 100-point wine. In retrospect, in fact, I wish we had bought one or two more bottles of the 1997 Insignia because it was undeniably incredible. Phelps Insignia now commands upwards of $250 plus per bottle, and I'm sure it's still quite amazing but given their attitude about pricing, I decided to never buy another bottle.

Although both wineries mass-produced their wine, Phelps was on a different level because they used premium grapes from first-class terroir-driven estate vineyard sites with an intense oak aging regimen (plus they had developed a loyal customer base, while Sutter Home used grapes from non-descript non-premium sites from all over California and maybe other places). Additionally, they didn't have to age their wine for several years in expensive oak barrels.

I was told by a friend in the industry that there is a simple equation when pricing wines, as I'm sure there is for beer and hard liquor as well. While supply and demand come into play, most of the time a three-tier system is used: COGs, or Cost of Goods, and transportation terms frequently called FOB, or Freight On Board, Distributor mark-up, and finally retail or restaurant margin. While I do understand that suppliers need to make a profit to make it worth their while (after all, would someone do it to lose money?), I've witnessed price gauging so blatant and extreme that I developed a disdain for certain brands.

The easiest way to know if your booze is overpriced: walk into a retail store (yes, even in Utah) and check out what's on sale. At any given time, there are always discounted products, and while they do generate higher overall sales, if the discount is significantly higher than its counterpart's discount, or it's "too good to be true," then it's overpriced – even if "on sale." Discounts are given in part to drive sales, but also to generate consumer pull over competitor brands – the impulse buy that will hopefully sway a person into being a regular customer, even when the product isn't discounted. Almost everything we buy in America has a frontline price – the manufacturer's recommended or retail price, which is whatever the market will bear. From butter to tires, to blue jeans and booze, most products will go on sale down from the front line in an effort not only to sell more cases/units but to catch the consumer's eye, and possibly a return buy. If a wine only sells when it's on sale (look for older vintages and dusty bottles), then it's a sign that the product is grossly over-priced, and a correction is needed on the front line. (More importantly, maybe you shouldn't be wasting your money?)

Pricing on imports can be also be misleading to inexperienced consumers. Aside from Bordeaux, importers usually have exclusivity with the brands they represent in America. With exclusivity and hopefully a decent rating from a wine publication, importers can name their price depending on supply and demand and competition from other products within the same shelf set. Just because a wine is foreign doesn't mean it should cost an arm or a leg. Importers search high and low for brands that they can buy inexpensively, then (with proper marketing and ratings) sell for a decent profit, many times even an obscene profit, depending on their scruples. One thing I've learned about imported wines is that the ratio of good quality terroir-driven authentic wine is higher than that of American made (often boardroom brand) counterparts under $15.

Then there is ego ...

A winery's ego can often get in the way of the ultimate goal – sales. For instance, at one point in my career, I represented both MHUSA and Pernod Ricard at the same time. MHUSA has the Champagne houses of *Veuve Clicquot* and *Moët & Chandon,* while Pernod Ricard imports *Mumm* and *Perrier Jouët.* I received a call from the Pernod Ricard rep one day asking for the current shelf price of *Veuve Clicquot Yellow Label* and *Moët Imperial.* After spouting off the prices, I said, "Why do you ask?"

To which he explained, "They're the market leader, so whenever they take a price increase, so do we."

I thought about it for a moment before replying. "Well, why don't you build sales up first by staying at a lower price then increase the price in a year or so after your customer base has grown?"

"Oh, we can't do that, we have to be on pace with them

at all times."

Confused, I said, "Umm... okay. Right now, you're five dollars less. The consumers will surely take notice. Wouldn't you rather sell a hundred cases at a lower price, building the brand against the leaders, rather than ten cases at the higher price?"

His final response? "I know it doesn't sound rational, but your logic is not part of the brand strategy. I'll be in touch regarding the increases once I finalize."

This sort of nonsense is confusing, in my opinion. I've watched hundreds of PowerPoint presentations regarding the launch of a new product, and they all say the same thing: "We want to be priced at and next to the market leader currently on the shelf." They're hoping consumers will pull their brand off the shelf rather than the market leader, and when it doesn't happen, the supplier is bemused (sometimes it's even attributed to the fault of the distributor or broker). The reality is, the position of the new product should be lower-priced, even significantly lower-priced, building sales to put the brand in a position to take over. Yes, incremental price increases are a turnoff, but the real consumer will stay with the brand – *if the juice is worth the squeeze.*

INNOVATION, TRENDS, BRANDS

FROM THIS POINT FORWARD, I've inserted tidbits on certain trends around the time they happened; a palate cleanser if you will, placed in between chapters to hopefully provide insight, a laugh, a breath of fresh air, or even maybe an a-ha moment.

Innovation occurs in every business. Creating something and capturing a segment or interest in a market prior to anyone else is how brands are made, and success is often measured. When successful innovation turns into a trend, the products that survive time become brands such as *Barefoot, Cavit, Ménage a Trois, Meiomi*, and *Josh Cellars*. As with other industries, the alcohol trade is notorious for introducing thousands of innovative products every year; taking chances by spending piles of money to grab market share in an attempt to create the next big trend. Each year, only a small amount of the innovation product that rises to the top will become a "true brand;" the rest will languish, unable to gain hold until finally discontinued by the very supplier that spent the piles of money to make an impression.

Trends often provide a quick jolt to the bottom line,

allowing an industry to capitalize on a hot new "must-have" craze that a large segment of the population eventually tries at least once. Trends encourage consumers to branch out from their sometimes-stagnant taste profile. Usually, the first to establish a trend collects the most market share until others arrive to undercut, over-deliver, and try to outdo the others. Depending on supply and demand, a trend quickly establishes what the market will bear price-wise. If a trend takes off, usually prices go up in an effort to slow down sales so supply can catch up. In the wine industry when prices go up, they usually don't come down, unless the trend becomes saturated, fizzles out, or gives way to another trend.

As a trend grows, quite often, most suppliers will begin to offer what are called line extensions within their other already established brands because it's an easy way to capitalize on a tried and true storyline instead of creating a whole new brand. A line extension is what it sounds like – simply taking an existing successful line or brand then adding the new trend, whatever it may be. The label and cache from the popular line or brand encourages consumers to try the new item because of the familiarity and trust they've come to have from buying the other wines within the line up.

Example: when Moscato took off, it seemed like everyone had to offer it – *Jacobs Creek, Barefoot, Cavit, Yellow Tail, Smoking Loon,* etc. The basic consumer did not really know or care that true Moscato comes from Italy, and Muscat is an ancient varietal, and that the wines are beautifully made, offering just a touch of sweetness but generally off-dry component. Because of the way Moscato was cleverly marketed, consumers only cared about the Americanized version that was shoved in their faces in every grocery store and wine shop – a cloying and cheap wine to get drunk on and satisfy their sweet tooth. A new trend can help stagnant brands boost sales, but at the end of the day, it's a lazy capitalistic approach to enrich and line a supplier's pockets. After line extensions come size extensions offering consumers smaller or larger versions to quench their thirst – never-ending exploitation.

The problem for both Utah and Wyoming when it comes to innovation is this: both state liquor control boards often react too slowly (and even sometimes not at all) to current market trends. Innovation and brand launching take place in the larger cities before making their way inland. Suppliers figure if they are successful in the larger markets, then it should eventually trickle into the smaller cities around the country. Since it can take quite a long time for a product to finally get listed and carried in either state, a trend could be dead in the big markets before they are even introduced in Utah and Wyoming and discontinued before even getting a chance.

I like to think of brands in two ways: "authentic" and "boardroom." An "authentic wine brand" comes from passionate, inventive, thoughtful, hardworking people with real stories, specific terroir, and techniques to create a product and literally make a living off the fruits of their labor. An authentic wine brand can be huge or small (or even "virtual" owning no land and possibly not even a winery.) But the one thing they have in common is the originality brought to the table. For example, take *Clos de La Fine Muscadet*, a very floral wine from the Loire region of France, five generations old – This wine, like other Muscadet from this region, is known for its acidity and structure pairing particularly well with local cheeses, oysters, and other shellfish; small brand and truly authentic. Or consider, *Fonterutoli Chianti Classico* owned by the Massei family since 1435, far and away one of the most prolific wines and wineries from Italy; this and its counterparts' pair specifically well with the local cheeses and their regional fare, bringing unmistakable authenticity to the consumers. People generally know what they are getting when they buy authentic brands – a reliable, tried and true test of quality, so the chances are extremely high it's going to be good. There are authentic American brands too, both large and small – most notably, colossal brand *Kendall Jackson Chardonnay*, a wine that everyone tries to copy but very few succeed in doing; a brand created with an accidental recipe built from a small foundation to become the best-selling Chardonnay in America. Since its inception, this wine has never lost its original authenticity, even after becoming a massive brand.

On the other hand, "boardroom brands," just as implied, are often created in a less-than-authentic setting by a group of marketing professionals with kitschy brand names and fake storylines. The juice is fashioned in a lab using a variety of additives to "enhance" the product, then flung out into the market in hopes a spark will happen resulting in capitalistic success. This equation also happens in reverse – a laboratory first manipulates and shapes a taste profile followed with clever names and marketing gimmicks. The product is then mass-produced in a factory setting along with other boardroom brands. This type of innovation is rampant in present-day America with no hopes of ever slowing down. Boardroom brands are developed with a specific recipe or taste profile in mind, and year after year, they try to reproduce the same taste profile and recipe regardless of weather or climatic conditions.

So, how does one know if they are buying a boardroom or authentic brand? The simplest way is to do some research on what you're putting in your body and don't be fooled by the glitzy websites, flashy labels, kitschy tag lines, fake stories, and cloying juice. Or, just try to call or book a visit to one of the wineries to sample products and enjoy their story and terroir; they simply don't exist. Boardroom brands are made for those not wanting to take the time to learn what they are consuming. While these brands may suit your immediate palate and budget and have a polished website and exciting story, they are often made using inferior juice manipulated with a variety of additives and chemicals to make it taste good, ultimately lacking true authenticity.

Boardroom brands give the consumer a false impression of what a grape varietal is really supposed to taste like – of what wine is supposed to be. Everyone wants to believe the wine they're drinking is made in a rustic vineyard countryside setting, but the reality is that the majority of wines under $15 are mass-produced in factories to keep up with supply and demand. While mass production is necessary to keep up with demand, fake brands with overly manipulated juice lead the consumer down a false path and deter them from authentic brands.

But consumers really don't stand a chance; the monetary power of the companies behind the boardroom brands allow them to saturate the market with clever mass media advertising along with deep pricing and discounting. This enables them to sell more product than many of the authentic brands with smaller budgets. Free enterprise is at its best with the creation of authentic brands, and at its worst when greedy companies ignore common sense by disassociating themselves from the nuances of vintage, terroir, story, and place for the sake of money; creating fake backstories and manipulating juice to help sell a line of wines is just a blatant lie to the consumer. When a company rips out vines from a vineyard that may not be producing the gauche grape of the day in favor of whatever is selling at the time, or they develop wines laden with residual sugar or laced with varietals and additives that shouldn't be in the blend, they become just another gluttonous pig. I strongly encourage all that read this to take the time to learn about the products they're consuming and their origin – support the smaller independent family-owned enterprises – it's better for your health and your conscience and keeps the system balanced by encouraging authentic brands.

TREND

AUSSIE WINES AND CRITTER BRANDS

FISH, DUCK, GOOSE, MOOSE, BEAR, GECKO, HOG, DOG, HARE. When I left the restaurant business, Australian wines and critter brands were abundantly displayed on the Utah state liquor store racks; the two trends seemed to happen almost simultaneously. A range of inexpensive, premium wine produced in Australia guaranteed a high-quality product at a reasonable price. Add a critter to the label like *Yellow Tail* or *Little Penguin,* and you've got a grand slam – for a while anyway. Aside from attractive low pricing and press, labels flat out help sell wine – period. Cute, lovable critters on labels appeal to the sentimental buyer just as edgy and quirky labels appeal to the experimental buyer. Traditionally, wine labels had always been a bit serious, stodgy, undecipherable, and even boring. Critter labels made drinking wine fun by swaying consumers from traditional wine brands, beer, and booze.

Sadly, however, a glut of decent but cheap bulk Australian critter wines and high alcohol jammy fruit bombs fueled by seemingly overinflated ratings from several publishers contributed to the decline of Australian wines in the United States. As sales slid, many companies altogether abandoned importing Australian wines. Nonetheless, several lower-priced Aussie imports, even some with critter labels, stuck it out, offering attractive everyday low pricing and large discounts, while a small contingent of serious mid-to-high-end labels maintained a presence in the U.S. for the unwavering

Australian fan. Trends can be a flash in the pan or long-lasting before they eventually wane. Critter brands didn't die; new labels continue to pop up to this day. However, one must prudently ascertain if buying the wine for the kitschy marketing on the label designed to grab attention or for the nectar in the bottle.

THE REVIEW

AT ADCO/SPIRITS WEST, employees were reviewed annually, beginning each February with a self-assessment first and then finished in March with a supervisor's grade followed by a meeting to discuss the outcome. I wasn't eligible when I first started, as I had only been on the job just under four months. However, after a full year plus on the job, it was time.

The assessment, which was probably standard practice around the world for many companies, was all new to me. I'd never completed this sort of employee review before, so it threw me into a bit of a panic for a few reasons: I couldn't for the life of me figure out how my boss could grade my work. I worked on my own with little or no supervision most of the time. Additionally, the two states in my territory were so different from any other of the states in the Northwest; I couldn't see how my work could effectively be judged. Add to this the fact that I'm not one who likes to talk about myself, and you can imagine how the dark clouds of dread began to gather.

Now, I'm not sure who comes up with the data and software for job performance appraisals, but I am sure several psychologists, motivational speakers, and team builders or coaches must be part of the equation. After a week of procrastination, I logged into the portal. The review required that I rate myself as one of the following: Top Performer, High Performer, Performer, Needs Improvement, or Non-Performer and I was to provide a written comment. Each rating carried a point value that was tallied at the end.

Naturally, we all like to think we're Top Performers and High Performers in every category, but if those ratings are entered in too many categories, then it looks conceited and cocky. I mean, after all, it was my first full year on the job. And by saying I was a "Performer" in too many categories, it could appear as nothing more than average. Surely, I couldn't say "Needs Improvement" or I was a "Non-Performer" in any category; that would send a signal to my boss that I needed constant supervision, or my self-esteem is too low, or I never left the home office! So, I decided I'd read through each category, rate myself, save my work, then go back later to provide comments and revise my rating if necessary. (I also found that after I saved my work and the point rating was revealed, it could be manipulated each time it was saved until the final copy was submitted.)

Somehow, I muddled through the review. Many of the topics and subcategories didn't relate to my job duties in Utah or Wyoming, so I just left them blank or not applicable. I rated myself slightly above par but not too close to the top percentages; I even managed to provide some drivel in each of the comments section about how I was a team player possessing reasonable enough knowledge to do the job; that I used strategic thinking to drive sales and create relationships; that I communicated and solved problems effectively, all the while, achieving my own sales goals. Blah, blah, blah - Bleh!

The very last section, however, caused me a lot of angst: "Name three areas of development and devise an action plan and a date to complete them."

Argh!! Okay, here goes:

1. *One – Take classes toward a Wine Certification.*

2. *Learn a foreign language.*

3. *Take continuing education classes in Excel, PowerPoint, and Word.*

God, it sounded like I was giving answers in a junior pageant, rather than on an employee review. But I couldn't think of anything else, so I went with it. And, as I found out later, the answers were fine. (In fact, my developmental areas were never discussed, so I used those same answers in the several consecutive reviews that followed!) After turning in the final, I felt relieved that it was over but also nervous about the one-on-one discussion that would follow with my boss.

The meetings began on Wednesday morning. I had flown in early so I could get to the office by nine o'clock. My two coworkers had arrived the previous day, so they had already completed their reviews. While I thoroughly enjoyed going to Seattle for the eating and drinking, I had come to absolutely loathe our meetings. When I first started it was exciting even though the material had nothing to do with my business. But each day was the same boring minutiae; sitting in a boardroom with my coworkers, listening to their problems, upcoming programs, numbers year-to-date, sales goals, and data. Occasionally, a supplier would stop in to show their products and talk about numbers and such, however, most of the time was spent surfing the web to study the wines and wineries I represented in my market. My only respite from falling asleep during these rah-rahs were numerous long trips to the restroom and company kitchen for coffee; taking my time, walking slowly the long way around the entire office and back to the boredom.

By Friday afternoon, I was barely hanging on. Two nights on the town with my fellow Spirits West sales reps and two full days sitting in a conference room were testing my limits. The view out of the window of Seattle's grey weather further played with my psyche as the meetings wore on. (And even though the meetings were painfully boring for me, it was still worth it to get out of Salt Lake City for a few days in January when Utah is faced with its own distinct seasonal anomaly - a polluted bone-chilling inversion so thick it's impossible to see the mountains on either side of the valley.) Late that afternoon, my boss Matt Tomlin dismissed the other two sales reps so we could go over my employee review. We started to go through each category first covering the portion I filled out, then his follow up comments. Twenty minutes later now at the end of the review, Matt abruptly said, "Look, Spartacus, I'd check off exemplary in each category, but I can't do that because no one gets all exemplary marks there's always something to work on, got it?"

"Got it," I stated firmly.

"I will say, as I've said before, that we have no idea what you're doing in your territory because it's so different from what we do in the open markets – But one thing's for sure: You're making money and the suppliers are happy, so keep up the good work!"

"Really? I'm not losing money in my two states?"

"You're making money in Utah and even though Wyoming

is a very small state, at least you're not losing money... So yes, you're making some money in both states – It's not a lot, but it's mind-blowing to us because we budgeted for those losses."

"Great, so what now?"

"Well, we didn't budget a bonus for you because the sales in your territory don't directly tie into our total business, and you're too new for a standard raise," he explained. "Next time around they'll most likely include you in the standard annual cost of living increase, however..." As I listened to him talk, I thought to myself: *Hell, I never even thought of a bonus. I was just thrilled to have a job selling wine and get paid to basically drink for a living. Whatever... I'm totally happy. No bonus or raise? Fine with me.* However, my ears suddenly perked up a bit as Matt said something I'd never thought of, "So, Spartacus, I'll tell you what I am gonna do. Next week, I'll contact the suppliers you've been working with to drum up some money for doing a good job; we'll call it an incremental bonus or something. Sound good?"

"Sounds great to me, thank you very much!"

"Just keep up the good work. Whatever you're doing, it's working, and people are taking notice." He paused. "Hey, you know, I do have one question..."

"Sure, what's that?"

"Do you think the state of Utah will ever go private?"

I laughed a little then replied, "If I had a dollar for every time I've heard that question I may be a little better off." We both laughed, after which I added, "I don't see that happening anytime soon. They make so much money off alcohol; it would be hard for them to give it up, even though they would probably make more money by going private. They could still tax alcohol, but at a smaller rate, bootlegging would slow down considerably, and they could get rid of all the infrastructure obligations that cost them money. But I think in twenty years, when more people move into the state, it might put enough pressure on the system that eventually the current organization would cave in and be voted out."

Matt leaned back on his chair lifting a finger to his chin. "Hmm, good to know. Just keep us apprised of any scuttlebutt you hear in Utah – Could be a good opportunity on the horizon."

"You know I will."

The rest of the afternoon was a blur, as I giddily thought about what kind of bonus I might receive – maybe $500? Or even $1000? Anything would be great! Funny thing was, I suddenly wasn't tired anymore!

Later the next week, my boss called to discuss a few issues and the results of the bonus hunt. "So, Spartacus," he explained, "I contacted all of your suppliers to talk about an incremental bonus for the work you've done for them during the past several months, and I was able to come up with $3,500. How does that sound?"

I gasped. I couldn't speak, my mind ran wild with what I could do with the money. I could barely breathe.

"Spartacus? You there?"

Shaken back to reality, I said, "Uh, yes, Matt. Sorry." I took a deep breath before replying enthusiastically, "Wow, that's fantastic! I really appreciate it. Thank you!"

"No problem - You've done a great job so far, so I just pointed it out to them."

Sitting in a stunned euphoria, chills went down my back as I hung up. It took me a few more minutes to process the short phone call. I couldn't comprehend a boss who would take time from his busy schedule and go out on a limb for me – it was something that had never happened before.

My dream job just got better!

ILLOGICALITIES:
Various Past Utah Liquor Laws – Part 2

Prior to 2009, the state required every bottle of alcohol over 4% by volume to be labeled by store employees with a small sticker indicating that it had properly entered Utah through the DABC, been recorded, taxed, then purchased in one of the state liquor stores.

If the bottle did not have a DABC sticker, it was considered illegal contraband and could be confiscated by law enforcement. It was also illegal for a restaurant to open a bottle of wine brought in by a consumer if it did not have a sticker.

Logicality? The stickers were supposed to dissuade people from bootlegging across state lines, however, it ended up only being a minor inconvenience. The stickers were easily transferable – they could be peeled off with a little care and concentration, then re-attached to another bottle. In fact, not only did I do this trick hundreds of times for patrons when I was in the restaurant business, but I had three or four rolls of stickers (equating to thousands of them) that somehow found their way into my coat pocket one winter while picking up an order in a state liquor store. And I wasn't the only one, there were a host of citizens with their own sets of stickers. I met one person who had several hundred applied to wax paper so she could easily pick them off and reapply them to her contraband bottles.

The biggest problem with the stickers: since every bottle had to be labeled, it required every case of product to be opened with box cutters in order to access the bottles and apply the stickers, resulting in numerous wounded employees requiring emergency room visits for stitches and Workman's Compensation claims.

Fortunately, in 2009, the state legislature did away with the stickers, saving almost $1 million dollars in the process – now it's virtually impossible to tell if a product has been purchased in Utah or not – bootlegging now encouraged!

 If you wanted to go into a bar prior to 2009 you had to "belong to a club."

"Belonging to a club" referenced the type of liquor license a bar had to have to serve alcohol: a "Private Club License." This meant a person over 21 years of age could imbibe alcohol without eating. Bars still had to offer food, but eating was not a requirement with this type of license. People under 21 were not allowed to enter the premises.

To gain entry to a private club, customers had to obtain a membership card by simply paying a fee and having their name and address recorded in a ledger. Temporary club cards were available for two weeks, or a full-year membership card could be purchased at a higher price. Bars had to remit part of the fee for the club cards to the state along with a copy of the ledger. A person with a membership card could "sponsor" or bring up to ten additional people into the bar – sponsored people did not have to have their own club card. It was not uncommon for a person to have five to twenty "Private Club Membership Cards" so they could visit different bars, and the membership cards had to be renewed each year. The extra cost just to have a drink in a bar could amount to hundreds of dollars, and because the ledgers went to the state, they could be profiled to boot.

Often, people with membership cards would sit at the end of the bar or close to the door. When the doorman or bouncer told a person or group they had to have a membership card to gain entry, the person with the membership would raise their hand, signaling the doorman that he or she would sponsor the person or group trying to gain entry – thus allowing them to enter as guests of the member. More often than not, the new non-members bought drinks for the member as a sort of "thank you." After all, if a person was from out of town, it was better to buy a beer or a cocktail for a stranger than buy a membership card. Members sponsoring guests sure saved a lot of money by not having to pay for drinks.

 The state required restaurants to install a "Zion Curtain."

A Zion Curtain is a spin on the term *"Iron Curtain"* and refers to a shield or a barrier of some sort on top of a bar within a restaurant so alcohol could be poured out of sight of the patrons, specifically minors. The act of bartenders mixing cocktails and pouring wine and beer was considered promoting alcohol consumption to minors by the LDS lawmakers. So, to protect the minors from observing the drink-making process, they required restaurants to spend an inordinate amount of money to erect the shields. Bars were not required to have the barriers because people under 21 were not admitted.

During the state legislative session of 2009, then-Governor Jon Huntsman recommended that the barriers be taken down to promote tourism and rid Utah of one of their weirdest alcohol laws. And in fact, the Zion Curtains did come down a short time later, much to the consternation of several Mormon lawmakers. However, after Jon Huntsman vacated his post as governor to accept an ambassadorship role from President Obama, the regressive state legislature restored the barriers in 2013.

Led by former Senator John Valentine (R – Mormon, Orem) who stated, "I'm concerned about the culture of alcohol. And, I'm concerned about changing the atmosphere of our restaurants to bars." (Romboy 2013) Now, something must have happened so bad as to rile Mr. Valentine into such a lather, he decided when the time came, and he got the chance – then, for the love of Joseph Smith, he was going to resurrect those barriers just as Christ was resurrected. I can only surmise after coming home after a long day at work, upon rounding the corner to his kitchen, there was his beloved 14-year-old son mixing martinis for all his friends while Frank Sinatra crooned in the background. He then cried out, "Holy potatoes! Why did I ever take my family to those restaurants pouring alcohol out in the open? Those rat bastards and their booze turned my son into a martini hound!"

Mr. Valentine's statement about alcohol culture was in fact, extremely dull-witted, for they were not his, nor any of the Latter-day Saint population's restaurants to pass judgment. His statement followed by the dominant LDS legislature's actions to re-establish the barriers displayed LDS Church influence and overreach by imposing their beliefs through the passing of laws to satisfy church hierarchy and the LDS population. Which, last time I checked, violates church/state separation.

In Utah, there are plenty of restaurants that do not choose to serve alcohol. If he and his Mormon cronies were so concerned about their families being exposed to alcohol, they should have asked the leaders of the LDS church to pass a "law" or "decree" or "revelation" or whatever they wanted to call it, at one of their general conferences stating: "If you are a member of The Church of Jesus Christ of Latter-day Saints, then you may not enter a restaurant that possesses and sells alcohol on its premises." *Voilà* – problem solved!

Utah restaurants are owned by professional people who spend fortunes on their business, providing a place that a person, religious or not, can go for a meal. If, by chance, the account has a liquor license, people are within their full rights to have a glass or more of wine, beer, or alcohol. And, if a restaurant happens to have a bar, then it should be allowed to serve alcohol over the bar whether the bar happens to be in sight of the dining room or not. This decision should be left to the restaurant owners, not the influenced LDS faithful from the state legislature. If Mormons are so worried about their children becoming boozehounds from viewing alcohol in a restaurant setting, then they have failed to do their job as parents, and the LDS religion has failed by not inflicting enough guilt to curb such attitudes.

The illogicalities with the Zion Curtains were, in fact:

- They were, and are, ridiculous-looking and expensive.

- With an international airport, five national parks and numerous ski resorts – to tourists, Utahans look like idiots!

- How is a person to know that the $8 Baileys and coffee they ordered is not being compromised by a less-expensive liquor?

- And, what if the bartender, God forbid, is having a bad day and spits in a cocktail or slips in a roofy? No one can see the person making the cocktail, so how does one know?

Except for the brief time during Huntsman's tenure, Zion Curtains existed for many, many years. And, during that time, it was never proven that Zion Curtains were effective at controlling whether minors are likely to drink or not after viewing alcoholic products poured in a restaurant setting.

 Utah residents can only buy alcoholic products through the state – either from a state-owned liquor store or what is called a Package Agency.

Package Agencies are usually located in private businesses out of convenience for customers in rural and resort areas. The entity agrees to house a small selection of alcohol in a corner of their business for the locals, then remit the proceeds to the state after purchase. The state pays a small fee for the entity to house the convenience.

- Grocery and convenience stores could only sell 3.2% beer, which is actually 4% by volume. All liquor above 4% alcohol by volume is sold in state-run liquor stores – so, imbibing consumers must shop at two different stores for their daily and weekly needs.

- Because the DABC decides what they will sell in their state-owned liquor stores, the selection is severely limited to the consumer because there is only so much shelf space, and not all state stores are the same size.

- Most state liquor stores are only open from 11 am to 7 pm and are closed on Sundays and state and federal holidays. Only a few select stores in the busiest areas are open until 10 pm. This often results in excessive lines out the doors, and out-of-stock products, especially around the holidays.

- Travel time is only an hour or so going east, west, or north of Salt Lake City, so the stores just outside the borders conduct a healthy business. Bootlegging is excessive because people can get the products they want for less across state lines.

 The state does not allow wineries to direct ship wine to households.

Memberships to wine clubs really don't exist, unless it is shipped to a relative's home in another state and bootlegged across state lines.

And why no direct shipping? The LDS lawmakers believe that if a minor is home when a shipment of wine arrives, they may open it and drink what is inside. Or, even worse – a minor could order wine online themselves then ship it home while their parents are working. Stupid? You bet! I highly doubt that little Jimmy desires a 92-point $25 bottle of Cabernet from Chile to help dull the pain of a mid-term math quiz. The fact that shipments of wine require large stickers on the side of the box that say: "Package Contains Alcohol and Requires a Signature of Someone over 21 years of Age," somehow does not resonate with the state lawmakers. If they treated their citizens as adults instead of prepubescents, they could be taxing and making money on said shipments. Instead, people bootleg, so they make nothing.

 Even if moving into the state, it is prohibited for anyone to import alcohol across state lines – other than the DABC.

Also considered bootlegging, relocating a prized wine cellar to a new Utah residence is illegal. There are two exceptions: If entering from a foreign country, two liters are allowed, and if relocating or inheriting alcohol from someone out of state, it may be brought into Utah by first notifying the DABC and paying a handling fee or a tax. Since state taxes are extremely high, this could mean paying for a product twice. Most people relocating to Utah do not notify the DABC that they are bringing alcohol with them. Moving is such a pain in the ass anyway, why would anyone spend the time to notify the DABC? I have heard of several instances of future Utahans being turned into the local police or DABC because a curious nosey LDS gospel fanatic next door observed the new transplants moving cases of wine and alcohol from their massive moving trucks into their new home. So appalled that their pristine neighborhood has been sullied, they report them. Ridiculous!

TREND

PINOT NOIR

SOMETIME DURING 2004, A LITTLE FILM called "Sideways" became a major motion picture and a cult classic. The main character rants and raves about how Merlot is easy to make due to the grape's plump, juicy, thick-skinned qualities in contrast to Pinot Noir, which is harder to produce because of the grape's thin skin and fickleness to weather.

The public, gullible as ever, jumped on the movie's unintended bandwagon downing Pinot Noir like water. The only problem? They never realized the dichotomy of the main character's ultimate prize bottle; a wine named Chateau Cheval Blanc - often made with a healthy dose of Merlot.

Well into 2005, the demand for Pinot Noir resulted in widespread outages and higher prices; wineries couldn't make it fast enough. In ritualistic fashion, capitalists producing wines from great grapes of every variety other than Pinot Noir ripped up their vines to replant with said grape. However, Pinot Noir was being consumed so fast that newly planted vines couldn't mature fast enough to produce ripe quality grapes. Many producers began to add Syrah and other varietals, and even additives, to their Pinot Noir bottlings to mask the inferior unripe or soft juice so they could stretch what they did have to make more wine and money. Many of the best Pinot Noirs became inaccessible because of demand and high prices – the California Pinot Gold Rush was on.

Consequently, the success of "Sideways" also drove

Merlot sales into the ground. Merlot began to disappear off wine lists and the Merlot section in retail stores shrunk dramatically, continuing for years to come. After the dust cleared and supply caught up with demand, a couple of dynamic results materialized – a lot of excellent Merlot on the market at reasonable prices and American Pinot Noir had now established itself as one the greats. Ensuing years showed improvement in the quality of lower-end bottlings in an effort to capture reasonable wine by the glass options for restaurants, but prices for high-quality terroir-driven Pinot Noir continued to escalate with the best producers.

THE ESKIMO

AT THE LAST COMPANY QUARTERLY MEETING OF 2005 IN SEATTLE, we were notified of a kick-off event for an up and coming supplier. Kick-off events usually introduce new wineries or suppliers and their products to the distributors or brokers that are tasked with selling them in a specific market. Since the event happened to be in Seattle and we'd be selling the wines at some point in the future, our small team was invited as well.

This supplier burst onto the scene with clever labels and marketing backed by one of California's oldest names in the wine business. Most of the brands were boardroom brands. However, they had the right combination of low prices, press, and consistent ratings of 86 to 90 points on several wines ranging from nine to fifteen dollars. The wines had already hit the major markets, so they had traction. They were on the cusp of steamrolling everyone that got in their way.

This particular kick-off was held at one of Seattle's best hotels. The event was so large it took up the entire expanse of one of the meeting room floors. Upon entering, the hotel staff greeted guests with a glass of one of their new white wines. Posters and pictures of wine country, brand logos and labels, and supplier logos filled the walls lining the hallway en route to the grand ballroom. Long tables lined one of the walls displaying all of their gear and POS (all the giveaway promo crap): t-shirts, hats, golf bags, wine keys, wine buckets, and other tchotchkes to be used in the market to help boost sales. Hotel servers with massive trays passed hors d'oeuvres. A large table in the middle of the room held several different kinds of the supplier's wines for the sales teams to sample. A massive screen displaying the supplier logo hung from the rafters over a gigantic stage complete with a podium facing the crowd. Music blared, but it couldn't overcome the clamor of the vast crowd sipping, swirling, laughing, and talking.

Our small division of four filed through the throng to sample the wines and food. Our boss Matt Tomlin knew everyone, stopping to chat, tell a joke, then continue on so as not to clog up the main artery. We planted ourselves at a spot not too far from the stage (or the wine), so we could view the presentation without interruption.

They were easy to spot – several people moving like a pack of wolves through the crowd, stopping every so often for photo ops and to shake hands. As the crowd parted for the pack, the multitude of salespeople clapped. Their entrance was so grand, I wasn't sure if they were a wine supplier or a rock band. As they neared, Matt greeted them then turned to introduce each of our small contingent. They were unimpressed, I could tell. Our little division was meek compared to the larger territories and these people had bigger fish to fry. Shaking hands with the patriarch of the group was like shaking hands with Don Corleone – arm out, slightly bent, palm down, as if he were royalty (I guess considering his winemaking heritage – he was). Moving past us toward the stage, Matt reached out to a gentleman closely following the pack. Although part of the entourage, he was not a familial member, but rather a wine mercenary brought in to oversee and execute sales in the Northwest. Matt tapped him on the shoulder, and he turned, smiled, said hello, then looked to us as Matt made introductions.

That is when I met the Eskimo.

Introduced as their Pacific Northwest Division Manager, the Eskimo was tall, athletic, somewhat balding, a bit younger than me, impeccably dressed as if straight off a page in GQ, with a slightly goofy but confident smile. The Eskimo extended his arm, and his paw enveloped my hand. "Are you Spartacus Falanghina?"

"Yes," I replied quizzically, unsure if we'd previously met.

"Are you from Salt Lake City?" he asked.

"Uh, yes, how did you know?"

"Oh... come on, man. I've heard of you – everyone's heard of Spartacus Falanghina!" he said somewhat mockingly, with a note of humor, all the while flashing a goofy, cheesy grin full of near-perfect teeth. Just before he walked off, he leaned in close as if to relay a deep dark secret. "Relax mannnn, I'm from Salt Lake City too. I'll be in touch. WE are going to burn that motherfucker down!" And with that, he was gone, disappearing into the crowd to rejoin the pack.

On stage, the lead wolf gave a rousing speech about the wines, winery, family heritage, and the joint task between the two companies of selling hundreds of thousands of cases in the Pacific Northwest. The salespeople (by now worked into a wine-induced froth) cheered loudly. The rest of the night was a blur as we drank, talked, and joked with coworkers throughout the room. Laying in my hotel bed that night I reflected on the Eskimo's words. I was quite sure he was messing with me, although maybe he was trying to put me at ease. Or maybe he *had* heard of me, but how? No... Impossible. No one in Seattle, besides my coworkers and a few friends knew me; he had to have been messing with me. With only a few years in the business under my belt, I still had plenty to learn, but even I can pick out a bullshitter – or maybe he was just building me up? Either way, I'd figure it out eventually.

I didn't hear from the Eskimo until a few months later, but from time to time, I thought about our first meeting. I supposed with large markets like Oregon, Washington, and Alaska he had his hands full. I knew he'd eventually contact me, so why push it? I had plenty to do; chasing new business wasn't necessary. When he finally did contact me several weeks later, I didn't even have a chance to say hello after answering the phone. "Sparty, what's going on in Utah, man?" he said.

"You know, just dealing with the state and selling wine," I replied. "How's everything in Washington?"

"Oh, it's sick man... This place is cool. It's a fucking gold mine. Sorry it took me a while to get in touch, but I had to move my family from Vegas and get shit going up here. But I'm back and ready to work on Utah and Wyoming."

"Sounds great to me, I need some new wines to sell."

"Excellent. So, tell me how Utah and Wyoming work?"

For the next hour or so, I went into detail about the DABC and the Wyoming Liquor Division. Periodically during the conversation the Eskimo regaled me with his prior experiences of selling wine in Vegas. His voice reeked of confidence – even though younger than me, he had several more years of experience; I just hoped to keep up. Neither state carried any of his wines so we would have to build everything from scratch. We devised a plan of attack that included him flying to Utah for an initial meeting with fine wine buyer Cliff Bradford. He asked me how he could send samples so I could work the market for special orders. When I told him it was illegal to send samples, he simply said, "So, how in the hell are you going to work the market without samples?"

"Well, technically it's illegal to sample alcohol with anyone in Utah. But –"

"But you do it, rrrrright?" he asked, cutting me off.

"Well… yes."

"Well, then we need to figure out how to get you some goddamn samples." After a brief pause, he said, "I got an idea. How long will it take you to drive to Twin Falls?"

"Uh… I dunno, maybe three hours."

"Okay, here's what you do…" He paused to think. "I want you to go to XYZ Distributors in Twin Falls – Write this down because I don't want it tracked in an email."

"Okay…"

"When you get there, ask for a guy name Jorgy B. I'll have samples ready. All you have to do is pick them up, sashay them back – And *boom*, we're in business. Sound good?"

"Yeah, sure, I can do that. I'll do it next week."

Before he hung up the phone, he said. "Oh, one more thing."

"Yeah?"

"My folks live in Salt Lake, so I'll throw in a few extra

cases. Can you drop them off for me?"

"Sure, no problem. Send me the address and I'll take care of it."

After the phone call, I made an appointment six weeks out for us to meet with fine wine buyer Cliff Bradford. I planned to drive to Idaho the following week. Bootlegging didn't bother me because I despised Utah liquor laws, especially the no-sampling law. Besides, it was just to pick up a few cases of wine – piece of cake.

The following week, after arriving at the distributor in Twin Falls, I found myself talking to none other than Jorgy B on the warehouse floor. While waiting for the wines to be brought out, he flung out a few choice words about the Eskimo – something about acting like he was the only supplier on earth and that he owed him some commissions, but I eschewed them, I didn't know enough of him yet to pass judgment. As the forklift rolled up, my jaw dropped. There packed on a wood pallet were several cases of wine.

"Uh, how many cases is that?" I asked.

Glancing at the clipboard in his hand, Jorgy B said, "Looks like thirty-two mixed cases."

"All for me?" I stammered.

"Yes, is there a problem?"

"Uh, no... I'll just back my SUV up to the loading dock. Gimme a minute." Walking to the parking lot I laughed to myself: *Thank god I have an SUV.*

Once loaded, I could barely see out the back window. I stopped at the local KMART to buy a dark sheet to cover the load. When bootlegging on this magnitude, it's very important to cover everything completely. (And of course, drive the speed limit; why give a state trooper cause?) Once back on the highway, I called the Eskimo. He answered after two rings. "Sparty! You get the samples, man?"

"Yeah, did you mean to give me so many cases?" I asked.

He snickered. "C'monnnn, mannnn! You got a job to do, righhht?"

"Well, yes, but I'm a little freaked out about driving thirty-two cases across the state line!"

"C'mon, CUZZZ! Settle down man! You'll be fine."

"Yeah, but thirty-two cases?"

He laughed. "Well, it's a long way to go to get more. This'll set you up for what.... six months?"

"Yeah, I guess."

"Then relaaax man. Look, lemme explain something to you. I'm not a fucking micro-manager. It's your market. You know what needs to be done to succeed. And I'll give you whatever you need to do the job. If you need to buy anything, like a gift or concert tickets, or you need to buy someone lunch or dinner to make a sale? If it makes sense and it's not astronomical, then do it man! I don't want you to bug me over every little detail. You're the pro. I expect you to work your business. Got it?"

Slightly relieved, I replied, "Yeah, I got it."

"Alright, drive safely, see you next month!"

Wasting no time after I returned home, immediately I started taking samples out to my accounts. The reception I was met with was remarkable. Low cost, press, and decent well-made juice was the right combo for accounts looking to set themselves apart from the competition. The first week

I collected eight special orders, and after signatures from all parties, I turned the orders in along with the necessary paperwork to set up a new supplier as a vendor to Utah. Purchase orders were generated about a week later (which, considering how fast the DABC works – could be some sort of speed record). With a stroke of luck, the wine actually made it to the state before the Eskimo, providing options for meetings and dinners.

The following month I met the Eskimo for lunch at a Salt Lake City restaurant prior to the meeting with the buyer. Standing in the waiting area, he cut quite a presence dressed in a dark tailored suit, French cuffs, and expensive fine Italian leather shoes with barely a scratch. I looked shabby in comparison with my slacks and sport coat.

"Sparty!" he enthused while walking toward me, swinging his arm from the side of his body, gathering speed for a roundhouse handshake followed by a resounding loud slap. (I almost missed it at the last moment.) "Great to see you, man! How you doin?"

"I'm doing fine," I said. It was hard to match his enthusiasm; I was still trying to read him.

"Fine?" he said incredulously. "Fine is for neophytes! You're alive, ain't ya?"

"Yeah."

"You sell wine for a living, don't cha?"

"Yeah."

With voice raised, he replied, "Well, wake up brother, and smell the coffee! We have the best fucking jobs in the world. We sell wine GOD DAMN IT!"

I laughed slightly at his bravado and rationale. "Well,

when you put it that way – FUCKING A! I'm doing GREAT!"

"That's what I am talking about CUZ! Now, let's have some lunch."

After sitting down, the Eskimo launched into stories about his childhood growing up on the east bench of Salt Lake City, then his college glory days. He inquired about my past, both personal and leading up to my position with Spirits West, but my stories paled in comparison. We had to get past the "getting to know you stage," so we could move on. He knew it, I knew it. The server could barely get a word in edgewise, but we did manage to order in between stories. Finally, personal information disclosed and satiated with food, he said, "So, tell me about the state buyer."

"Okay, his name's Cliff Bradford. He's been the fine wine buyer for decades in charge of Limited Listings –"

He looked puzzled, then cut me off. "Okay, well, these wines aren't really fine wines. We want to sell in mass. Maybe we need to present to the other buyer? You know, the General Listings guy. What's his name?"

"Dennis?" I replied.

"Yeah, him."

"Well, we could go that route, but they take so long to review products, it could take six months before they even taste them. Since Cliff tastes all the time, we could have some wines on shelves by end of next month."

"Okay, sorry for interrupting. I almost forgot you're the pro. Proceed." he said, smiling, bowing his head slightly, then leaning back in his chair.

"So, when you're talking to Cliff, don't mention promotion or samples, or bootlegging or any of that shit. In fact, don't mention it with anyone at the DABC – It's fucking illegal."

"Got it!"

"Just give him your story, tell him about the wines, the winery, and any press. Chances are he's heard of them already, so he'll probably be looking to deal."

"Oh, I can fucking wheel and deal with the best of em; I got plenty of money to play with!"

"Easy, easy... I know. Just don't show all your cards at once – okay?"

"So, how can we buy this guy?"

"Buy?"

"You know..." he said, throwing his arms up. "Can we buy him dinner?"

"No."

"Can we offer to set him up in wine country?"

"No."

"Concert tickets?"

"No."

"Blow?"

"Nooo!"

"Hookers?" he said, laughing.

"Nooooo! None of that; he cannot be bribed. I've watched suppliers offer all kinds of shit – He always says no - He's bound by state laws."

"Okay, I got it," he said, exasperated. "Let's go get this meeting over with so we can have some cockies."

"Some what?"

"Some cocktailsss mannn!"

I laughed. "Oh yeahhh… cocktails sound good to me!"

Driving to the DABC offices, I thought about the impending meeting; it would either be productive or a giant waste of time. At any rate, I had a front-row seat to watch the young gun up against the seasoned stone-cold buyer; it was sure to be quite a match.

After exchanging handshakes, we sat across from Cliff, now seated behind his large desk, seeming to be in a rather good mood. Leading up to actual business, they exchanged friendly banter. The Eskimo regaled Cliff with tales of his childhood in Salt Lake City, along with the fact that his parents still lived in Utah, trying his best to soften him. After noting one of his parents was a landscape architect, Cliff's eyebrows perked up as he too was an active horticulturist. Sensing an opening, the Eskimo flashed his signature goofy smile and slapped his leg as he tried amusing Cliff with tales of selling wine to the casinos in Vegas, but the conversation turned cold. Undeterred, the Eskimo rebounded by talking about his position with the new company, the winery heritage, and of course, finally… the wines.

The shift worked; Cliff began to pose questions about the products and finally, a breakthrough. With another chink in the buyer's armor, the Eskimo began to volley subtle sales pitches, but they were rebuffed each time. First, soft but assuming: "Just say the word, I can get all the wines here in two weeks," to persuasive but assured: "How about just listing two wines from each line to see how they do? I know my parents will drink them. If they don't sell, I'll pick them up, no questions asked," to factual: "I'm telling you, these wines over-deliver for the money – you can't miss. You can't find inexpensive, rated wine of this quality anywhere. What do you say?"

Out of pitches and breath, the conversation stagnated until Cliff spoke up. "Look, I'm sure the wines are great to someone somewhere. We only have so much room on state store shelves. Just work with Spartacus and go through the process. Ever since the movie "Sideways" escalated prices, decent Pinot Noir around ten dollars is of particular interest. I can't buy them all, but I'll look at the wines the first chance I get – Just go through Spartacus; he's your broker and he knows what to do."

The Eskimo took a deep breath. "Okay, if that's the way it has to be, then so be it!"

With the meeting over, we all stood, shook hands, then Cliff showed us out.

Back at the car, the Eskimo threw his hands up in the air. "Goddamn, that was painful. I've never met a buyer like that, ever!"

"I told you," I laughed. "Now, how about those cockies?"

"Abso-fucking-lutely! Let's go!"

We settled into a bar downtown to rehash the meeting. After several "cockies," we moved onto an early dinner across town at a restaurant featuring one of his wines brought in via special order. Once seated, the Eskimo perused the small wine list. After just a moment of study, he dropped the list on the table, "Great job on the placement Cuz, but this isn't going to work."

Surprised, I asked, "What do you mean? You don't want to drink your wine? Isn't that what all suppliers want?"

"Well, not me Cuz. You see, I can drink as much of that as I want anytime. And it's fine for what it is, but what I am interested in is exercising the expense account!"

"You don't need to ask me twice. Let's go. I'll smooth it over with the manager later."

Now, I was no stranger to exercising an expense account, but as I found out, the Eskimo was not only a skilled salesman, he was a connoisseur. The high-intensity workout began with bottles of Montrachet, then Single Vineyard Cornas, ending with high-end Super Tuscans. Numerous food courses accentuated the regimen, and by night's end, I was exhausted, fat, happy and... drunk! What a way to work out.

A few weeks later, we submitted the full line-up from two of the winery's flagship brands – about twelve wines in total. Six weeks after that we received five new listings – two from the entry-level label and three listings from the next level up. However, before purchase orders were cut and wine delivered, a short round of wheeling and dealing took place. Cliff wanted a certain price point on the shelf: $7.99 for the entry-level and $8.99 for the second label. After negotiating several back and forth price scenarios between the two, I finally convinced the Eskimo it would be worth his while to simply accept the low prices. They wouldn't ask for any discounts; the wines would be set at an everyday low shelf price. Besides, we had to start somewhere – some sales are better than no sales. (In Utah, half the battle is getting in the door and on the shelf. Once a wine is on the shelf, depletions are almost guaranteed; as long as the product sells, the listing can be retained.)

With time, I found that the Eskimo was more than just another supplier. Sure, when he came to the market we conducted a bit of business, such as visiting accounts or a few state stores, or even a follow-up meeting with Cliff at the DABC, but a market visit wasn't complete without working out the expense account, which often included a day of bar-hopping, fishing, golf, or skiing. In the factual sense, the Eskimo worked hard but played even harder.

As he told me in the beginning, he expected me to run the business as it related to my territory, and he would give me whatever I wanted – if it made good business sense. His style of management had its own psychology: by staying mostly hands-off, delegating, then providing positive reinforcement through rewards, he knew I would work hard to execute and deliver cases. And it worked. I felt compelled to deliver because I knew the hard work would pay off – literally. Plus, I liked and respected the guy (it was difficult not to). Behind his bravado, confident, goofy charm, and uncanny wit was a guy that in the truest form, epitomized a good time. He could walk the walk and talk the talk, whether sitting with Fortune 500 CEOs or hanging with the locals at a bar. He would always say, "Sparty, I may not be a millionaire (yet), but I certainly live like one!" There aren't enough "Os" in the words cool or smooth to describe the Eskimo. Sales professional, raconteur, connoisseur, athlete, party boy, family man, sportsman, businessman, aficionado – the Eskimo was all of those things and more.

With wine in the state stores and loads of illegal samples, business took off for this fledgling company. After initial impressions and decent sales as backup, eighteen months later, Cliff approved seven more wines, putting a total of twelve wines across four of the supplier's brand names on the state store shelves. One brand, in particular, the flagship brand from the company, accounted for seven of the listings and the majority of the sales. Nationwide, this brand accounted for almost two-thirds of the winery's business; it seemed to be that way in Utah as well. Order after order rolled in, and cases upon cases were bought up by content consumers. Though Utah is a small state compared to others, in just over three short years we had reached more than 3,000 cases in annual sales.

Along with the drinking, dinners, and adventure, the Eskimo had always given monetary incentives such as bonuses for met sales goals and new listings or wine list placements. However, after depleting upwards of 3,000 cases, the incentives took a different turn, moving up to trips. And not just any typical incentive trip either – wine country to see the winery or Vegas wouldn't do – rather Hawaii and Pebble Beach were on the table. Trips usually reserved for sales division managers, chain store buyers, and restaurant buyers from larger states were extended my way. The big advantage when it comes to incentive trips over cash? They often aren't taxed directly to the salesperson – and the Eskimo knew it. The Eskimo wanted to get to 5,000 cases in sales in Utah. For him, it probably meant a substantial bonus; for me, he offered a golf trip (all-expenses-paid to Pebble Beach, the equivalent of the *Holy Grail* in my mind). First and foremost, golf is my sport; I had to make that goal.

Shortly after the incentive was lined up, a bit of luck happened my way in the form of a phone call from Cliff Bradford. Now, usually a phone call from the DABC means problems need to be fixed, or I'm in some sort of trouble. With this phone call, however, I was informed that due to high sales performance from six of the wines, he would be recommending that they be moved to General Listing status, which meant that they could be put on sale. He also congratulated me, telling me no other broker had ever been approved for that many General Listings at one time. I was ecstatic, to say the least; this meant that hitting the 5,000-

case sales goal would soon be a reality.

The very next year I hit the goal, and true to his word, the Eskimo booked the trip to Pebble Beach. Deciding to fill out the group as a foursome, he invited two buyers from the Northwest to attend as well.

With bated breath, I waited for those four glorious days in June. Finally, when the moment arrived, I packed, then unpacked, then packed again to be sure I had everything needed. (Even in June, Pebble Beach can be victim to a full range of weather.) The flight was scheduled for late afternoon, and I tried my best to work before departing, but it was no use, my mind had already checked out of the office and into the Pebble Beach Hotel. Just before shutting my computer off, an email from the Eskimo arrived. It simply said, "Hey Cuz, hope you're ready to go! See you in San Jose. My flight gets in after yours so just wait in the airport somewhere until I land."

After retrieving my bags in San Jose, I found a little bar in the airport to watch TV while I waited. It was just after 7 pm; the Eskimo's flight was not due in until around 8:30. I figured he would want to get something to eat after he arrived, so I had a beer while watching the NBA Finals. Four beers later, 8:30 came and went and the Eskimo had yet to arrive. I checked the arrivals but found no inbound flights from Seattle. Worried I had the wrong airport or something, I sent out numerous texts to him, but nothing came back. So, I sat and drank more beer. Giving into hunger, I ordered some chips and salsa – It would have to suffice; the kitchen had closed. Finally, just after 10 pm, a text came through from the Eskimo: "Flight was delayed, just landed, be there shortly."

I staggered slightly on the way to the baggage claim. The

Eskimo was all smiles as I walked up, "Hey, Cuzzz, did you think I wasn't going to show up?"

"I was beginning to have my doubts!" I said.

"Flight was delayed in Seattle – fog. You already drunk?"

"Just about... Sitting for three hours in a bar is tough."

"No worries, I slept the whole way. I'll drive."

"Where are the other two guys?" I inquired.

"Oh, at last minute, they couldn't make it. One guy had to deal with a medical problem with his wife and the other couldn't get away from work."

"Bummer for them..."

"You know it. I guess it's just the two of us all weekend. I prepaid Pebble Beach ten thousand dollars for this trip, so I hope you're ready to have fun!"

"You what?"

"Yeah, man. It's cool. I had to use the money, so I had them invoice my company for 10k. After they get the check, they simply hold it until we arrive to spend it. Pretty cool, huh?"

"Hell yeah," I said, laughing to myself.

I waited with our bags on the curb while he handled the rental car. After what seemed like thirty minutes, a brand new shiny red Cadillac skidded to a halt in from of me, Eskimo at the wheel, window down. "Don't look so surprised," he called. "You didn't think we were gonna roll into Pebble Beach in a fucking Geo Metro, did you?"

"Uh, well no," I stammered. "Of course not."

With the car loaded, the next stop was a convenience store. I waited with the car while he ran in, minutes later emerging with a box of cigars, a six-pack of beer, and a few other amenities. He flipped me a can of chewing tobacco as he slid back into the driver's seat. After lighting up a stogie, he paused, then looked at me. "Ready?"

"Uh, yeah, but I quit chew a long time ago."

"It's going to be a long four days; you may need it. Just hang onto it. Hell, I may need it!"

"Are we going to get some food?"

"We probably won't find shit open at this hour. How about we just wait until we get to Pebble?"

"Okay, no problem," I said, a bit worried. I had a pretty good buzz, which on a semi-empty stomach, was turning into inebriation.

We smoked and drank, talked a little business, and told stories all the way to the now mostly dark Pebble Beach Hotel. After checking in, the Eskimo handed me a Pebble Beach credit card. "Just use this anytime you need something. Whatever you buy with it will come off the 10k I prepaid."

"Holy shit, really?"

"Yes, just don't get fucking crazy with it!"

"Okay, okay. What about the food! I'm hungry."

"They said the restaurant is closed, but room service is still open. Just order what you want."

"Great, thanks. I was beginning to worry."

Once in the room, I couldn't wait to unpack before calling room service. Not wanting to entirely fill up before bed (due to the fact we were playing golf in the morning) I ordered small: crab cakes, a tin of Caviar, and a bottle of single-vineyard *Talbott Chardonnay*. (Hey, it was Pebble Beach after all.) As I finished unpacking, the food arrived via a white-gloved room service attendant. Just as I was about to put that first bite of food in my mouth, came another knock at the door. After opening the door slightly, the Eskimo burst into the room, looked around, then said, "Nice order CUZZZ! I have a measly hamburger coming. Mind if I have some *Talbott?*"

"Go ahead," I replied.

The Eskimo poured a large water glass full. While taking his first sip he glanced at my tray of food, "Is that fucking caviar?"

"Uh, yes. Is that okay?"

"Absolutely," he said. Glancing up he added, "Mind if I try some?"

I laughed. "Be my guest."

The Eskimo plunged two fingers into the eggs, then brought them to his mouth. "Oh, those are fucking marvelous!" he exclaimed, laughing. Then, shaking his head while walking to the door, I could hear him laughing as he talked to himself, "Caviar, crab cakes, and Chardonnay. And I'm just having a fucking cheeseburger?" Before he closed the door, he said, "See you in the morning. I am going to kick your ass on the golf course!"

"That'll be the day," I shouted after him.

The next day at Spyglass, we met up with a caddy nicknamed Timmy T, who, after several rounds of questioning, turned out to be an old college associate of the Eskimo. With friends and stories in common, we had to take him on. He volunteered to be on the bags all weekend, and we obliged for what turned out to be a grand adventure. After golf that day, dinner, drinks, cigars, and late-night ping pong followed at Timmy T's house. We had gained a new close friend, with whom I remain in contact to this day.

The Eskimo and I would spend another two years selling the wines that got us to that point. Successive years would bring two more incentive trips (both times Hawaii but at least to two different islands). Just prior to the second trip to Hawaii, I received a call from the Eskimo – He was resigning to move into a similar position with a competitor in the same region. There were no tears though, because the company he was moving to just so happened to be a supplier that I also represented in my territory. But alas, those are other stories.

Not too long after the Eskimo resigned, I was notified that the company we had taken from zero to almost 6,000 cases in Utah and zero to 2,000 cases in Wyoming, canceled our contract to represent them in the Pacific Northwest to move to our main competitor. It was a bit unsettling that a company would just jump ship after all the positive business, but I realized that Utah and Wyoming really didn't factor into the mix. The under-performance of the bigger states of Alaska, Washington, and Oregon dictated where my territory ended up. They needed to reorganize after sales had stagnated in the larger states. I heard they put an end to all the incentive trips and cut back on all frivolous spending as well. The shitty thing about brokerage states? There are no contracts; with just a handshake and an appointment letter, companies and brands come and go.

I was told never to take it personal, but I had to get in one jab at my local competitor taking over the business. It happened about a year after they had fired us. I was in a state store when my rival's employee ribbed me about losing the brands that I had built up. I smiled, then said, "Yeah, but it was a good ride. Tell me, did they take you to Pebble Beach and Hawaii yet? They sure know how to party!"

His smirk turned to form a frown. "What? No... Really?"

I just smiled and walked away.

THE ANTI-SALES REP

AROUND THE EARLY SPRING OF 2006, it was announced that a major French/South American import company would be contracting us in the Pacific Northwest as their broker. I was elated at the time because it meant bolstering up the imported fine wines in the small portfolio I represented in both states.

Before business commenced, the importer decided that they would have a different sales representative from their company oversee each state as part of their territory, which was complete nonsense to me because Utah and Wyoming as control states operated in a similar fashion; Utah was just more tightly controlled than Wyoming. At the end of the day, it really was not a big deal, it just meant that I would have to meet with two sales reps from one company and it would be a bit more time-consuming. Darrel Winters, a tall, husky blond fellow with a great sense of humor and gentle demeanor based in Houston, would be my sales rep for Wyoming, and Harry French, a transplant from New York now based in Denver, Colorado, would be my sales rep for Utah.

Harry had sold women's shoes in NYC for many years prior to becoming a sales rep in the wine industry. We exchanged a few email pleasantries then set up a phone call to discuss the overall business. While I don't remember exact details from that first call, I do remember his voice distinctly – a rough, deep, slight western drawl that eased its way out like pea gravel mixed with Vaseline. As time would tell, Harry seemed to be more anti-business than pro-business, and no matter what, Harry was all about... Harry.

Harry was a braggart.

On his first visit, six months after our initial phone call, I introduced Harry to the buyers at the DABC. Meeting a new supplier for the first time usually means picking them up at the airport or at their hotel, and on this occasion, I picked up Harry at the Southwest terminal on a crisp fall morning. He told me he would be dressed in black pants, a black turtleneck, sports jacket, and cowboy boots. I easily recognized him and would find out in time that this was his official uniform (with a few color variances on the boots and sports coats). On the tall side with wiry black hair and a prodigious bushy mustache that would've made Wyatt Earp or any hipster jealous, Harry was slender and fit for a man who appeared to be close to sixty.

Since this was our first meeting, I exited the car and walked around to the passenger side to shake his hand and help him throw his bags into the back of my SUV. Driving away from the airport, we exchanged the usual gab about the weather in Salt Lake as opposed to the weather in Denver, the Utah Jazz versus the Denver Nuggets, the ski resorts, and so on.

Prior to his arrival, I asked Harry if he'd like to prepare and present a line of wines for consideration with the DABC, but he decided the initial meeting should be a meet and greet. (I guess maybe he thought the buyers would be so charmed by his presence they would automatically buy everything he had for sale, maybe even beg for the business.) Before we entered the DABC building, I cautioned Harry on what to say (and what not to say) to the buyers so as not to raise any red flags, and I explained that they'd allotted about forty-five minutes for the meeting. No talking about "promoting" alcohol, we wouldn't be tasting wine with them, and above all – absolutely do not tell them that any wine sampling would take place during his visit.

Harry chose to completely ignore the time as he blathered on and on about his life in Denver, his family, Colorado sports teams (his many season tickets), his Harley Davidson, and finally... the history of the import company, which, although fascinating, took so long to get to that both buyers had completely lost interest. Sensing their agony and knowing we had exceeded our time limit, I politely interrupted Harry, ending the meeting with handshakes and hopefully saving some face. As we exited the office, Harry led the way just out of earshot. The fine wine buyer laid a hand on my shoulder and whispered, "Make sure to bring a specific agenda next time that covers products."

I had just been gutted. Instead of making a good first impression, we'd wasted their time. I knew what he meant, and I whispered back embarrassingly, "Understood. I had no idea what he wanted to talk about. I promise to never let that happen again."

And, as it turned out, in due time, he would pull this shenanigan again with many of my restaurant accounts. In fact, every account I took Harry to had the distinct pleasure of hearing about the greatness of Colorado and his life in Denver.

Because professional sports are a common thread among

many, Harry would brag on and on about his season tickets for the Avalanche, Rockies, and Nuggets, even offering his tickets to some of the wine buyers and sommeliers if they were ever in Denver. However, on several occasions, when a buyer wanted to take him up on his offer to use the season tickets, to my dismay, he would decline, citing some lame excuse. Now, I don't care if the tickets were available or not; when the invitation is offered, follow-through is of the utmost importance, even it means buying another set of tickets for a game – Make the buyer happy; never miss a chance to build a relationship. If blowing part of the entertainment budget is necessary, so be it. Harry must have missed this in Sales Relationships 101.

Harry was cheap.

In this business, we're taught never to use the word "cheap," but to use "less expensive" instead. Less expensive sounds better and doesn't carry the degree of negativity that cheap does. However, less expensive wouldn't work to describe Harry, for he was the CHEAPEST S.O.B. I'd ever come across!

When suppliers pay a market visit, they expect to spend money on wining and dining. But not Harry. When Harry arrived in town, he asked me to take him to a state liquor store so he could buy a magnum of one of their bulk wines for his room. And instead of going out to dinner, Harry most often declined, choosing to hole up in his hotel room and eat pizza so he could watch one of his Colorado sports teams.

Harry would often call me in the morning before I picked him up to tell me to eat a big breakfast because he didn't have the budget to buy me lunch. When I told him buying lunch at an account was a good idea (and that I'd pay for my own lunch using my own expense account) and that I didn't care if he ate lunch or not. He often gave in begrudgingly, causing undue animosity throughout the day.

Not only was Harry cheap, he was unrealistic.

Harry asked what I needed to help propel business forward in my market. When I told him wine buckets and wine keys would help, he replied, "Okay, I'll see what I can do, but my company doesn't spend a lot of money on disposables. Our wines are so good, we don't need to promote them by giving out swag."

Later that year, on a follow-up trip to Salt Lake City, after we had picked up his magnum of cheap bulk wine and I was dropping him off at his hotel, Harry surprised me. After getting out of the car and he had gotten all of his bags together, he remembered he'd brought some wine openers. "I almost forgot," he said, laying his suitcase down on the ground, "here are the wine keys I brought for you." Harry then proudly held out a twelve-pack box of wine openers as if he were a surgeon presenting me with a newborn baby.

As I took them from his hand, he said, "These are the good double-hinge ones so make sure to stretch them out. You should be able to get quite a few new placements with these guys."

"Um, okay," I replied in utter shock. "Is that all there is – only one box?"

"Well, yes, that's all I've budgeted for the first half of the year in Utah. I guess you'll have to just get some from your other suppliers. We don't really operate that way. Those things are expensive; we'd rather put the profits back into the wine."

"Alright, I guess," I replied. "Just curious... How many

placements do you think I could get with twelve wine keys?"

"Oh, well... Try to get one placement for each wine key, but I think at least eight is realistic."

As I pulled away from the hotel, I was shocked by the silliness of such a statement. We typically would just hand a box of openers to our good accounts – not one at a time. I wanted to throw his wine openers out the window. I never asked Harry for another wine key or wine bucket ever again.

Harry was demanding.

Often, when visiting an account with a large wine list, Harry would say something like, "Wow, this is a big wine list. How many wines do you think they have listed in here?"

"I don't know; maybe 150 or 200 wines, I guess."

"Well, I think with a wine list this big we are severely underrepresented. Our wines deserve more attention at this account. What are you doing in the market? The next time I come to town, I want to see seven more of our wines on this list."

Harry wanted to do anything but work.

During one of his market visits in late March toward the tail end of ski season, I'd taken Harry to the liquor store to pick up wine for his room, followed by dropping him off at his hotel. As we turned into the hotel entrance, Harry asked, "Do you think you could come get me around 11 am tomorrow?"

"Yeah, sure. Is there something we need to go over?"

"Well, no," he said a bit awkwardly, "but there is an AA Callister here in Salt Lake somewhere – Ever hear of them?"

"Uh, no," I replied. "Is it a restaurant?"

"No, it's a country-western store," he said excitedly. "Supposedly, they have the best selection of cowboy wear in the state, but since this is Utah, I'm not expecting too much."

"Oh, I've never heard of them, but I'll Google them – shouldn't be a problem. How much time do you need?"

"Not long – just a quick walkthrough. I have a huge collection of cowboy boots. In fact, I have a room dedicated solely to my boots and belts. I'd like to see if they possibly have something I don't have in my collection."

In disbelief, I replied, "Uh…okay, see you tomorrow at 11 am." After Harry closed the door, I sat quietly, totally confounded. *I have a tight ass sales rep for a major wine company who wants to go shopping on a work with – absolute insanity.*

Driving to the hotel the next morning, I was still stunned that I was going shopping. My annoyance and resentment began to build, realizing that I would have to spend the next few days entertaining a cheap, inconsiderate moron; I'm sure my irritation exposed itself as we drove to AA Callister.

"Looks like another great day in Salt Lake City. How are you doing this morning?" Harry asked.

"Good," I replied curtly.

"Did you watch the game last night?"

"What game?"

"The Nuggets, of course."

"Uh no… should I have?"

"Oh, man, you missed a great game," Harry said, rambling on in detail about how the Nuggets came back in overtime to win the game.

"I watched a movie then went to bed," I replied. "Plus, I really don't follow professional sports. I did when I was younger, but I've just lost interest."

"Well, it was a good one," he said.

Wanting to – no, needing to, I changed the conversation. "I found the address and phone number for AA Callister; it's not too far from here."

"Good, let's go." Harry enthused as he began looking through emails on his phone and making calls on the drive to the retail store.

AA Callister, located on the west side of Salt Lake City, has one of the largest selections of western clothing, hats, rodeo equipment, farrier equipment, and accessories for men, women, children, and farm animals in Utah. My antipathy toward Harry turned to awe as I walked into the store; awe gradually turned into fascination at the quantity and quality within the store. Harry, walking in front of me, made a beeline to the footwear section, while I wandered around the store reading emails and marveling at all the "stuff." I'd lived in Salt Lake all my life but had never heard of this place.

After twenty minutes or so had passed, I grew tired of the situation; I'd looked through all the bolo ties, hats and silver, and turquoise jewelry, so I decided to find out how Harry was doing. Turning the corner into the footwear section, I found him sitting in a chair making his way through a stack of about six pairs of boots, trying them on one at a time, analyzing the fit. Pulling on one of the boots, he stood, then walked around, stopping in front of me. "Well, what do you think?"

"Uh, you know I'm not really a boot guy, so I couldn't say," I replied, bemused that he would ask me at all.

"Well, just give me an opinion."

Irritated, I searched for a way out. "I mean, they all look like very good quality, but you're the one that knows what you have in your closet already, so I couldn't give you a proper recommendation."

"Yeah, I guess you're right. Give me just a few more minutes to decide. I'll come find you when I am done."

"Okay," I said in disbelief, then walked out of the store to get some air.

I found a wooden bench made from a log close to the entrance next to a hand-carved wooden Indian statue to resume scrolling through emails. After twenty more minutes had passed, I decided to go see how the boot fitting was progressing. My lower back now ached, and my butt was sufficiently numb from the hard bench. I hobbled, trying to regain the blood flow to my nether regions.

Back in the boot department, Harry had narrowed it down to two pairs but appeared unable to make a commitment. Holding one boot in his hand, scrutinizing it from the side, he ran his hand over his mustache, twirling the coarse hair at the edges working it into a point. Harry looked up at the salesperson and then me. "I give up. I can't make my mind up. I guess I just looked at too many pairs and I can't decide. I think I'll come back another time after I have a better look in my closet at home."

The salesperson and I both sighed in unison as Harry put his own boots back on. We exchanged a smirk and chuckle before he could look up to catch us in the act.

Looking at my watch in horror, I realized it was now well after noon; we were late for lunch with our first appointment.

As I was leading Harry back through the store toward the front door, I realized that I was walking alone. I turned to find him stopped a short way back to admire a leather vest hanging next to the aisle. As I walked back to him, Harry looked up as I looked at my watch. "We have to go; we're late for lunch with a buyer," I stressed.

"Oh yeah, I forgot," he said laughingly.

Back in the car, I fidgeted with the phone to find the buyer's number while Harry buckled up. The buyer answered my frantic call as we turned out of the parking lot. I apologized profusely for keeping him waiting. I lied, telling him we got stuck in traffic, then told him we would be there in ten minutes. He said no problem, but also had to leave soon, so I had better hurry.

Not even thirty yards out of the parking lot, Harry all of a sudden pointed across the road to a strip mall. "Hey, there's another country-western store right over there. Let's swing in there for just a moment. I want to do a quick walkthrough."

"What?" I replied. "We're already late, we need to go."

"Oh c'mon. He'll wait, it'll just take a minute!"

I looked at him briefly, then asked, "Really?"

"I promise, I just want to walk through quickly. You can even stay in the car. I just want to get an idea of what they have so maybe next time we can go back."

Trying to fight the urge to ignore a supplier, I yielded to his whim, quickly making a U-turn to get back to the strip mall. I stopped in front of the store and Harry jumped out, then disappeared through the glass doors. I looked at my watch, realizing the rest of the appointments for the day would either all have to be pushed back or I'd have to cancel at least one. That was it... Now I was pissed.

As Harry promised, not more than two minutes later, he reappeared. "Okay, not much to see in there, let's go."

We made it to the restaurant in record time but realized after walking into the dining room, the buyer had grown tired of waiting and left. Sighing, I looked down, then up, then dropped my shoulders in anguish before taking a deep breath to stave off my desire to tell Harry he was a complete asshole. Trying to appease a supplier, I had probably tarnished my good relationship with a buyer.

Harry, who had disappeared after we arrived, now reappeared wringing his hands after visiting the men's room asking, "Did we make it? Is he here?"

"No, I guess he had to go," I replied angrily. "I'll call him later to apologize."

Harry looked at his watch. "We weren't that late, were we?"

"Uh - yes, we were very late as a matter of fact."

Harry looked around at the restaurant, then breaking his form of no lunches, stated, "Well, I'm hungry. Let's get some lunch, shall we?"

Completely astonished, I replied in a low growl, "Yeah... sure!"

Over the next four or so years, the Harry French bullshit continued. He complained non-stop of budget constraints, of being over-spent on discounts when he put wines on sale, and rarely, if ever, offered market incentives. I received little if any point of sale in the way of wine openers, buckets, support or samples. In fact, buying samples and billing them back became so difficult I just stopped asking or pushing the wines because I had other suppliers who were willing to work the market with their funds and resources.

My relationship, or "relation-shit," with Harry French eventually would come to an end due to territory restructuring by his company. Months later, a new market manager contacted me to schedule a trip to Utah to figure out the market. Over the phone, I could tell right away that this would be a welcome change.

On his first visit, we did the usual appointment with the state so he could do the meet-and-greet handshake with the buyers, then we went to lunch to discuss current business, opportunities, and needs. After going over sales figures and upcoming discounts, he asked, "What kind, if any, POS or promotional stuff could you use to help further the business in Utah?"

"Well, from my last sales rep, I understand that you don't produce or give away much in the area of promo material."

"Oh really?" he said. "I'm not sure what Harry did or didn't do over the last four years, but we do have POS, and I do have a budget for Utah, so we'd better use it."

"What?" I stated, "Harry always told me he didn't have any budget; that we were over-spent in sale discounts, and provided little if any money for samples or POS."

"Well, I'm not sure what budgets were in the past, but we have promo material at your disposal that I'll ship you."

I sat silently thinking for a moment before asking, "So, what do you have? We can't use printed material or anything in the state liquor stores, but if you have wine openers, wine buckets, t-shirts, golf balls, or any other stuff, I'm sure I can use it."

"Take a look," he said, as he opened a file on his laptop, turning it toward me, then proceeding to flip through slides on a PowerPoint presentation showing all the options. After a few pages, he asked, "How about some golf bags, balls, wine openers, and jerseys?"

"Jerseys? What kind of jerseys?" I replied.

"Soccer, or what they call in other parts of the world football jerseys. One of our South American wineries is a sponsor of the Argentine National Team, so we have some jerseys to give away for programs that support their wines."

"You're shitting me," I said incredulously. "You mean to tell me Harry had all this at his disposal but was too greedy to give any to Utah?"

"I guess, but like I said, I really don't know what type of budget he had to work with," he replied.

I went back to looking at some of the slides on his laptop then it hit me: *that sonofabitch kept everything for Colorado.* I looked up at the ceiling to gather my thoughts. "Now it makes sense. Since he lived in Colorado and it's a much bigger market, he used everything there to make his numbers and make himself look good to all his accounts."

"I guess that's probable," he stated.

"What an asshole! He broke my balls for over four years and provided hardly anything in support," I said, shaking my head.

We both sat silently while I calmed down. "Well, hell, if you're offering, I am going to use this to our advantage. I'll take six golf bags, a dozen jerseys, several dozen golf balls and wine openers."

We both broke into laughter for a moment, then he

replied, "You got it, not a problem, I'll get it ordered. Let's have some wine."

We spent the rest of the day seeing a few state stores and a couple of restaurants, eating, and drinking wine along the way. What a complete change from Harry French. I felt refreshed and excited at the new approach and attitude to the market. As I dropped him off at his hotel, he said, "Thanks for a great day. I'll give you a call later next week. The POS should arrive at your house by next Friday."

Sadly, he would only last just over a year, quitting to move to another state and company. Eventually, the company was reorganized into two divisions due to acquisitions, mergers, and the need to grow. With two divisions came two new sales reps I would have to deal with for both of my states; one that was actually very congenial and ready to help in any way and one rep that was just damn too busy with his bigger states to care about Utah or Wyoming.

Back to the drawing board!

TREND

NEW ZEALAND SAUVIGNON BLANC

OH SURE, NEW ZEALAND SAUVIGNON BLANC HAS BEEN AROUND FOR AWHILE, but even in this day, its popularity continues to grow, outlasting each new challenger, kicking them to the curb as another new opponent rises to threaten this stalwart fighter.

New Zealand Sauvignon Blanc possesses a taste profile all its own. Gooseberry, grapefruit, hay, lime, fresh-cut grass, and passion fruit offering a kaleidoscope of flavor, stun your senses with a flurry of lefts and rights. Intense aromas crinkle your nose as you close your eyes and wince, trying to single out a particular component of its multi-faceted fragrant bouquet. Each sniff awakens your senses as if given a dose of smelling salts. Then, the one-two punch as the liquid passes your lips, unapologetically assaulting your taste buds with such veracity that your mouth reels and waters. Weeping from the attack, the wine flagrantly drags you back into the ring for another round of sensory abuse.

"We were the first, we were the first!" each supplier exclaims, bragging to anyone that will listen, each claiming they own the title and belt of this highly regarded prizefighter. With such a bevy of choices and an array of prices to satisfy every pocket, it really doesn't matter, for in the end, the consumer usually wins this fight.

"THE DISEASE"

THE INVITATION WAS FOR A 50TH BIRTHDAY; it said semi-formal and to bring a date, which was tricky, for I was in the middle stages of a bad breakup with a drama queen I had been dating for six years and in the early phases of a new relationship that was mostly at the informal stage of, "See you when I see you – okay?" Plus, I just really wasn't up to going. After driving around Wyoming the whole week prior, working and entertaining suppliers and clients – too much wine, whiskey, beer, and not enough sleep had taken its toll. In fact, I had been going full bore for years, and I was now overweight and run down. I needed rest, and more importantly, diet and exercise. Nonetheless, the party was in Park City at the home of a friend who had a terrible problem with money – He had too much of it. It was sure to be a barn burner. The friend took his food and wine seriously, so I knew he would pull out all the stops – It was a party that one should not miss. After consulting with the host, I found out that some of the guests on the invite list were mutual friends of the drama queen, so after considerable apprehension, I ended up taking her.

It was an absolutely beautiful Saturday evening in August when I arrived to pick up my date. We had a cocktail while she finished primping. After the twenty-minute drive to Park City, we arrived at the party, now well underway. I brought two bottles of very nice wine for the host (which in retrospect was probably stupid because upon walking through the massive house, I found that there was no shortage of booze to be had). Wine bottles, both full and empty, lined the kitchen counters, the living room held a pop-up bar where spirits were copiously being poured, and the hot tub on the deck was no longer a hot tub, but rather a cold tub filled with beer and ice. The place was packed with people drinking, toasting, and eating food elegantly displayed on a 20-foot-long table catered by one of the best local restaurants.

The party raged into the night. By midnight, half the guests were gone; the die-hards, including myself, were still going strong. The house was not a complete wreck yet, but it was well on its way; I was sure it would take a week to get it clean again. Then, someone yelled, "TACOS!" and the remaining partygoers staggered and stumbled out the front door to a taco cart the host had arranged to arrive just after midnight; a smart move considering the condition of the guests. My date and I ate, then sat on the front lawn regaining our composure before making the drive home (which, I will admit, was probably a bad idea).

I drove home without incident while she slept. After parking in her driveway, she invited me in for a drink (one I didn't need, another bad idea that I voluntarily embraced), followed by yet another bad idea – the removal of our clothing. One smart move was made that night on my part: I did stay at her house, as driving at that point would surely have been a mistake. I awoke at 6 am in a panic, realizing I forgot I'd volunteered to play in a golf tournament that morning. At least it was a scramble; my teammates would have to carry me. I was so hungover I could barely walk straight – I was pretty sure a considerable amount of alcohol was still in my system. In fact, I was so sick, it could've been possible to get pulled over for DUI on the way home or even on the way to the golf tournament.

I rushed out the door, then drove home to change and grab my golf clubs. It was going to be miserable day; not only was I sick, but dark, ominous clouds were rolling over the western mountains of the Salt Lake Valley. I contemplated no-showing but couldn't let my teammates down (some of whom were wine buyers at a couple of local restaurants); I couldn't lose face with them. The foul weather was just hitting the area when I arrived at the golf course. Just after unloading my clubs, one of my teammates informed me the tournament had been canceled. I was relieved. Many of the golfers were going to brunch for Bloody Mary's, which upon hearing, made me throw up a little in my mouth. I took a drink of water and politely declined – I couldn't wait to get home.

Back at home, I showered quickly, then laid on the sofa napping periodically while flipping channels well into the afternoon. Around 3 pm I went to the gym to try to sweat out my hangover; it helped a little, but I still felt like crap upon my return. So, I drank a couple of beers, then ordered a pizza (surely that would do it), thinking good old-fashion hair of the dog and grease would solve my problems. Both offered some respite as I once again lazily flipped through the channels sprawled out in my leather recliner with sleep arriving at some point shortly thereafter.

I don't remember if I was dreaming that evening or if it was complete blackness, but around 11 pm I suddenly awoke. The TV was blaring. It took a minute for me to get my bearings. Tilting forward to a seated position in the chair, that's when it hit. My ears began ringing loudly, followed by what I can only describe as a feeling of being pulled through a time warp – it seemed like everything in front of me was pulsing – the room felt as if it was being sucked by some imaginary force in and away from my face. Then the room began to tilt and spin violently. I grabbed the arms of the recliner trying to steady myself. I became nauseous. My mouth watered; puke was sure to follow. Bouncing off the walls through the hallway into the bathroom, I fell to my knees, grabbing both sides of the commode and expelling what had to be everything in me. The shaking started in my arms, then flowed through my body as my brow broke out in a sweat and my heartbeat accelerated. I couldn't catch my breath. I needed water, so I crawled to the sink a few feet away. With the cold water running, I splashed my face and cupped my hands, filling them so I could drink, only to fall back to the floor. Ears still ringing, room still spinning, I managed to sit propped against the wall. My mind raced. *What the fuck is happening to me? Am I dying? Oh shit – I have to throw up again!* The water I drank, along with internal juices projected from my mouth. I didn't know what to do. It was almost midnight, and I stayed in the bathroom for a few more hours, laying on the cold floor, occasionally drinking water only to throw it up soon after. I cried.

At some point, exhausted, cold, empty, ears ringing, shaking with fear and panic, I mustered enough energy to make it to the bedroom. I fell again to the floor, however, this time to my knees to pray. (Seems we all pray in times of need, suffering, or affliction. This was my time, and I begged God for help.)

Once finished, my mind continued to race. *Sleep – yeah, that's it – I just needed a good night's sleep,* I thought to myself. Without making any sudden movements, I slowly slipped into the sheets. My usual position, fetal on either side, worked for a moment, but the room would spin and tilt, resulting in another dash to the bathroom to furiously dry heave. Once again, slowly I eased back into bed, now on my back, this time propping my head up in between two pillows so I wouldn't accidentally move to one side or the other. As the remainder of the night wore on, I drifted in and out of sleep, jerking awake from time to time, steadying myself, checking the clock. Morning seemed so far away.

Around 7 am Monday, I awoke. Lurching side to side, I walked to the kitchen still shaking. I needed water and food but feared I wouldn't keep it down. It was worth a try, but ten minutes later the toast and banana were violently evacuated. Though it was early still, I had to call someone, and that someone was my mom. Clutching my phone with one hand, the kitchen counter with the other, I made the call. She could hear the pain and fear in my voice as I explained the hell I had just been through. She wasted no time arriving at my house soon after. She made oatmeal then started to make phone calls. First plan of action – the emergency room.

We made several stops on the way to the hospital; the nausea was unbearable. I called my boss from the waiting room simply explaining the need for a sick day without all the gory details. "No problem," he said, "hope you feel better tomorrow."

The doctors shook their heads after the initial examination. "Seems like an inner ear problem – which is mostly a mystery." To rule out a brain tumor or aneurysm they scheduled an MRI first, followed by a CT scan – it would get expensive. That long day at the hospital yielded no concrete results. I did, however, have fluids pushed through me with an IV, which seemed to help a little. All the doctors could say was: "It may be Ménière's Disease – go see a specialist." And so, I went to the family doctor who had treated me since childhood. An exceptional doctor, his specialty was ears, nose, throat – there was hope (or so I thought).

The first opening in his schedule was two days later - an eternity if you're sick. The thought of lying down, let alone sleeping, was terrifying. Nights were mostly small stretches of light sleep followed by bouts of vertigo, dizziness, ringing ears, praying, and heaving over the toilet. The days were a little more tolerable; I held food and water down for longer periods of time, providing me with the needed nutrients before hurling everything up. Since I could work a little from my home office, my company was none the wiser to my plight. On the third day, my mother asked my brother in law, the bishop from her LDS ward, and my uncle to administer a blessing: something that's performed within the Mormon religion to help council, comfort and heal. Since I was still a baptized member of the LDS Church, I still qualified, I guess. Even though extremely far from the fold, I would take any help I could get at that point.

The following day, the family doctor poked, prodded, listened, and peered through a multitude of tiny instruments into my ear cavity. He had several thoughts on the issue: tinnitus, a virus, possibly a crystal imbalance, but firmly landed on Ménière's Disease. "It has to be," he stated.

"That's what the ER doctors said," I replied. "What is it and how do I get rid of it?"

Deep in thought, his eyes squinted as he rubbed his jaw between his forefinger and thumb, then shook his head. "Become a good Mormon."

"What? You're kidding me, right? What does that mean?"

He told me the story about Ménière, a Frenchman, for whom the affliction is named, then said, "Basically – give up caffeine, alcohol, nicotine, and salt. Essentially, do what the Mormons do."

"No way, that's not an option. I tried that already. If you recall, I grew up Mormon," I stated. "How am I supposed to do my job – I sell wine for a living for hell's sake?"

He thought for a minute. "The only thing I can tell you is that diet seems to work – try to modify your intake. It probably wouldn't hurt to go to the Hearing and Balance Institute downtown to be examined. They may be able to help. I'll make an appointment for you, okay?"

"Sure, I may as well exhaust all options."

He left the room briefly and I panicked. Again, my mind raced, *I finally had a dream job selling something I truly love. Now if I can't find a cure, I may have to quit.*

A short time later, he reappeared holding a few papers in his hand. "Here's the address. They can get you in tomorrow afternoon, so I booked it for you. This other paper is a prescription to help with nausea. Remember, modify your diet for now."

Dejected, I thanked him and left.

My diet wasn't a problem (at least not now - it was a forced diet – I could hardly keep anything down), the mere thought of drinking alcohol was repugnant. I was mostly repulsed by food as everything seemed overly seasoned and offensive. I had to force myself to eat. The symptoms continued day and night. Unable to get a good night's sleep, I was physically, mentally, and emotionally exhausted.

Next stop: The Hearing and Balance Institute, which for me, was a waste of time. While I'm sure they've helped many people, the visit only resulted in extreme discomfort as they put me through a battery of tests (which, if you have vertigo, is probably akin to being a prisoner at Guantanamo Bay). First, they had me lie on one side, then the other, then slanted slightly downward, followed by a very brief episode upside down with my feet locked into some kind of inverse exercise machine. Then they put me through a series of tests that could have passed for a DUI assessment. Walk a straight line – nope. Hop on one leg – nope. Now the other – hmm, nope. Then, pick up items from the floor while balancing on one foot, with and without my eyes closed (out of the question). Extreme vertigo and dizziness followed with bouts of throwing up – pure agony.

When day six of my new malady arrived, I was starting to own it, so I did what most people do: turn to the internet, spending the whole weekend researching my dilemma. Between bouts of sickness, I read, watched TV, and answered phone calls from worried friends and family; some offering advice, but mostly consoling me as if I had one foot in the grave. A few people came to visit, some bringing home remedies, homeopathic medicine, and even food that sadly went to waste.

Deciding to not notify my company of what was going on was probably doing them a disservice, but I did manage to work some each day; just enough to get by – no one the wiser. Luckily, no business trips, supplier visits or meetings with accounts were scheduled, so I just shored up in my condo working from my home office. I was asked to meet several times by some of my accounts to taste through some wines, but I declined politely, telling them I would catch up after I felt better.

A significant amount of weight loss followed; by the end of the third week, I had lost close to twenty pounds, going from 195 to around 175. I will say, weight loss as a side effect was the only benefit from having Ménière's Disease, or whatever the hell I had, but it's not something I'd recommend to anyone, or even wish upon my enemies. I have had some terrible illnesses throughout my life; there was even one stretch with the flu that sidelined me for two weeks. I was so sick, I had to relocate to my mother's house as I was sure I was going to die. But nothing could have prepared me for the endless days of ear-ringing torture laced with vertigo and dizzy spells that I was now enduring. I wondered how long it could last. I couldn't live the rest of my days suffering in despair and misery. At one point, I actually prepared for the worst – a fairly young death.

Into the fourth full week, one of my sisters called to check on me. After listening and consoling, she offered an option that had not been considered – acupuncture. She told me of a place on the east side of town owned by a Chinese doctor; she said he was supposed to be a miracle worker. I called immediately and he was able to get me in the following day.

Toward the back of an insignificant strip mall, landlocked behind some other businesses is where Dr. Ling headquartered his small but busy practice. Upon entering, as one might expect, little bells and chimes sounded when opening the door, a subtle alarm that someone had arrived. Soft music permeated the air of the tiny waiting room decorated in soothing pastels. A video about the many benefits of Chinese medicine looped over and over. Completing the waiting room were several chairs (a few of which reclined), diagrams of the human nervous and muscular systems, and a couple of electric foot massagers. I waited among several other patients, each of whom had their own special set of ailments needing to be remedied. After a short wait and finishing the requisite paperwork, Dr. Ling appeared and escorted me back to his office. He offered a cup of water and a chair. "Mista Fawanghina, very good meet you, please have seat."

"Thank you," I said, slowly sitting down in obvious distress and discomfort.

Dr. Ling read my paperwork, periodically looking up at me. When finished, he asked, "May see hands, please?"

Leaning in slightly, I held out my arms, laying them across his desk. Dr. Ling took hold of my wrists to measure my pulse, then told me to stick out my tongue - which he examined top and bottom – followed by my eyes and ears. Reflecting for a moment, he began a sequence of questions about my job, family, and lifestyle, then he returned to his thoughts. "I fix you," he stated, "but will take time. You must come two-three times week for treatment until allllll symptom finish."

Elated, I replied, "Great, thank you." I knew it would take time, and would probably not be cheap, however, at that point, deep in misery and depression, I would've paid just about anything to end the hell I was going through.

The doctor showed me into one of the examination rooms. I was face-up under a sheet, almost completely naked, as Dr. Ling proceeded to insert what felt like forty or so needles into various pressure points and nerves – several around my ears, jaw, head, then down my arms, hands and even legs and feet. Slight discomfort accompanied the treatment but that was to be expected. A heat lamp was placed just above me providing soothing warmth. Waterfalls, waves breaking, and bird sounds intermittently played through a small CD player in the corner. A kitchen timer was set, and I drifted off for what seemed like several hours – the best sleep I'd had in weeks. I was awakened by a small ping signaling the end of the session. The needles were removed, and after dressing, I went back to meet the doctor in his office.

"So, Spatta-cus," he said, handing me a list of tasks which I read through as he spoke in a very serious broken tone. "You need do following til treatment finish. Very, very import - nooo coffee – only green tea! Reduce salt!" he stated firmly and abruptly, shaking his finger back and forth to get his point across. I just nodded as if I were one of his kids. "Eat vegetable, lots vegetable – raw, very good. If you need cook – only steam! Only two or three serving meat each week! Noooo refine sugar – very important! Noooo tobacco!"

"Okay," I said, "no problem."

"Last thing very important!" he stated adamantly, "NOOOO ALCOHOL, for at least one month. Then after, only little wine. Two-or three-times week. No beer, no booze!"

Looking up from the list of "don'ts," I paused briefly before asking, "How long will this take?"

"Til all symptom gone."

Sheepishly I replied, "So, um, my job is selling wine. I need to get back to work."

"Yes, but very important follow direction!"

"Uh, yes, I will – okay." Switching gears, I asked, "How do you think this happened to me?"

"Ahh, yes," he paused briefly. "Western civilization always go, go, go – very stressful. No yin, no yang – no balance! Too much one thing put life out balance!" I thought about what he was saying as he continued. "Too much salt – out balance! Too much sex – out balance! Too much work – out balance! Too much alcohol – out balance!"

"Yes, but wine is good for you. Do you drink wine?"

"Ah... yes, but small amount. Spatta-cus, Spatta-cus, Spatta-cus... Too much one thing – no Yang! Alcohol – form of Western medicine – too much – no good!"

"Okay, okay – I got it."

"One more thing," he stated as I laughed (which was probably the first time since becoming sick) "Wear warm socks, good shoes. Very important – keep feet warm!"

"Okay, anything else?"

"Yes, yes, yes – almost forgot. Very important," he said, disappearing into a back room as I laughed discreetly. Moments later, he reappeared with three large plastic bottles filled with Chinese supplements and handed them to me one by one reciting the directions. "This one - take one morning, one lunch, one bedtime. This one, take three each morning – with food – yes, with food – very important. This one, take three at dinner – each night – yes, with food – yes."

"I got it, thank you."

Dr. Ling then showed me to the door. Holding it open for me, he added, "I have one more question for you.

"Yes, what's that?"

"If you have any extra, 'Western Medicine,' you want me

sample…I'm good – how you say…?"

"Guinea pig?" I asked.

"Yes, yes, yes – guinea pig," he replied, laughing heartily.

Laughing with him, I turned to make my way from his office. "See you in a couple of days… I'll bring you some 'Western Medicine.'"

I faithfully visited Dr. Ling for six more weeks, two to three appointments each week, then once a week for a few months. A few thousand dollars, needles, and supplements later, I began to heal. At my worst point during the whole ordeal, I weighed just over 145 lbs. I was gaunt, ashen, and weak, but I persevered. Luckily no one from my company, not even my boss found out about my dilemma. Due to my ability to work from home and the fact the whole ordeal happened during the communication era probably saved my job. At numerous times during the treatments, I provided Dr. Ling with some "Western Medicine," and ultimately, we became friends. Though expensive, it was worth it. Chinese medicine did something Western medicine could not – it cured me. The symptoms gradually declined each week and I got my life back by mid-December.

After that experience, I've tried hard to find balance each day, a Yin Yang flow – trying not to take life for granted. It does not always work, but I try. So, what did this story have to do with selling wine? I guess the point would be, don't let excess tear you down. I let my job take me to a point where I became unbalanced. Even though selling and drinking alcohol were part of my job, the overindulgences were simply too much – not enough balance. In retrospect, I was burning the candle at both ends; late nights, excessive drinking, countless rich meals, dehydration, and not enough sleep – all were factors. It was a valuable lesson, one that would play out in a life-changing decision, many years later in the quest for Yin and Yang.

TREND

WE'RE GOING GREEN BABY

OUT OF NOWHERE, momentum built rapidly to capitalize on the green movement that seemed to begin with specialty grocery stores and restaurants featuring non-GMO farm-to-table products grown organically and sustainably by small producers.

Many wineries already practiced some form of responsibility, be it sustainability, alternative energies such as solar, wind and water, organic, and even biodynamic. But the movement within the wine industry grew dramatically as consumers demanded alternatives to wines produced without regard to their health and to that of the land. Soon, a supplier presentation wasn't complete without some information (whether true or not) that the wines they represented were "green" in some sort of way.

Needing to sell wine, the capitalist spew flowed:

Ours is organic!

Ours is bio-dynamic!

Ours is SIP certified!

Our winery has solar panels!

Ours is sustainable!

Ours is all of those things, plus the bottles and labels are made from recycled products!

We have owl boxes!

We have sheep!

Our female winemaker doesn't shave her armpits!

We employ raptors and anteaters with night-vision goggles to consume all the pests!

We only irrigate with the tears of our consumers!

Wait, wait, wait... What? Okay, the last few were a stretch, but you get the point. Looking for any edge, any opening, suppliers created stories to praise, and in most cases, validate their wines.

I must applaud a winery's effort to "go green" in some form or another. In most cases, going green means spending a pile of money to produce a product with social conscience. Respect for the land and the environment results in respect for their employees, the product, and ultimately the end consumer. A common misunderstanding is that products should cost less without the added expenses associated with using pesticides, fertilizers, fungicides, and herbicides. However, sustainable, organic, and bio-dynamic products often cost more for a reason: they require an extreme amount of time and care to ensure the land, and or the environment in relation to the land, is prepared in a specific manner to produce said products. Due to location, some wineries need to use some sort of pesticide or fungicide, and that's okay if used sparingly and other efforts are made to ensure responsibility to the consumer. The sad truth is that many American consumers don't care what they put into their bodies, so giant petroleum-like factories owned by powerful corporations without a conscience continue to exist, pumping out inferior, inexpensive juice with clever gimmicks to claim their share of the almighty dollar.

THE UTAH "WINEMAKER"

SOMETIME DURING 2007-08, I was approached by a gentleman named Jorge Perez regarding representing his new line of wines from Perez & Palmer Winery. I thought he was a bit crazy at first because Jorge had what seemed to be a great position working for my largest competitor. Although I despised my rival, I liked Jorge because I knew him from his previous years as the owner of his own wine brokerage, Passito Wines. Even prior to that, I knew him as the owner/operator of his own restaurant. At some point, Jorge had sold his wine brokerage to my competitor but retained a job heading a division under their umbrella. A family man, extremely knowledgeable, affable, and driven, Jorge was very well-liked in our industry, and he was a formidable competitor.

"Why don't you ask if they'd like to represent you?" I inquired.

"Well," he sighed, searching for the correct words. "After telling them I wanted to start my own label and winery, they basically kicked me to the curb. It seems that if you don't toe the company line 100%, they blackball you."

"Tell me what you've got, the concept and story, I'll have

to run it by my boss first to get approval, but it's possible, I guess."

Jorge launched into his spiel while I sat back and listened. "Spartacus, this has been a dream of mine for a very long time. I have a couple of partners – a gentleman named Chet Palmer owns the majority of shares, and his lawyer, acting as our lawyer for the winery, has a small number of shares, and I have the balance. Do you know Chet?"

"Sounds familiar, but I'm not sure," I replied

"Well, back when I owned Tavola Restaurant, Chet Palmer was one of my regulars. At the time, he didn't know a lot culinarily, but as he kept coming in, I exposed him to different foods and wines and how they interacted and complemented each other." As Jorge continued to talk, he became more animated, using his hands and arms to help tell his story. "Chet's a self-made man; he's designed bridges, developed real estate, taught scuba, and done an array of other things. Needless to say, he has a significant amount of money invested in this venture, as do I, so we're going for it. This is my dream. It's time for me to give it a try."

"So, where is the winery?" I asked, still skeptical but warming with his enthusiasm.

"Well, we make the wines in California with a winemaker friend of mine. We have our own labels, codes, and story. We get the juice from what we perceive as the best areas – mainly Central Coast, but if we can get Napa or Sonoma fruit at a reasonable price, we'll do it. We produce two lines at this time – a lower-tier called Trois Chiens and a higher tier called Perez & Palmer. We've already approached the state buyers; they've agreed to bring on a couple of wines to sell in the state stores."

"Well, that's fantastic Jorge!" I said, feeling a little jealous, because in the back of my mind, I wanted my own winery too. "But if you already have some listed wines in Utah, why do you want me to help you? Sounds like you're on your way?"

As Jorge continued, I could hear the excitement in his voice and see the sparkle in his eyes, signaling a fire burning within his soul. "We'll definitely help get the word out, but with your sales team, you can reach more accounts than we can. And since you also have Wyoming in your territory, we'd like to try to get our products sold in that state as we continue to grow. Part of the deal I have with Chet is that I meet distributors in other states in an effort to sell our wines in other markets. Ideally, we'd like to be in about five to eight states within the first few years, then continue to expand."

"Okay, fine. Sounds like some good case volume, and we don't have anything like this in our portfolio. Plus, I'd rather take a shot at representing you before any of our competitors. If you could do me a favor? Just put the presentation in an email along with brokerage fees and such. I'll get it to my boss for approval. Once I have the approval, we can get started. Sound good?"

Jorge's face lit up with a big smile. "I'll get the email over to you by end of day tomorrow. Thank you, Spartacus!"

Just as he said, Jorge sent me the presentation, which I reviewed then forwarded to my boss for approval. He questioned it a bit, but when he found out they already had some wines listed generating case volume plus commissions, he approved it. After I notified an elated Jorge, we set his new winery up as a new vendor with my corporate offices and, we were off to the races.

The next step was to set a date for Jorge to present his

products during a lunch with my wine team so they could sample the wines and hear the back story of the brands. Also, I wanted to meet his partner Chet to find out more about his side of the deal.

We gathered at one of the local restaurants for lunch, sitting away from the crowd in a corner off the main dining room. Jorge and Chet had arrived before us so they could set up the wines on the table along with an easel and technical sheets at each place setting.

When I entered the restaurant, Jorge eagerly jumped up to greet me and to introduce me to his partner. "Spartacus, I'd like you to meet my partner in the winery, Chet Palmer."

Chet was a single man, twenty years Jorge's senior, about six feet tall with thinning dark hair and a fake tan. His face was full of deep but warm character lines from years of hard work and fun. Chet walked to Jorge's side, extending his hand to me. "Glad to meet you, Spartacus. Jorge has told me many wonderful things. We are very happy to be doing business with you."

"Thank you," I said, laughing for levity's sake. "I'm quite sure Jorge embellished a bit, but I'm glad to be working with you too. Hopefully, we can turn this into a long, productive relationship."

I introduced the rest of my team, we ordered some food, and the new partners began to tell their story and talk about their wines as we tasted.

A good portion of selling wine is its history (or back story), the significance of the region, winemaker, vineyard, or some other bit of minutiae. A good story can sometimes help make or break a product when a brand is launched.

Just a short time span will tell immediately if the brand will make it – often products are discarded before they can get legs. The Perez & Palmer line, along with the Trois Chiens wines, had just enough story with decent juice to get some good traction.

With Trois Chiens, the story was simple; the French name for "three dogs" came from Chet's three dogs, Healy, Mabel, and Beau. The label was decent (a watercolor of three dogs playing in a field), and the juice was good for the price, so that was a plus. The other part of the story that they wanted to use was that of the actual winemaker (for credibility purposes), including his name. His condition, however, was that we could not use his name when selling or promoting the wines, as he did not want to dilute his own namesake label. Difficult, but not insurmountable.

They had chosen their last names as the label for their upper-end tier; their names directly positioned at the label's center below a made-up family crest for the new partnership. The type of wine and vintage was listed at the bottom. The crest was comprised of a bunch of grape leaves with a shield, and on top of the shield, a sword, a chef's knife, and a ladle were all crossed over the top. The story behind the crest: after doing some research, Chet found he was a very distant descendant of Louis the IX, an old European king – hence, the sword. Since Jorge was a chef prior to the wine business – the knife and ladle. The story was a little loose regarding the higher-priced upper-end tier, but like I said, the juice was pretty good, so we hit the market doing our best to get the products on wine lists.

Now, a couple of the best ways to promote a product is by holding winemaker dinners or having the products served at events and fundraisers. After a few months, we had our first winemaker dinner at an account close to downtown Salt Lake City. About 40 people had signed up for a four-course meal paired with Trois Chiens and Perez & Palmer wines. Jorge and Chet both attended, and both talked about some aspects of their partnership, the wine, and what was available for sale in the state stores. Chet had brought framed prints of his animals to display in the room for all to see while they were eating, which, in his opinion, helped sell the wine. And as cute as they were in their own way, I found it a little hokey. I'm not sure that it really added to the dinner, however, maybe a few of the older ladies liked the soft touch.

The next event was a charity event called Labrador Rescue. I had been contacted by a gentleman who was deeply committed to this breed of dog, and he wanted to have a wine tasting/fundraiser to raise money for rescuing Labs that had been abused or were old service dogs and such. They held the event at an old bar known for years as the local meat market; off to the side of the main bar, they were given a large private backroom sufficient for a small crowd.

Jorge couldn't attend so I went to the event with Chet. I asked Chet to donate a couple of cases of Trois Chiens wine, which, along with a few cases of wine from one of my other suppliers, helped further the cause. While the wines were poured, we took turns talking to the crowd about each varietal, pairings, availability and answering questions. A silent auction was held along with a live auction while videos about Labradors were played. Between talking to the crowd, Chet and I spoke about business and the event in general – and it was at this time that I got my first glimpse into Chet's true character.

"Check out the legs and ass on her," he said, leaning into

my left ear while gesturing to a middle-aged woman at the food table.

Now, I'm not immune to a little guy talk, but I barely knew this person, so I halfheartedly went along. "Yeah, that's one fine looking lady."

"She's no lady. I bet she was on her knees at lunch and on her back before she came to the event!" he exclaimed.

I faked a little laugh at his candor as I briefly glanced her way, then playing along, asked, "And, how would you know that?"

"Did you check out those fishnet stockings with the seam up the back?"

"Uh, yeah – so?" I asked, slightly amused.

"That's a sure sign of a sex addict."

"Oh, I had no idea," emphasizing my disbelief. "Hmm, maybe you should go introduce yourself?"

"As a matter of fact, I will, as soon as the presentation is over."

True to his word, as the crowd began to mill around, I noticed that Chet had disappeared. I had to hand it to the horny old bugger, at least he still was making a go of it.

I sat quietly for a moment sipping a glass of wine, taking in the sights of the mixed attendees, then joined the crowd browsing the silent auction items. After a half-hour, I hadn't seen or heard from Chet, so I decided it was time to go home. I found the event coordinator to shake his hand, congratulating him on a well-attended show and said I hoped we had helped him out. He thanked me, and as I made my way out to the open area of the bar, through the darkness, I spotted Chet walking toward me angrily, looking a bit disheveled, his shirt soaking wet, his hair in a tousle.

"What the hell happened to you?" I asked.

"Well, I introduced myself to the fishnet stocking gal," he said – as liquid dripped off his nose and eyebrows. "She turned me down, so I went out to the bar to get a drink. I sat down next to a couple of women at the counter, and after a bit of small talk, I told them I was a winemaker. They were thrilled." His voice lilted a bit, and his eyes widened as he continued, "I told them about the wines, gave them my card, then asked them if they wanted to come home with me for a threesome. It was then that I found out they were lesbians – I called them a few names and told them they didn't know what they were missing. That's when they threw their drinks in my face."

I began to laugh uncontrollably as tears filled my eyes. Patting Chet on the shoulder, I consoled him. "Well, how were you supposed to know?"

"I don't know," he replied, throwing his arms in the air, eyes still wide with disbelief. "They looked like normal everyday women to me. What in the hell is this world coming to?"

"I guess you tried," I said, advising him. "You better get yourself cleaned up a bit in the men's room before you say goodbye to the organizer. As for me, I'm out of here, I've got to get home. Please let Jorge know the event went well. At least the first part of it, I guess! I'll see you later."

"Okay, Spartacus. Thank you – I'll see you soon," he said as he turned to walk away.

I laughed hysterically the whole way to my car. On the drive home, I thought about what Chet said to the women at the bar – that he was a "winemaker," which he really wasn't. I mean, I guess technically speaking, Chet was a winemaker, but in truth his role was simply that of an owner. But whatever, I guess winemaker sounded sexier than winery owner, and whether he was using it to sell more wine or pick up women probably didn't matter in the long run – or so I thought.

When Perez & Palmer began their business relationship with us as their broker, they had two wines from the Trois Chiens line and two wines from the Perez & Palmer line state-listed and carried on the state liquor store shelves in Utah. The Trois Chiens line retailed for around $12.99 and the Perez & Palmer line retailed for around $20 - $30 depending on the grape. We presented Trois Chiens Zinfandel, Sauvignon Blanc, and Chardonnay, but the DABC denied them, so we had to wait for a year to re-present. I knew it was not likely that they would get listed as the other wines were still getting their legs, but as brokers, we had to present everything at the behest of the supplier.

After six months or so we decided to try to get a couple of their wines state-listed in Wyoming. We sent samples to my state manager so she could taste her accounts across the state. Right off the bat, she secured several decent quantity special orders, which would help when it came time for us to present the wines to the state for listing; a decent backlog of special orders from the licensees is one of the criteria the Wyoming Liquor Division reviews when they decide to buy. Jorge Perez even came to the biannual listing meeting to present the wines to the Wyoming Liquor Division. Since we could show some movement with special orders from the private licensees in the state along with his presence as one of the winery owners, we secured two new placements - Trois Chiens Cab and White Blend.

Back in Utah, we continued to pound the pavement, working hard to secure wine list placements, lining up wine dinners, and hitting as many events as possible.

As the months went by, it was business as usual for the Perez & Palmer winery. My staff and I worked the market with the wines the state carried on their shelves, driving placements on wine lists and in the state-owned retail accounts. Though Chet contacted me frequently, I noticed that Jorge was spending a considerable amount of time out of town trying to secure distributors around the country to carry their wines, leaving him little time to work the market. When Jorge was available, he still went with us to some local account appointments here and there.

Then one day I received a phone call from the GM at Ruth's Chris Restaurant in Salt Lake City, stating that Chet had attended a private dinner hosted by a winemaker from Napa Valley. A little over halfway through the dinner, Chet started to uncork bottles of Trois Chiens and Perez & Palmer wines under the table, then offered them around the room during the private dinner in front of the other winemaker.

"Holy shit," I said, "what the hell was he thinking?"

The very agitated GM said, "I have no idea, but it was a very classless thing to do. In fact, I kicked him out, and he's banned from coming into Ruth's Chris again. I just wanted you to know since you're their broker. We were going to bring in their Cabernet to serve by the glass, but then this happened, and I can't allow it."

"I see. Okay, no problem," I replied. "I'll let his partner Jorge know what happened. Thanks for the phone call."

After hanging up, I immediately called Jorge, who apologized profusely, telling me that he would talk to Chet about his behavior. He went on to explain, "Chet has become very passionate about the wines, and since he's the primary partner funding the venture, he's doing everything he can to ensure its success. This, however, is not acceptable."

A few weeks later, I was invited to a private dinner for the soft opening of a new Italian restaurant in Salt Lake City called Fritto Misto, along with about forty other guests. After entering the restaurant, I spotted Chet Palmer sitting quietly at one of the tables, so I went over to talk to him. He explained that he was invited by the owner; they had been friends for a long time and had even traveled to Europe together on a cooking immersion trip. Chet invited my date and me to sit with him, but the owner had already assigned the seats, so we declined politely then sat down at another table to wait for the dinner to begin.

About halfway through the evening, the owner came over to talk to me about the food, which was very impressive even though it was the first night the kitchen staff had prepared it for guests. I gave the owner my impressions about the food and decor, and even though I wasn't the broker for the wines, I told him they were very good, then thanked him for the invitation. He went on to explain the nuances of the course paired with the white wine, when all of a sudden, he abruptly stopped to look up at a table across the room. Shaking his head, he said, "Can you fucking believe it? Chet Palmer is opening his own wines and offering them to the rest of the table!"

"What? No way," I said, pivoting to get a better look over the heads of the people sitting across from me.

The owner took it in stride, halfheartedly laughing

it off. "I go to all this trouble and expense to invite him here and he opens his own wines, which aren't even Italian? I can't believe it. This is an Italian restaurant; the wines are supposed to complement the food, and vice versa. I'm not even having American wines on the wine list – only Italian. Those wines don't even pair with my food!"

"Do you want me to say something to him?" I asked.

"No, he's my friend; we go back a long way. I'll go talk to him."

I could see them talking across the room. After much discussion, I guess they came to some kind of understanding as the Trois Chiens and Perez & Palmer wines stayed on the table for anyone to try, but in the end, it was a tough sell as everyone wanted Italian wines with their food.

Back in Wyoming, with inventory in the state warehouse, Trois Chiens white and red were ready to make their debut. We pulled cases of samples from the state, then my team began to hit every retail account they could from Jackson to Gillette and down to Cheyenne. We needed the wines on retail shelves, so we could get out of the gates fast, then hopefully onto wine lists as time went by.

Both Jorge and Chet made several trips to Wyoming to work the market with my staff, which definitely helped get the word out. They also held a few wine-maker dinners and helped pour at wine tasting events throughout the state. They certainly put in the time and energy to try and get the brands out in the market.

Everything seemed to be going well, and after the first year, we had enough points of distribution to generate the sales required for the Wyoming Liquor Division to maintain the listings. Then something happened over the course of the second year. Sales began to slow, and we began to lose the placements we had worked so very hard to obtain. I started hearing from my Wyoming staff that most accounts wouldn't even taste the wine or consider bringing them in. When I asked why, I was told that the sales reps from our archrival and Jorge Perez's former employer were telling accounts not to buy the wine. I don't know what they told the accounts in Wyoming – whether they said the wine was terrible or lies about Jorge - it really didn't matter. Whatever they were doing was working and the licensees weren't buying. By the end of the second year, we had lost one of the listings with the state of Wyoming due to low sales; special orders also had dropped off significantly. We desperately tried to hold on to the one existing red wine listing, doing our best to promote the wine to maintain adequate sales.

Conversely, in Utah, everything was going along fairly well for Trois Chiens. We still had four wines state listed on the shelves in the liquor stores and sales had grown. Although our rival also did business in Utah, they couldn't do anything to kill the brand in the liquor stores because the DABC decided what would be on the shelves, not independent buyers. If a product continued to sell, then it would stay on the shelves. The only place they could engage in any type of negativity with the brands would be in the on-premise restaurant accounts. And, it's possible that some negativity made its way out into the market, but we were still able to get many restaurant accounts to buy the wines.

Then out of the blue, something bizarre happened in the middle of the third year. I received a frantic call from Jorge asking me to meet him for coffee because it was an emergency. Sensing his anxiety and hearing the worried tone in his voice,

I agreed. An hour later, I was sitting in a coffee shop listening to Jorge, shocked, and beside himself, as he tried to explain that he was no longer a partner in the winery with Chet. I asked him how something like that could happen since he, too, had invested a considerable amount of money in the project along with all the time and energy. "Well, Chet's the primary investor, and along with his attorney, he holds more interest in the company, so they forced me out."

"Wow, that's unbelievable. When did this happen, and why? What are you going to do?"

"It happened about three weeks ago," he said. "I have no idea what to do. Part of my job was to get out to the other states to sell the product to distributors and expand the business. I guess it just wasn't happening fast enough for them."

"But you have money invested, right?"

Jorge looked extremely pale and on the verge of tears as he dejectedly looked down, then gasped, "I emptied my 401(k) and invested all my money to take a shot at owning my own label. Now, I can't even make the mortgage payment on my house and provide for my family."

I sat sickened and shocked for a minute, then Jorge added, "I've already put my house up for sale. I guess I'll have to start looking for a job; I may even have to move out of state."

"Wow," I said. "I'm stunned. I really don't know what to say except I'm sorry this has happened to you. I just can't believe it."

We both sat in silence for a moment before I asked, "So, I guess I just have to deal with Chet from now on?"

"Yes. I thought he would've called you by now."

"No, I haven't heard from him. He's probably waiting for you to tell me and for the news to die down." My anger began to build. "This really pisses me off, Jorge!"

"I know, I just wanted you to hear it from me in person rather than from Chet or someone else."

"I'm not sure if I can fire him as one of my suppliers," I said, "but I'm definitely going to try."

Jorge stood to excuse himself before leaving. "Thanks, Spartacus. I appreciate all your help and hard work. This had nothing to do with you; this was just something I never imagined would or could have happened."

I stood to shake his outstretched hand. "Good luck, Jorge. If I hear of any jobs around town, I'll let you know."

He thanked me again, the once-gleaming sparkle now gone from his eyes. After a deep breath, he turned and left the building. That was the last time I saw Jorge Perez in person. Sometime later, I did hear that he landed on his feet; it seems after selling his house, he relocated to California to work at a winery as an event coordinator.

Upon my return to my home office, I immediately emailed my boss to explain what had happened and that I wanted to terminate the relationship with Trois Chiens and Perez & Palmer wines. He said he would consider it, but he had to check their profitability. As it turned out, they were caught up in commission payments, and even though it was less than $10k per year in commissions, he wanted to keep doing business with them. Realizing I was stuck, I accepted the situation, and from that point on, did my best to keep my disgust in check when dealing with Chet.

The years following the partnership split became increasingly difficult. I received periodic emails and phone calls from Chet accusing our company of not doing enough to promote his products, and he adjusted pricing and booked events without consulting me. Calming irate owners and restaurant managers, and even a few enraged husbands became the norm for me. Chet continued to help with winemaker dinners, but it seemed more about his ego rather than the wines. Sure, he was passionate about the wines, but he used and abused the winemaker moniker extensively, all in the name of partying. Chet's candor and approach to business soured our relationship, resulting in my team and I doing the bare minimum to push his wines. Instead of firing us, Chet soldiered on, pushing, prodding, and making an ass of himself.

Progress in Wyoming was not much better, in fact, it was regressing. The Wyoming Liquor Division eventually delisted the only label Chet had left in the state, and unfortunately, the brands pretty much ceased to exist in that market.

On a positive note, each year Chet and his lawyer Clay McNutt helped pour wine at some local events and even volunteered to pour the wines during several of the Park City Food and Wine Festivals, which was a welcome respite because my staff and I didn't want to man a table of products we no longer believed in. Forcing a smile and agreeable face was too difficult; it was too hard to take Chet and Clay seriously. It appeared that all they wanted to do was party and act like lewd assholes. In fact, even the Park City event organizers had a hard time dealing with Chet because all he did was bitch and moan about where his booth was located. Plus, he was obscenely loud and obnoxious during the event, over-pouring people, and making passes at the women, married or not.

The straw that broke the camel's back for the Park City organizers came in the form of an unexpected set of wines Chet decided to introduce during the Saturday grand tasting at their annual summer event.

Staged in the plaza at Canyons Resort just outside of Park City proper, the event typically ran from three in the afternoon until seven pm. My local team and visiting suppliers usually showed up around one-thirty or two to set up our tables in preparation for the onslaught of drinkers. However, on this particular day, the Trois Chiens and Perez & Palmer table sat empty until just around 2:40 – only minutes before the tasting started.

The event organizer came over to ask who was pouring for Trois Chiens, and most importantly, he wanted to know where they were? Frantically, I called and texted Chet to track him down and see if he remembered the tasting that day. Even after several attempts, there were no replies. Then, just prior to three o'clock I heard faint rap music in the distance. Glancing toward the front gate, I noticed someone from Chet's entourage (of about seven or so people) carrying a boom box on his shoulder. The crowd parted as they made their way through the plaza reminiscent of a heavy-weight prize fighter heading to the ring; everyone gawking at the parading circus.

With a sigh of relief, I returned to the task at hand of organizing and preparing the table I was pouring at that day. Just moments before the gates opened, I decided to check in with Chet. Looking off in his direction I was speechless at the sight before me: Chet had hung a banner easily measuring 4 x 10 feet long across the tented top, corner to corner, directly above where his wines were being poured. The red banner read: "XXX Doggy Style XXX" (or something to that effect) in black and yellow – obviously, an attention grabber.

As I walked across the lawn on the lower plaza to get to his booth, the growing crowd stood pointing, whispering, and even snickering at the banner. The event organizer rushed up to me, wanting to know what the hell Chet was up to. Quickly evading him, I slid behind the already crowded table next to Chet. Mortified, I searched for the words. "I don't have the foggiest idea what the hell you're doing... I haven't been told about any of this or heard anything about it before now. What's going on?"

Chet laughed but couldn't elaborate, for the Trois Chiens table was already at a high level of chaos. His entourage, an array of odd people that I'd never seen, tried to get the table ready for the crowds, but it was too late, they were inundated. Three of the members of Chet's entourage were very young women, scantily clad in a sleazy assortment of stockings, heels, garters, and bustiers; their makeup applied in layers reminiscent of a stripper or streetwalker rather than that of a wine pouring assistant or aspiring wine geek. Two others in Chet's support team, there to photograph and film the event, scrambled to set up the perfect shots, jockeying for position while Chet smiled and chortled. Clay McNutt, dressed in a Hawaiian shirt and cowboy hat, frantically popped corks and arranged bottles on the table; the labels emblazoned blatantly with XXX Doggy Style XXX White and Red. Not one to be outdone, Chet Palmer himself also wore a Hawaiian shirt, but instead of a hat, he had shaved what was left of his hair into a makeshift Mohawk, bleached bright blond from its usual color.

Chet politely acknowledged me, shook my hand, then began to launch into the story of Doggy Style Wines. Stunned, I stared at his Mohawk while listening to his spiel, then one of his slutty "models" appeared by his side to reinforce his ego and speech and show her support for the brand, the wine, the doggy-style position, or whatever he was trying to do.

Knowing that my table across the plaza was probably full of patrons wanting wine, I stopped Chet before he could get started. "I'm just glad you made it. I have to get to my table to pour wines; we can talk later about this later – okay?"

Chet nodded, then said, "Very good, Spartacus. We'll visit you at your table."

Utterly floored, I shook my head incredulously, even talking to myself as I made the walk back to my table to help the hordes of wine drinkers, now pouring through the event gates.

Within minutes of returning to my table, I had five or six people in front of me – some looking at the wines deciding what to drink while others just held their glass up for me to pour. Just as I started to question my guests about what they would like, Chet and one of his "models" blatantly butted in front of the paying consumers, who stood by staring in disbelief. The young provocateur spoke in a sultry tone. "Hi Spartacus, I'm Veronica. So nice to meet you."

Baffled, I shook her hand as I tried to pour wines for the patrons.

"So, tell me, Spartacus, do you like Doggy Style?" she asked. Chet snickered, as did some of my patrons, while others recoiled.

"Um, umm, I really don't have time for this right now. How about I come over to your table when it slows down, and you can tell me all about it?" I replied, doing my best to remain calm while continuing to pour wine.

Instead of acknowledging me, she launched into the spiel again. "Spartacus, Doggy Style wines are not just wines, they're a lifestyle. Are you ready to try Doggy Style?" The crowd laughed and cajoled as she bent over slightly, pushing her barely covered fishnet-clad legs and butt in the air while filling my glass with the wine.

Angered, and now red in the face with embarrassment as I now had more than a dozen patrons at the table watching the spectacle unfold, I glared at Chet. Exacerbated, I said firmly, "Chet, when I get a minute, I'll come over to hear all about it." Chet laughed and took his helper by the arm, escorting her back to the Trois Chiens table.

I took a deep breath then went back to the task at hand, pouring wine for the masses. Though I was extremely busy, I glanced up from time to time to look at the Trois Chiens "Doggy Style" table. It looked more like a strip club than a wine tasting. They had a steady crowd, but it was mostly men trying to get a glimpse of the slutty helpers.

I never made it back to the Trois Chiens table that day because I was just too busy. I was told they ran out of wine, so I guess I was somewhat glad for Chet and Clay, but I was extremely uncomfortable and deeply resented the fact that I was associated with them and still represented their wines.

When the tasting was over at seven that night, the organizer found me to inquire how everything went. I told him all went well, but I offered an apology for the Doggy Style situation, to which he said, "Oh, it wasn't a big deal, but next year it wouldn't hurt if we left them out of the festival. Besides, it's not like they add anything anyway."

"Fine with me," I exclaimed. "I really would like them to

 244 | page

just go away." He nodded and laughed as we shook hands, and another event came to a close.

With sales in Utah sluggish at best over the next few years, Chet and Clay decided to try their hand at selling their wines in Europe. They put a lot of time, energy, money, and travel into their new venture. I guess they became somewhat successful because I rarely heard from them. As the old saying goes, "Out of sight, out of mind," which held true as it was toward the end of 2015 when the state started to delist the Trois Chiens and Perez & Palmer wines, citing lack of sales. After their last wine was discontinued, it took about a month before Chet Palmer emailed me to ask if the delisting was true. Relieved that the relationship was basically over, I replied, "Yes, thank you for everything, it would be best if we went our separate ways at this point in time."

I never heard from Chet again, but it was mentioned that he had to liquidate hundreds, maybe thousands of cases of cheap aging wine at huge discounts that translated to a massive monetary loss.

I like to think of it as karma.

AND... IF YOU DRINK BORDEAUX, YOU ARE MY FRIEND

MY FIRST TASTE OF BORDEAUX WAS IN 1997, after starting as an assistant manager at one of Salt Lake City's hottest restaurants. A customer had sent a fairly expensive bottle of Bordeaux back, opting for a well-known California Cabernet instead. At that point in time, I knew just a smattering about the wine regions of France – enough to get by or get me in trouble. Sure, I had tasted Champagne, Italian Chianti, and a few wines from France such as Cotes du Rhone and several from the Languedoc region, but due to Utah's westerly locale, the gravitational pull favored domestic west coast wines.

The bar manager, a well-traveled, well-spoken guy named AV, poured me a liberal glass. AV had been offered my job but had turned it down for one reason or another, so there was a touch of animus in the air as we got to know each other. After swirling the glass, the first odor hit me with a lateral blow. Pulling the glass back, I winced, then reluctantly tasted the wine, looking at AV for any indication of a hoax. Laughing at my uneducated nose and palate, he swirled and inhaled the pungent bouquet, then sipped the opaque wine. I followed, however, this time studying the components intensely to gain a better understanding, it was unlike anything else I had ever tried. "Smells like a stinky barnyard or dirty Frenchman's boots, huh?" AV asked.

"Yeah, that's crazy, I've never tried anything like it," I replied. "So, there is nothing wrong with it?"

"Happens all the time: some dumbass customer thinks he knows everything about wine, but he's just another poser. Joke's on him; his loss is our gain! Want some more?"

"Hell yeah," I said, holding out my glass. I was hooked; I had to know more. The next day I bought a book on the wine regions of France and a mixed case of wine to help further expand my own nascent informal education.

Eventually, AV and I moved past the adversarial stages of our relationship. After all, we were both managers; it was just that I had a bit more responsibility than he did. Soon he had me purchasing Bordeaux wine futures and buying somewhat expensive wines in six-packs. His reasoning: "When you buy in six-packs it allows you to taste the wine over time to experience its evolution." Waiting two years for the Bordeaux futures to arrive after shelling out what I considered big bucks in those days was not easy to stomach, but he assured me it would be worth our while. He purchased them in California through a big retailer and smuggled them back as if it was high-grade cocaine, and it was worth it. The wines were magnificent! Many late nights were spent in AV's cellar sipping, swirling, smoking cigars and listening to eighties music while lambasting and telling stories about restaurant clientele and our unsuspecting coworkers. We still had our differences, but mutual respect and a strong friendship was borne over stinky, expensive French wine.

Now, flash forward many years later, and as a wine broker, I relished the fact that representing Diageo meant almost 90% of the Bordeaux on the store shelves were in my portfolio. At the time, Diageo was the largest single importer of Bordeaux in the United States housing vast inventories in massive warehouses on both coasts. Back vintages were always available, so keeping the state store shelves stocked was a relatively easy process. I was now passionate about the wines of Bordeaux, taking every opportunity to taste, explore, and educate my accounts so they could make the right choice for their wine programs.

The Bordeaux region just about has it all: dry white wines with bracing acidity and seductively opulent Sauternes, excellent in their own right, flanked by the incredible reds from the various AVAs and communes that stretch along the mighty Gironde River. Cabernet, Merlot, Cabernet Franc, Petite Verdot, and even a bit of Malbec each contribute individual qualities and characteristics to complement a range of impressive cuvées from the region's famed producers. Cassis, blackberry, vanilla, leather, coffee, spice, graphite, tobacco, mint, smoke, rustic, rich, earthy, tannic, powerful, and concentrated – What's not to love? Since my first tasting many decades ago, I've noticed that much of the Bordeaux now produced has evolved, bringing a richer fruit-forward palate rather than their earthy and tannic predecessors. Nonetheless, though I still brood over the slightly Bohemian qualities of old Bordeaux, I equally appreciate the richer, more approachable style.

Just when I thought I'd started to figure out the DABC processes, something new popped up that I was not too familiar with – in this case, how to sell Bordeaux futures to the state fine wine buyer.

After fall harvest was all but over in the Northern Hemisphere, my sales rep at Diageo notified me that futures would be offered for the previous year's 2005 vintage. Wine futures, like investment futures, are contracts that obligate the buyer, the seller, and an asset to be purchased at a lower price than when the actual product is released (in this case, about two years later). With Bordeaux futures, the buyer had to make a down-payment with Diageo; they required half. Since Bordeaux is the most commercially successful wine region on earth with prices to match, it's usually considered a very good deal, especially when they report an excellent vintage. By buying futures, in Utah's case, specifically, because their taxes are so high on alcohol, it allowed them to obtain the most expensive classified growths right on down to many of the sought-after Cru Bourgeois at a lower price, then pass it along to the consumer through their state stores. Since state taxes are set, the shelf prices can often be a better deal than in an open market. I've heard stories from state store managers about wealthy easterners buying up several cases of Bordeaux and Burgundy because the prices are better than anything they could get back home.

I emailed the fine wine buyer Cliff Bradford, explaining that Diageo was offering Bordeaux futures each week for a period of two months. He simply told me to send him a copy of the tasting notes by Wine Spectator or Robert Parker's Wine Advocate along with the prices broken down to the bottle including state taxes and freight. He would send me confirmation as to how many cases he wanted of each offering that week. Each week after I received his order, I sent it back to Diageo so they could keep a running tally. After the two-month futures offerings were complete, Diageo emailed me a spreadsheet showing how many cases of each wine were ordered by the DABC with instructions that half of the total owed was due by the end of the following month. If Diageo did not receive the payment, then the futures were canceled, and the state would have to wait until the release of the 2005 vintage in 2008 and pay a higher price. Fair enough, I thought, and simple too.

I had not been keeping track of the tally, so when I opened the Excel spreadsheet at the end of the futures drive, I was shocked. Cliff had confirmed that the DABC would buy 496 cases of 2005 Bordeaux for a grand total of $286,626. Holy shit, this was a first! I had never sold an order of that size to anyone. Giddily, I made an appointment with Cliff to go over the futures the next morning.

Meeting in Cliff's office at the DABC, he greeted me and asked how everything was going.

"Everything is going pretty well, as a matter of fact," I stated. "I have the final tally and spreadsheet for the 2005 futures. They told me to tell you this is the final, so if you want more or less of something, please write it down now so the order can be modified."

"Great, let me take a look," he said, holding out his hand.

I handed him the four pages and waited patiently while he perused the documents. After several minutes, Cliff handed them back to me, "Looks like I'm getting everything I asked for, so tell them it's a go."

"So, how does the state pay them half upfront?"

"Oh, we won't be paying half upfront – and the state won't allow me to sign anything because we won't officially receive the product for two more years."

Dumbfounded, I sat thinking about all the time and effort

I had put into this task. "Well, that's what they require; the terms are outlined on the contract. Don't we need to get this on a purchase order so it's official?"

"We can't put it on a purchase order either. When a new PO is created for a new product within our system, it's automatically entered into the price books we publish as a new item for sale; since we won't have the product for two more years, we can't create a PO."

"Oh, I see. So how do we make it official?"

"Just email the spreadsheet back to Diageo and copy me. I'll confirm that we want the Bordeaux when it's released in 2008. They'll take it."

"Are you sure?"

"Yes." Cliff laughed assuredly. "I know the Bordeaux buyer at Diageo, and he knows how we work; we've done this before."

I thanked him for his time and stood to leave his office.

Now, that's power! I thought to myself, driving back to my home office. *The state fine wine buyer has so much clout; he can just say he'll buy nearly 500 cases of Bordeaux worth $300k without putting any money down, and it'll just happen in two years as if it was just business as usual. Crazy.*

As the years progressed, I would learn just how much power Cliff wielded, as well as the fact that suppliers had the weak bargaining seat at the table. In subsequent years, Cliff bought 2006 Bordeaux futures then skipped 2007 because that year was not particularly great.

Then the largest financial crisis since the Great Depression hit at the end of 2007, resulting in immediate push-back from consumers who had a taste for expensive wines. Slight panic and uncertainty crept into every American's life as they pulled back, unsure of what the future would bring. The media storm didn't help much either, preying on the fear of the people by creating social distress. Yes, we had problems, but we couldn't hide. Bombarded with dismal news each day necessitated alcohol just to get by. Everyone from housewives, laborers, and businessmen hinged on the monthly economic data hoping for news signaling the end of the depressing times. Sales on wines over $40 slowed to a crawl and many sat on shelves while back vintages stacked up. Deep deals were made just to move product. The word "allocation" became a thing of the past.

Everyone took notice, including Diageo, shocking the industry by announcing the end of their relationship with the Bordelaise, even walking away from the 2009 futures campaign. With warehouses full of product and lackluster sales, they slashed prices on existing inventories in an effort to liquidate their holdings. I immediately notified Cliff of the subsequent sale, sending weekly offerings to his attention. Cliff, astute as always, cherry-picked the best products, buying enough to hopefully get by until another importer took their place.

I fretted and grumbled about losing such a valuable tool in my portfolio. It made me realize that in this business, indeed, everything changes, sometimes on a dime. Several months later, after most of the Diageo Bordeaux inventories had been sold off, I began to look for new suppliers. It was difficult at first, many suppliers sensed an opportunity, however, they didn't want to step up during the ongoing recession to outlay tremendous amounts of cash to import and warehouse expensive Bordeaux. Several suppliers came and went. It would take years to overcome.

A NEW PLAYER IN TOWN

ALMOST SIX YEARS HAD PASSED IN MY NOW NOT-SO-NEW CAREER, and I was hitting my stride (or so it felt). Aside from some necessary corporate minutiae, I was having fun. Drinking on the job, receiving decent wages, incentives, bonuses with an expense account, and wining and dining mixed with a bit of travel while comfortably working from home, life was good. My friends were jealous. My portfolio had grown slightly; just enough to keep busy but not enough to cause strain. I had developed relationships with a solid base of accounts, the DABC, and the suppliers. Everything was moving along smoothly.

Then one day, as most things do, there was a change. At first, it was nothing more than a rumor rippling through the sales force. It was mostly speculation within the lower ranks, the buzz growing daily, even if untrue. Word on the street was that the company was being sold and there was talk about us losing our jobs. I kept my mouth shut until the dust had settled a few weeks later when it was confirmed by my boss that the company had indeed been sold. He said not to worry; it would be a smooth transition; that is, until he was fired. Bracing myself for the worst, I considered my alternatives, but a phone call after the fact from my now "old" boss telling me my job was not in jeopardy calmed me before I could commit hari-kari.

Our parent company, Alaska Distributors, had lost a major supplier; a supplier so big the loss equated to a huge shortfall in revenue. So, ownership agreed to sell the business, including the Spirits West division, to rivals The Oaks Corporation and Sojourner Spirits & Wine, now new partners in the Northwest. I heard the venture was fifty-fifty, but I'm sure one of them had a slight edge (my bet was on Sojourner).

Shortly thereafter, Sojourner Oaks Spirits West, or SOSW, was born. Gone were the quarterly meetings and trips to Seattle, the almost non-existent presence of my supervisor, the incremental bonuses, and the casual business dealings. Conference calls and dealing with human resources, including new training, drug tests, and incessant reports, were the new norm. And my new boss arrived soon thereafter doing what most bosses do – analyzing my position, my pay, my contribution, and how I could contribute even more. He wasn't all bad; after six months of analysis, I was pretty much left alone once again. Aside from the new reporting methods, business was status quo.

In just over a year into the new company came my third new boss and another round of, you guessed it – analysis, reviewing my pay, my contribution, and how I could contribute even more. But this time there would be some cutbacks. "Make the suppliers pay for everything," was the new mantra – cutting, saving, improving profitability – that's what managers do. And he wasn't all bad either; after things settled down and I got to know him, I found that through his hard-ass tough exterior was a decent person just trying to do a good job. After some time, with money coming in and expenses in check, something unexpected happened: he asked me to hire a new salesperson that I would oversee in the great state of Utah.

Wait. What? I was a one-man show for God's sake. Say it ain't so, please... With only myself to manage, I was loving life, and as a matter of fact, I had become good at working on my own! I had managed people during my restaurant days, many of them, in fact, most of whom could barely function on their own in society. I thought I was done playing parent to a fleet of unruly miscreants. I didn't want to manage another person. There would be no argument and I would later learn why. Two new suppliers, Palm Bay International, followed by E & J Gallo, would come on board bringing in a pile of new commissions.

Days after finally digesting the news, I set my sights on hiring a person I had known from the restaurant industry – a bar manager I'd been selling wine to in recent years with plenty of wine knowledge and a good work ethic. He was a shoo-in. However, I was overridden, as he was rejected by the higher-ups in favor of a gal who had been working within our Utah liquor division. Tired of late nights and bar promos, she opted for a slower lifestyle selling wine. It was difficult at first, as she was behind the curve. Although she had sales skills, she knew very little about wine; it took a lot of time, but she eventually figured it out. I even found that supervising a new salesperson really wasn't all that bad, plus it increased our overall market penetration enabling us to see more accounts.

Palm Bay International fit into the portfolio like a glove. One of the largest importers of fine wine from Italy, France, Spain, Chile, and Argentina; the brands had cachet, decent pricing, and ratings to back them up. Like all suppliers, Palm

Bay has its share of value juice, but the bulk of the portfolio outweighed the smaller, less desirable products in their collection. Palm Bay held legendary week-long conferences in some pretty decent places, which I particularly enjoyed. However, due to all the presentations, meetings, wine tastings, and nightly dinners, attendees hardly ever made it out of the hotel. In my estimation, they spent hundreds of thousands of dollars (maybe even over a million) to pay for hotels, flights, food, alcohol, meeting space, and audio/visual for over a hundred salespeople and support staff each year. The last day of the conference usually concluded with a motivational speaker like an athlete, a business guru, or a celebrity of some sort – and they aren't cheap! The whole thing was first-class. Aside from the dawn-to-dusk death march each day, the meetings were actually fun.

Gallo, on the other hand, held a vast empire of domestic wines including a small portfolio of imports. The behemoth that they were, and still are today, required them to employ a sales rep in each state – a person residing in Salt Lake City and one in Cheyenne. To say I was apprehensive when I heard we'd be representing Gallo is a major understatement. I was petrified. I didn't want to sell Gallo wines, period. We had a decent portfolio of wines, including Champagne and Bordeaux, and I didn't want it sullied up by the likes of *Turning Leaf* and *Barefoot*.

However, I learned long ago to take the good with the bad and made it a point to never bad-mouth a product, knowing that one day I may have to sell it. I swallowed my pride, moved forward, and a funny thing happened: I found that selling Gallo wines was really not half bad. Like most giants, Gallo never rests; it is consistently moving forward – shifting, creating, buying, entering new partnerships, evolving – striving to stay one step ahead. I found wines within their portfolio that practically sold themselves, and I even enjoyed selling. With a bevy of new products consistently introduced each year, business stayed fresh, as did our sales pitches. Since the local Gallo reps handled all the paperwork and presentations with each respective state liquor board, all we had to do was obtain placements on wine lists and help merchandise products in state stores. Not a bad gig.

With increased commissions and Sojourner's backing, it was time to grow yet again, this time by adding two new employees: a state manager based in Jackson, Wyoming, and a merchandiser in Utah to help with the state stores; both of whom were under my supervision. As the years went on, I came to realize that working for Sojourner Spirits & Wine meant a few things - more and more responsibilities (including non-stop paperwork) while the pay stayed about the same.

The first state manager I hired in Wyoming turned out to be a bust. He could talk the talk, but miserably failed when it came time to walk the walk. Since he was based in Jackson, one of the few bright wine-selling spots on the Wyoming landscape, it seemed he had an aversion to actually working. He was very good at "putting on the dog" while I was in town, but aside from a few nice placements around town, overall sales in Jackson were flat as was the rest of the state.

While visiting the market on a few different occasions, I ventured out on my own to see some old contacts and accounts I had sold to in the past. Both asked who the local rep was and if I could steer him their way. Upon further inquiry, it seemed the word on the small Jackson streets was that my new rep had a major gambling problem subordinated by an alcohol problem. After several missteps, the final straw came when I asked to meet him at his townhome so I could drop off some wine buckets and wine keys. And as the garage door opened on the side of his house - a revelation. Stacked from floor to ceiling in some places were every wine bucket, boxes of wine openers, t-shirts and hats, display racks and case wrap that I had ever sent his way. In the middle of the floor sat fifteen cases of unopened wine samples, most of which had accrued since day one. That was all it took; after a short call to my boss and human resources, he was "set free," a term I've used since my restaurant management days for its lack of negativity. Somehow it conveys a sense of hope that out there, somewhere, something bigger and better awaits.

It took six more months to find a suitable new state manager for Wyoming. But the wait was worthwhile as I was fortunate enough to hire a former competitor from another brokerage.

This gal was everywhere all the time; she knew everyone, and she knew wine. Basically, she was kicking ass and taking names all over the state. Each time I showed up at an account, she was walking out, sales already made, smiling all the way. She was at every trade show working her table like a pro while I was getting my ass handed to me. What was fortuitous for me, was a result of unfortunate circumstances for her, as her boss had let her go for reasons other than professional.

"I have to have her on my team," I told my boss. "Please give her what she wants – she'll be worth it!" She was hired and as time would tell, proved to be an exceptional employee.

It is said that part of being successful is hiring people that make you look good. I would have to agree, for I was lucky enough to have worked with her for more than ten years with nary a problem.

My small team of four forged on for several years, until it was time to grow once again.

TREND

MALBEC

I BEGAN HEARING FROM MY SUPPLIERS that a new craze was coming in the form of Malbec from Argentina. However, unbeknownst to them, I was aware of the grape, I knew its origins, I already had several state listings in Utah before the craze started. I was ahead of the curve when the wave crested, crashed and enveloped the United States in a sea of inky purple juice. However, even I was ill-prepared for the ocean of Argentine Malbec flowing in to overtake the American market. Due to the insatiable overnight demand for Malbec, keeping the state in stock became an immediate problem. Like the feeding frenzy for Pinot Noir prior, Malbec, the new flavor of the day, became the rallying cry from every supplier, who all of a sudden had one or several new labels to offer, and of course, ratings to back it up.

It's hard not to like Malbec, with its deep dark color, mouth-filling, juicy, plummy goodness, and reasonable prices. The in-vogue wine of the day was avant-garde, fresh, and sheik. Malbec was different. Since most were imported, drinking Malbec conveyed a feeling of exotic worldliness to the consumer, but not for me. Don't get me wrong, I'll drink it if I must, but for me, Malbec under $18 it just too one dimensional – It all tastes the same. Call me snobby, I don't care. I've tasted too many inferior wines to waste my time on lower-end Malbec. There is a noticeable difference when paying a price for Malbec over $18; the wines become brooding, a bit earthy, multi-faceted, and even terroir-driven, which I like. And, I may have one or two wines hidden away that I most likely forgot, but you won't find a collection of upper-end expensive Malbec in my cellar, there are far more interesting wines in the world.

But for all my poo-pooing the grape, I do owe a small debt to Malbec, for it was the several state listings that escalated sales, resulting in a grateful supplier, putting me on the invite list for an all-expense-paid trip to Argentina. Spending four days in Buenos Aires followed by four days in Mendoza during their summer just after the new year was comfortable relief from the cold winter days in Utah. Led by market representatives from the import company, the group consisted of two dozen mostly well-behaved salespeople from various parts of the southwestern United States. Once in Argentina, a representative from one of the wineries was put in charge of us. Acting somewhat as a chaperone, his job duties consisted of educating, entertaining, and corralling the group to ensure no one died on his watch. His name: Diego Albana – an ex-footballer now making a living as a winery rep. He was a well-travelled, truly amusing guy with curly dishwater blond hair and a dry wit. Naturally inquisitive, he wanted to know everything currently happening in the United States in general, as well as in each market from each member of the group. His favorite endearment while raising his fist in the air: "Niiiicccce!"

Aside from miscalculating the number of people in the group after one late-night dinner in Mendoza, Diego did a great job. It was on this busy Friday night that I found myself stumbling around drunk on the downtown streets after having returned from the restroom at the end of the meal and discovering my group had left. Frantic, I ran out the door, but it was too late, the bus had already left. Nervous and a bit worried, I walked the streets trying to figure out how to get back to the hotel. I knew it was close by because it hadn't taken more than ten minutes to get us to the restaurant, but I couldn't get my bearings, so I waved down a cab. The driver didn't speak a lick of English, so I employed the very limited kitchen Spanish I learned during my restaurant days, but he just stared at me blankly. Finally, after several minutes of drunken "Spanglish," he appeared to understand. I anxiously looked out the window for any sign of the hotel while he sped down the streets of Mendoza, then onto the freeway. Soon the city lights faded, giving way to the cold blackness of the Argentine night. After twenty minutes, I panicked. I asked the driver to stop, which he did, on the side of the road in the middle of nowhere. Once again, I desperately tried to explain where I needed to go. Searching my pockets, I found the key card to my room with the name of the hotel on one side. After examining the card, the cabby realized his mistake and flipped the car around, whisking me back to civilization and the comfort of the hotel.

The next day I was too embarrassed to tell the group about my adventure. But years later, I recounted the story to Diego during lunch while he was in Utah for a market visit. Listening intently, his eyes grew big as he covered his mouth with his hand. He leaned back in his chair and apologized profusely, "Oh, my friend, I'm so sorry. I thought I counted everyone that night. You are extremely lucky; you could have been killed or had your internal organs taken. That's big business down there!"

I sat speechless while he continued to apologize. I'm sure the color drained from my face upon hearing the gravity of the circumstances. Shaking me back to reality, Diego raised a glass of wine in one hand, then held the other triumphantly overhead, hand balled into a fist as he exclaimed, "Niiiicccce!"

ILLOGICALITIES:
Utah Liquor Laws – Part 3

 It is illegal for a licensed broker or industry member to sample their products with anyone.

This law is probably one of the most absurd in Utah. The state legislature doesn't want restauranteurs, let alone anyone, drinking alcoholic beverages for free because, in their expert opinion, it encourages consumption and entices someone to buy. However, contrary to their beliefs and the law, sometimes it does occur by those who choose to taste. And the reason is simple: they want to try the products to ensure they'll complement their food and theme, and it's priced for them to succeed. The LDS faithful in the legislature want brokers to simply present pricing and information, then have the account make a sound decision, which is utterly impossible, especially when a product is expensive. An account will not take a chance on a $50 or higher priced bottle of wine or alcohol, only to have it sit in inventory, especially if they have to buy a full case via special order. They want to taste it to make sure it's a sound business decision.

The state is authoritarian when it relates to alcohol. A very long time ago, a group of brokers held a private event in Park City tasting and showing products with accounts. One of the brokers who didn't get invited to participate caught wind of the party, so he told the DABC, which in turn set up a sting operation with the local authorities and busted them. All the brokers were fined significant amounts of money, some lost their license for a period of time, and all were put on probation.

Nonetheless, not everyone may abide by this law; it could be done in offices, back rooms, residences, wine cellars, and even sometimes brazenly out in the open. It's all about being careful, because in this day and age, smartphones with cameras have become a weapon on the battlefield. Another broker or sales rep could easily snap a photo of you carelessly tasting with an account, then report it to the DABC, putting your job and license in jeopardy. Next thing you know, you're sitting in front of the compliance division, a DABC-appointed attorney present as you're brought up on charges. So, is the possibility of getting caught sampling worth it? Sampling should be a normal aspect of our job because it moves our business forward by helping adults make sound decisions. Brokers and sales reps provide a valuable service by informing accounts of the benefits and availability of the thousands of competitive products out on the market. It's no different than buying a car or a golf club – a person wants to try it before they decide. If a broker chooses not to sample alcoholic beverages with accounts (therefore not break any laws), it may not be a level playing field. So, it remains an unfair law in an unfair state created by unintelligent elected officials imposing their morality on the masses.

Around the spring legislative session of 2012, my main competitor took it upon themselves to introduce a bill to allow brokers the right to taste alcohol legally with restaurant, hotel, and bar owners and managers. Now, I must hand it to them, it took moxie and a great amount of time to formulate a bill. Most of the brokers, including myself, along with several in the hospitality industry, backed the bill.

The bill backfired, as most of the state legislature (if not all them), were in fact, freaked out; they had absolutely no idea that wine and alcohol brokers existed in Utah. After they found out what our roles were regarding working with the DABC, they decided that maybe they should regulate our tiny industry. They couldn't fathom that sampling wine, liquor, and beer could be handled by mature brokers, business owners, and managers, so they decided to treat everyone as a prepubescent. Instead of realizing that it may be already going on, and it was simply the right thing to do, they demanded sampling be conducted only at the DABC offices under supervision and that everyone should blow into a breathalyzer before leaving the premises. Wait, what?

As the bill progressed, sensing another opening, one of the Mormon lawmakers bandied his own stipulation stating that if sampling were to occur, all alcohol-branded materials would be banned, including all apparel, wine buckets, wine openers, key chains, etc. Stupid? Hell, yes. Violation of rights? Damn straight. But there's more... He also wanted all alcohol signage banned, including neon bar lights and billboards (which is against the right to Freedom of Speech, by the way). In fact, as I was told by credible sources, this lawmaker particularly wanted billboards and branded products produced by local beer brewer, Wasatch Brewing, taken down. The root of his problem: He was offended by their slogan for one of their beers called Polygamy Porter. *"Polygamy Porter, take some home to the wives!"* He was either a religious extremist, just plain dull-witted, or he was embarrassed for his polygamous ways.

But the final dagger included a provision that if a broker were caught sampling wines improperly, the penalty could be losing all their state listed products for a period of time, license suspension and fines. After hearing the demands of

the legislature, it was decided the bill should be pulled. Aw...
screw it, back to square one.

 *Happy Hour in Utah (and some other states)
is illegal.*

Reason: The consumer is encouraged to over-consume
during a set amount of time leading to quick intoxication. In
Utah, the only Happy Hour allowed is what's called "Appy
Hour," meaning discounted appetizers. This can be quite a
bargain and helpful in getting people through the door at times
when a restaurant isn't typically busy. Consuming food with
alcohol decreases the chance of a quick buzz. I must say, I'm a
little ambivalent about this law. Each time I return home from
traveling to "real states," part of me wishes I could get the
great deals offered during Happy Hour, but I can understand
the logic behind regulating irresponsible consumption. I have
experienced and partaken numerous times when abroad
during Happy Hour, which usually has amounted to a very
quick buzz before moving onto something else.

 *The state will only grant liquor licenses in regard to
population – and they use very old figures.*

Licenses are not always available, so an entity must
wait for one to be relinquished or they may buy one from a
licensee going out of business, under the supervision of the
DABC, of course. Month in and month out, new bars and
restaurants, often already built and ready for business, vie
for liquor licenses at the monthly DABC Liquor Commission
meetings, only to be told that none are available. While some
are able to obtain banquet permits or even temporary event

licenses, most show up each month, hoping that their name is called – until then, no booze may be sold!

There are many different types of liquor licenses, and the confounded liquor laws are so poorly written that it seems no one knows what's legal or not on any given day.

I recall eating at a restaurant in Cedar City with a friend one night many years ago. I called the restaurant beforehand to ask if I could bring in a bottle of wine, to which they agreed for a $10 corkage fee. Upon entry to the establishment, the hostess immediately grabbed the bottle of wine from my hands, informing me she had to take it into the backroom before other patrons could view the bottle. Disbelieving, I told her that was fine with me. After sitting down, I informed the server that I would like it opened. She retrieved the wine and presented it to us, but after confirming it was our bottle, scurried back to the kitchen only to return a few minutes later with the now-opened bottle of wine. While she poured, I asked, "How come you had to open the bottle in the back?"

"Because it is illegal for you and the other guests to see me open the wine."

Now, I had been in the restaurant business for decades and a broker for years and have never heard anything so ludicrous in all my life. This clearly was a misinterpretation of one of the many idiotic laws. We laughed (she did not), but we were tired and hungry, and I decided not to pursue an argument.

Furthermore, it seems even the DABC misinterprets the law from time to time. For instance, a debacle transpired in 2014 when the Liquor Commissioners, along with the director of the DABC (some of which have law backgrounds) decided that single event permits handed out willy-nilly over the previous years were granted too loosely. Specifically, the intricacies written within the law regarding the permits: *Events must only last a few days at most and the events must be used by civic or community groups to promote the common good.* Whatever that means.

To send a message, they decided to get tough with Snowbird Ski Resort over a permit for their annual Oktoberfest held each year on their ski plaza under a tented-off area. The DABC said they may not grant the permit allowing Snowbird to hold the event because they didn't believe the event was for the good of the community, but rather just another way for the resort to make money. God forbid a company make a profit on alcohol in Utah.

Aside from skiing, Oktoberfest has been a staple at Snowbird for decades and is probably one of their top events as they host over sixty-thousand people annually. After the folks at Snowbird did some serious digging, they found the statute did not mention anything about *for-profit businesses* being disqualified. The shakedown was merely something for a few failed lawyers to do as they interpreted and enforced their version of the law.

Word got out immediately and the state became the laughingstock of the country yet again. Instead of backing the decision by the Liquor Commissioners and DABC Director, several members of the state legislature took a different stance. Embarrassed and enraged, they publicly chastised the DABC, some even calling for the DABC to be disbanded. After the froth had fizzled out, the commissioners and director, tails between their legs, consented the permit to Snowbird.

THE ACQUISITION

IN MY ESTIMATION, about 50% of the time after a large corporation or company buys a winery or a brand, they downright bastardize the shit out of it on behalf of money. There are of course, instances when the process is done correctly – thus, creating a win, win, win – for the company, the winery or brand, and the consumer, but these instances are few and far between. There are even occasions when a winery or brand is rescued from bankruptcy, resurrected from slumber or even death by an entity with enough capital and vision to revitalize or resuscitate a brand to new successes – such as when *Francis Ford Coppola* purchased the almost forgotten *Inglenook Winery/Niebaum Estate* transforming it back into a very viable product.

This little chapter, however, is about the bastardization of a wine brand, then inflicting the negligence and carnage onto the consumer. What typically happens is this: a winery or brand started by hard-working, smart individuals is developed into an appealing, well-regarded, even sought-after must-have product. Along with established vineyards or contracts with vineyards, they have a formula = excellent juice, competitive prices, decent wine ratings, and clever marketing. Years or even decades go by with steady growth, turning the brand into success across many states or geographical areas, all the while maintaining quality, heritage, and appeal. The big corporations take notice because the brand possesses strength and decent market share in a segment they desire, or it's in direct competition to the brands in their portfolio. Or more likely yet, they smell money. Several of the big guys float bids to the winery/brand to buy them out, often millions of dollars. Unsure but not unwise (because at some point everyone has a price), the winery/brand sells out to one of the large corporations. The corporation then proceeds to exploit or "grow" the brand exponentially. Case volumes are dramatically increased, inferior juice is bought, and additives are used to supplement their need for growth and profit. That being said, quality goes down even as prices go up. They figure that the naïve consumer won't miss a thing, for they are already hooked; they will not possibly figure anything out; that there is a new owner; the label has slightly changed or the juice is now being made differently (maybe even from different vineyards). The corporation must capitalize on the existing name with loyal followers while expanding to new consumers. New spinoffs, brand extensions, and pricing often follow, so the brand can be further exploited for their greedy needs. Year in year out, volumes must grow to realize greater profits so they can pay themselves back from the original investment. However, quality suffers in their quest for success. At some point consumers take notice, sales and profits decline, massive discounting ensues to keep volumes and profits up. Sales continue to decline to a point that the brand or winery is now considered a failing asset. The winery or brand is sold, dissected, or even rebranded in hopes of revitalization. Happens all the time – a futile short-sighted game whose biggest casualties are the winery, brand, and ultimately, the consumer.

Case in point: During 2008, behemoth company Diageo offered to buy Rosenblum Cellars for $105 million dollars. Rosenblum Cellars, founded in the late '70s by Kent Rosenblum, a veterinarian from Minnesota, specialized in Zinfandel and Syrah.

Kent and his family had relocated to Alameda, California, where he found himself making wine as a basement hobby from purchased grapes. He started giving bottles of his excess wine to his neighbors and friends who always asked for more. Realizing he had a knack for making wine and that he was running out of space due to growing demand, he and some investor friends found a larger space so they could expand production. The winery itself was just that: a winery, no land, no vineyards. Just a winery. The grapes were brought in from select vineyards throughout California. In fact, most of the purchased fruit came from long term growing contracts sealed simply with a handshake between Kent and the vineyard owners. A few decades later, Rosenblum Cellars had grown into one of California's sought-after niche brands, producing over 80 thousand cases per year. Now, $105 million was just too good an offer to pass up, so he and his investors elected to sell the winery. Diageo, now the owner, asked Kent to stay on as a consultant winemaker for five years, which is how I met and became friends with Kent.

One of my competitive brokers, Libations, represented Rosenblum Cellars in Utah for many years. During those years, the owner worked hard building a presence with the Rosenblum brand to a tune of around fourteen state listings. Since I represented Diageo in Utah and Wyoming, Rosenblum Cellars moved over to my brokerage after the sale. A loss for Libations, but a nice gain for my small portfolio.

With the state as a loyal supporter of Rosenblum Cellars,

Diageo decided to send Kent to the market for a "work with" to pour wine with me at a tasting during the Sundance Film Festival. Prior to Kent's arrival, I found out he was an avid skier and that he would also be bringing a friend, who was also one of his original investors. Aside from the skiing, I lined up a few winemaker dinners plus a meeting with DABC buyer Cliff Bradford as part of the trip. Kent Rosenblum was one of the best winemakers to have in the market. Norwegian and Minnesota jokes, veterinary stories, and love of wine and food are some of the highpoints of this very affable human being; plus, even in his sixties and into his seventies, he could out-ski just about anyone.

With Kent's desire to ski, and with an excellent following in Utah, I convinced my Diageo sales representatives to allow several more market visits, and even a few visits to Jackson Hole, Wyoming. Even though we worked the local markets hard, we somehow managed to fit in some fun and occasionally a buyer or two would come along for the trip. Skiing with Kent and company usually involved breaking out several bottles of Rosenblum wine accompanied by requisite charcuterie and smuggled into one of the mountain restaurants (we were even reprimanded for breaking local rules). Hey, hard work, but someone had to do it. Guilty as charged!

As per usual in sales, Diageo handed out sales goals for their new acquisition. To say that the goals were extremely aggressive would be a colossal understatement. The email said the goals were "a must make" and that they were "non-negotiable." Along with the goals came sales trackers that needed to be filled out each month by a certain day to ascertain if the plans were being executed. With plenty of wine to sell the first year, business was status quo; all the lines and ranges were left intact, and the wines were still excellent with a strong following. And although the first year's goal was narrowly missed, sales were still brisk, so Diageo was mostly pleased.

Just a few short years later, it appeared that Diageo began to butcher the line-up by eliminating several of the single vineyard and varietal offerings to focus and drive sales on the "core-brands" within the portfolio. It could also be entirely possible that some of the handshake contracts to buy certain vineyard fruit had expired, but that's just speculation on my part. I began to hear stories that even though Kent was overseeing production, he was kept at arm's length, so the quality of the wines began to fade. Volumes were increased and the goals became larger in successive years – the Diageo recipe began to backfire and sales began to decline.

After five years were up, the contract was complete. Kent had paid his due diligence involving the non-compete period, so he bought some vineyard property along the Russian River in California, naming it Rock Wall. Along with the vineyards planted to Chardonnay and Pinot Noir, the property boasted an outdoor pizza oven, bocce ball, and a volleyball court. (I will add that bocce ball must be considered one of the ultimate wine-drinking sports – there aren't many games that allow the competitor a full glass of wine in hand during play.) The sights and sounds of the beautiful vineyards overlooking the Russian River Valley accompanied by some killer cheese, salami, olives, and homemade pizza fresh from the oven are a blissful formula for respite and reflection, away from the hectic unforgiving world. In fact, it's difficult to pry oneself away once nirvana takes hold.

With a vineyard comes a new winery. Chardonnay and Pinot Noir from his vineyards were just a few of the offerings that Kent and his daughter Shauna, a stellar winemaker in her own right, used to make several wines at their Rock Wall Winery located right down the street from the old Rosenblum winery, now a competitor. The winery is housed in an old naval hangar previously used to paint military planes. Experience, excellent staff, stunning juice, marketing, and an event center complete with a quaint tasting room with views of the San Francisco Bay and the city on a clear day, highlighted the recipe for the new venture.

Lucky for me, Kent asked if I would represent the new brand in Utah and Wyoming. And just after the start of the new venture, I was able to obtain state listings for two of their great Zinfandels – Jesse's and Monte Rosso vineyard designates. Along with special orders for many of their other wines, Rock Wall was steadily making a name for themselves. They may not have had as many listings as Kent's previous winery, but it was a start.

Fast forward several years, and it was during the fall of 2015 when Diageo decided to sell its entire wine business to focus on its liquor and beer holdings. The majority of the wine interests were purchased by Treasury Wine Estates, which included Rosenblum Wine Cellars. Treasury decided to sell off several brands in favor of the brands they wanted to focus. Rosenblum turned out to be one of the wineries up for sale. Now here is the crazy part: *I heard through the grapevine* (sorry, I had to get that cliché in there) that Treasury offered Kent Rosenblum the chance to buy back his namesake winery for the sum of $5 million; a winery that he sold for $105 million around eight years prior. However, one of the caveats was that the sale included around 200,000 cases of substandard wine - wine that was made well after the great juice and use of the successful system Rosenblum originally sold them.

But wait, there's more... While Mr. Rosenblum was taking his time to consider the offer, Treasury, as it would appear, floated the discounted winery past several other buyers as well; the successful winner would turn out to be Bronco Wine Company. Rosenblum Wine Cellars had finally found a new home. However, the ultimate coup de gras was yet to come – Bronco Wine Company asked Kent Rosenblum to come back as the consulting winemaker.

And that is Corporate Business 101 - wine style!

TREND

CARMENERE

I MEAN NO OFFENSE OR DISRESPECT to red-heads or stepchildren anywhere when I say that poor little grape Carmenere could be the red-headed stepchild of modern-day viticulture (in the U.S., anyway). From day one the grape has had a rough go.

Thought to be wiped out by phylloxera in France during the mid-1800s, the grape luckily survived due to Chilean growers returning from Bordeaux with cuttings that over time were unfortunately confused with Merlot in the early 19th century. And so, for almost a hundred years, the Chilean wine growers cultivated and vinified Carmenere as Merlot, or a hybrid of Merlot. Since Carmenere was often grown right alongside Merlot, the final wines were regularly a field blend of two or more grapes. The main problem with this equation? Carmenere needs more time on the vine than Merlot to fully ripen; picking it early results in an unappealing hint of bell pepper and astringent notes. It was not until the mid-1990s that clonal research was completed on the grape to confirm its true genealogy.

Carmenere gets its name from the deep red veins of its leaves; it's soft like Merlot and medium-bodied with smoky cherry, spice, and earthy tones, even including notes of tobacco and fine leather. Finally, after more than a century of unwarranted dormancy, Carmenere was celebrated, vinified and exploited for its own merits. However, the grape suffered yet another crushing blow before fully getting its legs, for it followed far too soon on the heels of the dynamic Malbec trend. Although Carmenere possessed the unique exploitive attributes desired by salivating capitalistic suppliers, it was not enough to rival that of the powerhouse Malbec, so sales never completely reached their full potential.

A STAR GOES DARK

DURING THE SUMMER OF 2009, Champagne house Moët decided to discontinue staple "White Star" in favor of *Moët & Chandon Imperial Brut*. White Star, produced using a sweeter dosage, was made specifically for a prominent cruise line and the neophyte American palates, while every other country consumed *Moët Imperial*. To streamline production, Moët decided to only make one non-vintage Brut to be enjoyed throughout the world.

With a large base of loyal customers in Utah, Moët White Star was among the top-selling Champagnes listed in the state. I was cautious the new package and taste profile wouldn't be embraced by the state and ultimately the consumer.

Without a choice, I compiled all the necessary paperwork to present to the DABC as a trade-out of products. At first, the buyers at the DABC didn't believe me, as they are the ultimate skeptics. Nonetheless, after all the information had been reviewed and confirmed, they took a stance. Instead of allowing a trade, they would simply delist White Star and require me to present *Moët Imperial* as a new item. Not wanting to lose six or more months of sales including a general listing, I fervently argued, even throwing in a few white lies, stating that it wasn't a new item, but rather a label and code change for an old product. And although the new wine was slightly drier in style, the profile was close to White Star (which it was not). I also pointed out that they needed the item to ensure their Champagne selection didn't have a black eye during the holidays and that they could possibly be the only state in the union that didn't carry the new label.

Finally, after a month of debate, I secured the claim, and the head of purchasing accepted the trade with one caveat: all the White Star Champagne inventory had to be completely sold out before they would issue a PO for the new product. That was fine by me because I firmly believed that all inventory would be sold out of the warehouse by October, enabling Moët to ship in the new product just in time for the valuable holiday season.

To help move the product, it was decided by MHUSA to put it on sale during the late summer and early fall months, thus guaranteeing the state would run out. Each week I paid careful attention to the warehouse inventory, and finally, at the end of September, all the White Star had been depleted from the central warehouse. Notifying the DABC the task was complete, I emailed the purchasing director and his assistant asking for a purchase order for the new product. Their reply soon after read, "Great job, however, every bottle in every state store must be sold as well before we will cut the new PO."

Dumbfounded, my urgent reply followed. "Since the busy holiday season is fast approaching, wouldn't it be better to have the product in the main warehouse ready to go after the last bottle of White Star is sold? That way we could circumvent possible out of stock issues?"

Their reply: "We are aware of out of stock issues. Every

bottle must be sold before we will issue a PO for the new product."

I notified MHUSA of the problem, and I was met with chagrin and disbelief. We had no other choice but to sell out the product in the state stores. At the time, the state owned and operated 39 liquor stores border to border. I obtained what was called an open-stock report from the DABC showing the open inventory in the state stores. Since the majority of the population resides within a 60-mile radius of Salt Lake City, White Star had sold out in those stores first, leaving a smattering of bottles sitting in the state stores in the outlying rural areas. October and part of November came and went. The monthly updated open stock report showed approximately 47 bottles scattered around the state. With Christmas only five weeks away, the busiest selling season for Champagne, and the fiscal year end for MHUSA, it left little time to spare. Finally, MHUSA had had enough and asked politely but insistently, "Please have your staff drive to all the state stores that still have White Star on the shelves to buy what's left. We need to get a purchase order for *Moët Imperial* before the end of the year."

Since this would require paying retail for the product at $40 plus tax per bottle, it would cost MHUSA over two grand. It would also cost productivity with my sales reps being out of the main market, as well as expenditures for gas, food, and in some cases, overnight stays in motels in the most rural areas. With Moët agreeable to reimbursement of all expenses, my team went into action. Sales reps drove as far south as St. George and Moab – each almost four hours away. At week's end, the task was complete.

I asked my sales rep at MHUSA what I should do with the bottles of White Star. "Drink it, give it away, we don't care," he said. So, the booty was split among my very grateful sales reps. We drank well that holiday season.

Now, with every bottle depleted in the state, once again I asked the buyer at the DABC for a purchase order. After checking the state store inventory, a purchase order was finally generated, eight days after I asked. Since the DABC waited so long to cut the PO, the product would have a slim chance of making it to the state liquor stores before Christmas, signaling an end to the quest to have the product in Utah before the busy holidays. MHUSA rushed the order for 50 cases of Imperial to the state, which undoubtedly cost extra in shipping charges to expedite. After the cases arrived (in six-packs no less), the DABC took their sweet time receiving and shipping the product out. One six-pack was sent to the smaller stores and two six-packs each to the larger state stores leaving approximately five cases in the main warehouse. By the time the shelves were stocked, it was January 2nd – missing the busiest Champagne selling day of the year.

CHOPPING the NOSE OFF to SPITE the FACE

DURING THE 2011 SPRING LEGISLATIVE SESSION, a proposal to cut 2.2 million dollars from the DABC operating budget was introduced. At the time, Senate President Michael Waddoups (R- Mormon, Taylorsville) said: "every agency must make cuts to make up for state revenue short-falls, including the liquor department." (House, Cuts Would Force 13 Utah Liquor Stores to Close 2011)

Mr. Waddoups and his other Mormon legislative pals believed that cutting store hours, closing state stores, and laying off people was the best answer to recoup overall lost revenue in an economy that actually faired pretty well after the financial meltdown of 2007. Even though the DABC continually remitted record profits year in year out, these idiots wanted to close down stores providing profit to the state. What they didn't understand is that people drink just as much, if not more, in troubled times.

To those that reside in Utah, news such as this is really not a big shock. The cutting of budget dollars from a sinful business by a bunch of Mormon lackeys disguised as unbiased lawmakers is exactly what we have come to be accustomed.

However, closing state stores that were profitable was the big shock. A list of state liquor stores up for closure was created, ten stores in total. All the stores on the list generated profits, high profits. Even though the state already has the least amount of liquor stores per capita in the nation, the argument was made that consumers could buy alcohol at neighboring stores across town.

The reality of the situation was that it was actually just an LDS lawmaker's cream dream – A loss of revenue in other agencies so they could impose their religious beliefs onto the masses and chop a sinful business up for the love of church and God – Fuck the state! If the elected lawmakers, on the public dole, were so worried about the budget, then why didn't any of them offer to cut their own salaries. Most of them are very well off from outside interests anyway; maybe they should have given their salaries back or made cuts in another division or department rather than the money-generating machine of the Department of Alcoholic Beverage Control.

Apropos, on April (Fool's Day) the 1st of 2011, the first of many state liquor stores slated for closing boarded up its doors for good. (House, Hope Ends as First of State Liquor Stores Closes 2011) Although the store only employed seven clerks, it was still painful for them; most went on unemployment hoping to find other jobs while others hoped to be placed at another location within the liquor store system. The store generated in excess of $3 million in sales, contributing around $1.3 million in profit to the state.

The fact that the first closure actually happened proved the legislature intended to go through with closing all ten liquor stores – businesses producing tens of millions of dollars in profit to save $2.2 million dollars – asinine! What kind of dimwit masquerading as a businessman would close very profitable businesses instead of building them into higher profit generating successes? I'll tell you who – A bunch of religious zealots pandering to their church. As rumor became reality, the news quickly spread. The public now outraged, banded together generating thousands of signatures on petitions and sent mass emails, letters, and even phoned their disapproval to the DABC and legislative body.

With the public livid and the state legislature running for cover, emergency meetings were held with the governor and other state leaders. The outcome: spend $100,000 to conduct an audit to find *"efficiencies within the Utah DABC,"* (House, Liquor Store Outcry: Utah Lawmakers Having Second Thoughts 2011), thus placing a moratorium on any more closures.

Notoriously, government and other entities use audits to steer away blame and outrage from their constituents or employees anytime shit hits the fan or they feel they need to make a change. If people are unhappy with something, an audit by hiring an outside, unbiased person or team to get to the bottom of problems will help an entity duck and weave the disenchanted. Usually, the word "audit" calms the masses because they now feel the problem is recognized and something is being done to rectify the issues. However, by the time the audit is complete, most people don't give a shit any longer about whatever problem they were mad about in the first place.

Of the liquor store closure audit findings, the most significant stated that by closing outlets, the adverse effect would happen. Rather than curb drinking, or profits increasing at other liquor stores, pissed-off residents would likely drive the one hour in any of three directions to

Nevada, Idaho, or Wyoming to buy their booze, adversely affecting business. The audit also recommended no further closures take place. No more liquor stores were closed after the audit, however, the DABC budget was still cut, so they had to find ways to save money elsewhere. The ensuing years amounted to nothing more than constructive prohibition; store hours were slashed, employees laid off, and products and inventories were butchered all in the name of saving money.

However, there's an asinine part of this story the state doesn't want anyone to hear. I was told by reliable sources they are still paying the lease on the building that housed the store they closed in 2011.

THE TOWN HALL MEETING

I MUST HAND IT TO SOMEONE in the state legislature or whoever set up the town hall meeting in Salt Lake City – it was indeed ballsy, but I'm sure I'll never know. They came from all parts of the state - students, homemakers, white-collar, blue-collar, no collar, restaurant owners and managers, bartenders – Utahans from all walks of life. The meeting was held on the third floor of the new city library, and even many members of the local media were in attendance filming, recording, writing notes. The panel consisted of several state legislative members, staff from the DABC, and a few restauranteurs seated behind a long table in front of the crowd.

With no issue off-limit, frustrated citizens stood to voice their displeasures and desires and even offer the panel advice. Topics such as privatization, product outages, grocery stores selling wine, removal of the Zion Curtain, home brewing and winemaking, wineries direct shipping via mail, bootlegging, store hours, and much more were all discussed. Passions ran high, voices were raised, anger spewed forth as criticism mounted. The panel listened and jotted down notes as they backpedaled; they asked questions to start friendly conversation and debate; they consoled and counseled as they tried to calm the masses, but each time they were shut down by the furious crowd.

Just as the meeting ran past its allotted two-hour time frame, a gentleman serving as the moderator stood to address the crowd, cutting several citizens off in the process. The list of issues was long (too long), and the meeting had to be cut short. He offered an email address for those who were not heard, then asked another gentleman sitting to one end of the panel to stand and be recognized. The man worked for an independent auditor. The crowd hushed while he explained that they had just completed an audit and they would like to share the results to conclude the meeting. Reading from his notes he pointed out revenue dollars, state-owned infrastructure, and profit. After his short speech, came his final message: "Basically, the state has become so dependent on the profit they make from selling alcohol that they can never give it up. We recommend a few changes but nothing drastic."

Most in the crowd groaned and snickered incredulously while several pointed and yelled obscenities as they stood to leave the building. What began as a somewhat promising acknowledgment from the state government to actually listen and possibly do something about the liquor laws, ended in a decisive blow to the unruly sinners of Utah. Aside from minor tweaking recommended by the auditors, there would be no major changes for now.

I thought about the meeting as I drove home, deciding to send an email offering my advice on how they could maintain control as well as a revenue flow. The outline demonstrated how to eliminate all of their infrastructure while increasing revenue. I never received an acknowledgment or a reply from anyone within the DABC or state government.

THE ESKIMO RESURFACES

THE ESKIMO AND I CONTINUED TO DEAL WITH EACH OTHER for several years after our heyday introduction as he took another job with a supplier already established in my territory. And since this little story involves bootlegging on a grand scale, I'll just name this supplier Plush Wine & Spirits or PWS for short. This supplier owned a few wineries in California but was better known for its imports, including products from Argentina, Italy, Spain, and France. For several years we literally crushed it, obtaining goal after goal set forth by the upper-ups.

However, during one particular ski season, we were presented with a problem so big, I was skeptical it could be pulled off. One of the sales and marketing minions at PWS decided to partner with several events during the Sundance Film Festival to increase awareness with one of their Champagne brands. But there were two big problems: the wines were not listed by the DABC, and they needed sixty cases for the events, and they notified the Eskimo and me with only five days left until the events took place. Emails flew back and forth between the festival organizers and PWS trying to figure out how to get the product they needed. Just days before the event I received a call from the Eskimo. "Hey SPARTY, I figured it out!"

"Oh, yeah? Tell me," I replied cynically.

"I'm going to overnight the product to you."

"What, really? *UPS or FedEx?* That's going to cost a fortune!"

"No, no, no... Check it out. I have sixty cases of Blanc, thirty cases of Rosé and ten cases of Champagne mini-bottles ready to be shipped overnight on Delta Air Cargo. It'll be there tomorrow morning. All you have to do is sashay over to the airport, pick it up, then deliver it to the events in Park City."

Completely stunned, I sat silently, jaw hanging open. "What? Are you out of your fucking mind?"

"This will work, I'm sure of it. Relaxxx, man."

"So, how the hell do you think I'm going to be able to pick up that much product and not get caught?" I exclaimed. "What if someone at Delta Air Cargo calls the DABC and turns me in? I could lose my license or get thrown in jail. Or both. Not to mention the fines I'll have to pay. What'll I do then?"

"Don't worry, brother, I got you covered," he said calmly. "If you get caught, you may have to move, but I'll get you a job."

"Oh, that's just great!" I exclaimed, visualizing the front pages of the local newspapers with my picture; the headlines proclaiming: "Utah Wine Broker Busted Bootlegging 100 Cases of Champagne into State!"

"This'll work, I'm sure of it," he replied.

"I thought they only needed sixty cases?"

"They upped the number, my apologies. Relaxxx, Cuzzz, I got your back. Nothing's gonna happen. Call me as soon as you have the product. You're probably going to need some help. Can you get a rep to help you or something?"

"Yeah, I guess. Remember our caddy from Pebble Beach, Timmy T? Just so happens he arrives tonight to hang out for a few days. He wants to snowboard and check out the festival. He's staying with me, so I'll get him to help."

"Awesome, tell him I said hello. In fact, take him out for dinner on the town and bill me for the cost."

"Okay, thanks," I said nervously. My mind was racing as I thought about all that could go wrong. My hand shook as I wrote down the confirmation numbers for Delta Air Cargo. The Eskimo repeatedly reassured me that nothing would happen. However, all I could think about were the consequences; anxiety took over and I felt sick. After several deep breaths, I realized I had another problem. How would I transport 100 cases of Champagne from the airport to my house then to Park City? I decided to ask my neighbor since he had a truck big enough to haul.

I slowly walked over to my neighbor's house, trying to figure out if I should tell him the truth. After knocking, I opened his door a crack. "Hey, Darren, you home?" I yelled.

"Yeah, what's up man?" he replied from the other room.

I walked into his kitchen. "Do you feel like doing something illegal and slightly clandestine?"

"Sure," he said. "Does it involve booze?"

"Of course, and I'll make sure to make it worth your while."

An avid outdoorsman from Alaska, Darren spent countless hours mountain biking, camping, and boating. He was always up for adventure even if it involved some slight law-bending. I knew I could count on him. I nervously explained the situation, proposing we could load it into my basement. Darren, however, volunteered his garage, as it was closer to the driveway than mine; we could back right up to the door rather than traipse through the snow and down the stairs to my basement. I told him I'd call him the next day after I had confirmation that the product had landed and was ready for pick-up.

Later that evening, after picking Timmy T up at the airport, I took him out to dinner. While we ate, I told him about the black ops going down the next day and that I needed his help loading and unloading the products. Timmy was unfazed, slugging back his beer. "No problem. What'll it take, a few hours maybe?"

"Yes, at least," I replied.

"Wait, is any of this illegal?" Timmy asked.

I paused for a moment. "Uh, yes, bootlegging is a misdemeanor in Utah, I think, but on this scale, it may be more serious. It could even be a federal crime."

"So, what could happen?" he asked.

"I'm not sure, maybe a ticket, a fine, a night in jail? I know one thing for sure... I'll lose my broker license with the state."

"So, why are you doing this? Can't you just tell him no?"

"Well, I could, I guess. If it were anyone other than the Eskimo, I probably would, but since he needs this favor and he takes such good care of me, I need to make it happen."

"That motherfucker better be buying us some dinner and booze!"

"Yes, he said I could bill him back for a nice dinner somewhere."

We both took deep breaths letting the realization sink in before he stated, "Okay, let's do it."

Tossing and turning, I hardly slept that night. Tired and nervous, my usual Wednesday morning gym routine was a waste of time. Timmy T went snowboarding for a half-day while I tried to get through the morning working on other projects. But, my mind kept drifting back to what was about to transpire. The day dragged as I waited for a phone call from the Eskimo with the confirmation.

Finally, at about one o'clock, I received the call. "Hey CUZZZZ, the product has landed and it's ready for pick up. The detail has your name on it. All you gotta do," he said in a calm drawl, trying to put me at ease, "is slide into the airport real nonchalant-like, pick up the product, take it back to your house, and I'll call you later with names and addresses to deliver the product in Park City. Piece of cake!"

"If this goes wrong, man," I said sternly but excited and somewhat terrified, "You better come bail me out and find me a job because I'll be ruined in Utah!"

"Don't worry, CUZ, I got your back," he said once again, adding, "Tell Timmy T I said hello."

I sent Darren a text asking him if he was ready. "Yeah, let's do this!" he replied.

Since I had no idea how much room we'd need we decided to take my SUV also just in case. Once saddled up, Darren followed me and Timmy T to the airport in his GMC long bed.

It was bitterly cold and grey that day in Salt Lake City as a long winter inversion had settled in; the perfect day for getting arrested. Once at the airport, we followed the signs until we arrived at a massive hangar with rows of garage doors large enough for eighteen-wheelers to back into. After several deep breaths, Timmy T and I entered through a bulky metal door while Darren waited and watched.

Fresh fish boxed up in Styrofoam from both coasts waiting to head to restaurants, pets shaking nervously in their travel cages, tires, packages, mail, and other assorted items littered the cargo bay. Sitting directly in the middle of it all sat a huge pallet of Champagne shrink-wrapped in cellophane revealing boxes adorned with large logos. Everyone knew. Gathering my nerves, my voice shook as I recited my name to the man at the receiving desk. The burly clerk in his tan Cargill overalls, stained from weeks of work without washing, breathed heavily as if on a ventilator while his giant dry cracked hands thumbed through the day's manifests.

"Oh, yes... one pallet from Washington. Sign here," he said as he slowly looked Timmy and I up and down.

I was sure his next move would be to call the police (or possibly the DABC) or some other law entity. My hand shook as I scribbled something resembling my signature. Then after showing him my ID he stated, "Back your truck through the middle doors up to the loading dock and we'll get you on your way."

My heart raced as I opened the metal door, quickly

scanning the parking lot for police or security; surely jail was eminent. I hurriedly walked to the truck, butt puckered and legs shaking. It was twenty degrees outside, but I was sweating. Once the GMC was backed up to the loading dock, the massive bay doors were shut, sealing us apart from the cold world. I couldn't help but think the sound resembled jail cell doors being closed. My heart pounded in my ears and my mouth was dry.

Walking around the pallet, we assessed the load. The receiving clerk leaned against his metal desk while another large dock hand sat in his forklift waiting for me to verify the contents. Several other workers in the warehouse stopped what they were doing to watch.

Breaking the silence, Darren said, "I think this whole thing will just fit right into the back of my truck." After some rough measurements, he instructed the forklift driver to slowly set the whole pallet into the bed, making sure it didn't catch on the wheel wells. With the product lifted in the air, ever so slowly the forklift inched forward, hovering the valuable merchandise over the bed. As gently as a butterfly with sore feet, he lowered the pallet, and the truck creaked under the weight. Once the full heft was realized, the back end dropped almost six inches.

Timmy and I looked at each other in disbelief.

With the truck fully loaded (lump still in my throat), I took a deep breath as the bay doors opened once again revealing the melancholy day. Relieved not to find not even one police cruiser waiting in the parking lot, I released the breath I'd been holding. Darren jumped into the truck to begin exiting the cargo bay; the diesel engine growled, flexing its muscle as it strained up the ramp. I quickly glanced at the clerk and forklift driver; they just watched and shook their heads, smirking in disbelief. They knew they had just witnessed something, that in Utah, slightly resembled a bank heist. The ice-cold air smacked me in the face bringing me back to reality. Elated, a calm rushed over me as I breathed another sigh of relief.

The first step complete, we now had to get the cargo back to the house, but there was one small problem. Okay, an enormous problem: the pallet rose almost four feet over the walls of the truck bed exposing the clear shrink-wrapped boxes that read PWS Champagne. Someone could surely make out the cargo driving back on the I-80 and through Salt Lake City in the middle of the afternoon. There was nothing we could do. A few people honked and waved as we drove through town. At a stoplight, one smart-ass rolled down his window to ask, "Where's the party?" Other than that, we didn't run into any problems.

With the truck backed up to Darren's garage, we laughed and joked in the cold afternoon air as we unloaded the cases in a fireman's line, one after the other, person to person, stacking them neatly in the middle of the garage.

It was only then, as we unloaded the cases that I noticed a large sticker emblazoned on each box. *Delta Air Cargo, Spartacus Falanghina, Broker, Utah.* Slightly taken aback, I laughed at the new problem. Grabbing one of the boxes, I looked for an odd edge to try to peel the sticker from the box - no luck; each one seemed as if it were superglued, making it impossible to peel away with just one tug. Each time I tried to peel the sticker it just ripped away in small patches. I had to get those things off before delivering the product the next day or surely someone would become wise. With time running out, I elected to try and cover up as much of my name as possible with a black Sharpie. After about an hour,

I stood admiring my work, fingers streaked with black ink, slightly buzzed from the smell, a few dozen Sharpies lay on the garage floor.

Over the next few days, Timmy T helped me make the deliveries. I notified the Eskimo once the job was complete. During the several months that followed, I cringed every time I received a call from the DABC or my doorbell rang, even looking over my shoulder once in a while, certain I'd be arrested at some point. I slept terribly each night, reliving the experience before finally drifting off. As each new day passed, I became more and more relieved. One thing was for sure, I'd never do that again.

BECAUSE, IT'S WHAT
MONOPOLIES DO
Part 1

THERE HAVE BEEN HUNDREDS OF ISSUES AND problems regarding how the state of Utah handles alcohol since they were given control just after prohibition. If a private business were run as poorly as the DABC is operated, then surely it would be out of business. However, since the state operates a monopoly, it leaves the public with little choice other than to bootleg and put up with their bullshit. The lawmakers know this, so they just keep the hammer down. The state legislature is the very root of the problem. Aside from letting their Mormon ideology interfere with the biased laws they pass, they grant the operating budget for the DABC. Because of the extreme budgetary constraints, the imbibing public and the entire DABC staff suffer due to the shorthanded, underfunded Department of Alcohol Beverage Control. Consequentially, the DABC suffers from an alternate deficiency as well, that of no competition, which has led to a general could-care-fucking-less attitude permeating the whole organization.

The factual compilation of events, policies, inefficiencies, and foibles by the state legislature and DABC that follow illustrate just how inept the system has become since the beginning of 2011 up to the time of this book's writing. Instead of properly funding, developing, and fostering a system that continually increases and returns profits for the state while satiating the public with a legal product, the Mormon-run legislature abuses the system, the public, and the state employees through blatant neglect and disregard. It's no wonder that imbibing Utahans despise, publicly ridicule, and joke about the legislature and the DABC at every opportunity.

Big Changes at the DABC Equal Years of Turmoil and Disruption

I heard it through a couple of suppliers first, then floating around the DABC offices: Dennis Crossland from the purchasing department had announced his retirement. Typically, people that work for the state government tend to hold their positions for a very long time, often until retirement, so Dennis' departure was really big news. I think he could see the storm clouds swirling and budget cuts coming, so it was a good time to get out of the game. Questions, rumors, and speculation ensued from my company, suppliers, and the other brokers as to who would take over the position – one that essentially oversees the entire purchasing department; even fine wine buyer Cliff Bradford would have to answer to the new boss. It was a big deal.

There was a short period of time while the right candidate was being selected. I dreaded the rumor that Betty Hansen may take over. She had been there for decades and probably deserved the position, but in my estimation, her demeanor and unbending quick-to-react judgment would not only be extremely tough to deal with but may hinder her from getting the job.

After several weeks it was announced that Don Tomovich would take the position. "Don Who?" everyone asked. Who was this guy? No one knew. Turns out Don had worked for the DABC in capacities other than the purchasing department for several years. Some of the reasons he was chosen included his tenure within the system, and from what I heard, his prior experience in another state working for a large grocery chain.

During the transition, one by one the brokers and suppliers scrambled to meet Don to gain a better feel of his style and hopefully instill a good first impression. After all, chances were high he would be in that position for a while. However, Don was older than expected, even close to retirement age himself. Tall and sturdy with wavy salt and pepper hair and a big bushy mustache, on the surface Don appeared to be genial and good-natured, but he was also hard to read because he rarely gave inclinations one way or another regarding his direction. In fact, during his first full year it appeared to be business as usual. He simply sat back, watched and learned – which is smart management in my opinion; not making any judgments until necessary. And so, for a while I liked him.

As I stated earlier, governments love audits. They will audit anything – paperclips, computer printers, booze, etc. If there is a value and taxpayers are involved, you can bet that it'll be audited at some point. Often audits help save money and/or streamline a way of doing business, but every so often they uncover dirt. Shortly after Don was hired, one particular audit at the DABC proved to be a major shakeup with the news that the director who had hired Don was involved in some type of wrongdoing involving state funds and hundreds of questionable payments to a company owned by his son for a machine that shrink-wrapped pallets of product. He immediately was let go, leaving the DABC headless.

Soon after the big news, several other top officials resigned or were dismissed from the DABC as well. Without a leader, the governor sent the director of the Commerce Department to fill in on an interim basis. With the Commerce Director now at the helm and the debacle still fresh, more audits soon followed covering every angle at the DABC, leaving no stone unturned; reform would soon follow.

Some of the immediate changes were a little over the top. A notice was sent out that the manufacturer sales representatives (meaning brokers such as myself) were no longer allowed to give swag or anything of monetary value to anyone employed by the state. No longer could we send Christmas cards, cookies or anything else to the DABC or the state liquor stores ever again. (And, it is here that I must confess – I am guilty but far less than other wine brokers and suppliers; but I must admit to sending a few cards and even gifting some popcorn, or cookies, or candy at Halloween, Christmas, or other holidays. Cuff me now and throw away the key.) The new mandate also meant we couldn't give swag to any of the employees working at the state stores. No hats, jackets, t-shirts, posters, etc. – all the stuff usually sent to us to give away; the stuff adorned with company logos and slogans from suppliers and the makers of alcoholic products; stuff that, to an employee getting paid around $8-$9 per hour barely getting by, meant a great deal. Also – no pizzas, sandwiches, or other food could be dropped off to help them get through a shift. The silent message the DABC sent to their employees: We already abuse you with low pay and little opportunity for advancement – we're taking this free stuff away that costs us nothing, so screw you!

While I do understand the fact that maybe free gifts could imply preferred shelf space and maybe a better place to stack products that are on sale, I never witnessed any favoritism. Maybe this happened, maybe it didn't, and probably shouldn't, but seeing the face of an employee light up because they didn't have to pay for a meal or were on the receiving end of a cheap t-shirt, hat, or winter jacket that said *Jacob's Creek* or *Sterling Vineyards,* was worth breaking the law.

Monopolies Squeeze Their Customers for Every Bit of Profit

One day, out of the blue, I received a phone call from new purchasing department head Don Tomovich asking what I thought about "going from five sale months per year to three sale months per year on general listed products."

"Well, that would mean reduced volumes and sales; people will be more apt to bootleg from other states. I think customers are used to the sales being five times per year, particularly some restaurants," I replied defensively.

"What do you mean?" he asked.

"Well, restaurants have to pay the same price as retail customers. They may only buy a product during the sale month and they may buy big to get them through to the next sale month. They bridge buy."

"I understand. However, the problem that I see is that many products only generate high volume when they're on sale. The rest of the time, they languish, which tells me they're overpriced, and the public has gotten used to only buying a product when it's on sale. When the product they usually buy is not on sale, they buy the competitor's product that *is* – So it's a bad mix."

I thought for a moment, then added, "I can see that as well. However, the same thing happens with other products; it doesn't matter if it's butter or blue jeans. When a product's on sale, volume increases."

"Thank you, I'm just asking the brokers to gather information before a decision is made. Have a good day."

"Oh, okay... thank you," I replied.

Several days later, it was announced: the DABC would cut the sale months down to three times per year per product. Phone calls and emails volleyed. The brokers and suppliers were irritated with this new policy and we weren't about to let it stand. Several suppliers and brokers made appointments to plead the case for having five sale months per year. After the air cleared, it was decided the difference would be split, allowing for four sale months per year. The decision was final.

Next, Don instituted a new modification to their delisting process. Prior to his arrival, when the DABC delisted products, they simply reduced the shelf price to what they actually paid for the product so they could blow it out within days. Since the state mark-up on alcohol is around 88%, the products being delisted were a considerably good deal. By blowing out the product within a few days, the DABC ensured they made room for new products the following month.

However, Don decided that the DABC was leaving too much money on the table. To increase profitability, delisted products were put on a sliding price reduction percentage over a period of time. During the first few months a blue discount shelf talker was put up notifying the public that a product had been delisted. The tag stated, "Last Chance" but didn't offer any type of discount. If a person lifted the tag, they could see the old shelf price on the regular shelf price tag. As time went by, depending on how much of a product was still left, the DABC would offer a small discount to encourage sales until it sold through. With the new policy, it often took several months to get rid of a delisted product's inventory rather than the old way of just blowing it out at cost. While I can understand a manager's decision to try to increase profitability slightly, and ultimately still get rid of a product, this new process clogged up shelf space. New products and trends couldn't be approved or bought until shelf space was freed up.

Monopolies Do Not Care About Their Consumer's Choices

Soon after, more changes followed by numerous cuts starting with the products they carried at that time. It was decided that fine wines did not need to be sampled any longer by the brokers or buyer Cliff Bradford. Any new Limited Listed wines could be bought simply by presenting press and ratings given out by the major wine publications. So, if a broker came across a wine with an excellent rating, all we had to do was print off the press and submit it to Cliff with one caveat: the shelf price had to be equal to or lower than the price provided on the rating. Cliff would decide if there was room or not within the shelf set. No big deal – I could live with that – so far, so good.

Also, Limited Listed wines that were already carried by the state did not have to be re-tasted each vintage – as long as they sold, the new vintages would be purchased. This was certainly fine by me because it was a pain in the ass to have every new vintage tasted and approved and I was getting tired of introducing new wines through the tasting and sampling process.

Then despite Cliff's opposition, Don began to actively delist products each month to reduce the number of items on the store shelves to in his eyes, a more manageable level. No category was safe as the butchery escalated. Cliff Bradford reportedly was told the products he oversaw would be reduced by two-thirds. Essentially handcuffed, dejected, and disgusted, Cliff resigned as the "Fine Wine" buyer, citing that he was no longer able to do his job effectively.

Don did not understand, nor did he seem to care that the state store system needed a large, diverse selection from all over the world to satisfy the demands of the retail consumers and the restaurant trade. He was only focused on sales, how fast a product sold through, and profitability. Don, even though well-educated, knew very little about the necessities and nuances of expensive Champagne, Bordeaux, Burgundy, Barolo, or Cognac, etc., to fill out a wine/liquor store in a state with a very high international tourism trade. It appeared that he wanted to change the dynamic of the state stores to that of a chain store mentality focusing on products under $25 rather than that of an independent fine wine store, which was Cliff Bradford's vision. Prior to Don, it was not uncommon to walk into a state store to find highly rated wines, liquors, and beers of every price from almost every nook and cranny of the planet. After the carnage, many wine racks and store shelves sat empty.

Now, I may have disagreed with Cliff Bradford from time to time or even bad-mouthed him under my breath for not buying a product that I thought was outstanding, but I understood the difficult part of his job was to review and buy products for the very limited space within the state store constraints. He had to cover as many categories and specialty items as the small store spaces would allow. That is what made Cliff Bradford an outstanding buyer. Cliff's vast knowledge of fine wine, fine liquor, and even beer allowed him to make sound decisions to satisfy the diverse tastes of the Utah population and the tourists that come to ski and visit the five national parks annually. I think some people rejoiced at the news of his retirement, but as time would tell, we didn't know what we had until it was gone. Cliff's office sat vacant for almost two years.

Monopolies Are Not Progressive

Desperately in need of a new director for the DABC, the Commerce Director filling in promoted Don Tomovich to the role of Deputy Director to help ease her workload. Brokers and suppliers held their collective breath, hopeful the new promotion would signal the end of his reign in the purchasing department. With a bit of luck, maybe they would put someone in charge of the purchasing department who would get back to treating the state stores as specialty stores rather than just another grocery chain with low-end swill. But optimism was crushed as he decided to maintain control over the purchasing department, scrutinizing inventory and every PO to make sure all was in line with his vision. In my opinion, Don's demeanor changed after the announcement; he waltzed around the offices as if he walked on water. He appeared to be untouchable. With only six months or so under his belt as Deputy Director, Don threw his hat in the ring to become the next Director of the DABC.

In June of 2012, almost a year after scandal brought down the previous director, the governor publicly thanked the Commerce Director for helping during the time of crisis and introduced Ted Petriole as the new Executive Director of the Department of Alcoholic Beverage Control.

Monopolies Don't Care About Stagnation

Audits can be helpful in pinpointing and addressing problems, but they can also be harmful because business may actually suffer. One of the audits analyzed the state's route to market – or how they sell the products of which they are in charge. When the audit was complete, it basically said: Sell only products that turn or sell frequently; there was too much inventory in the back rooms of each state store, and too many expensive wines that didn't sell within a defined time period tying up dollars, further cementing the chain-store mentality.

Immediately after reviewing the audit, Don and Ted, armed with facts and figures, set a plan in place – There was to be a moratorium on the purchase of any new products until the system was completely revamped. They decided that the state liquor store managers were ordering a surplus of too many products from the main warehouse, resulting in excessive inventory sitting in the back rooms.

The IT department was tasked to create a new way to order – a centralized ordering system within their present system using algorithms to analyze the daily inventory at the state stores at any given time. The program took place of the store manager's task of placing weekly orders by automatically taking the inventory on hand then recommending a replenishment order from the state warehouse. While this dramatically reduced the number of cases in the storage rooms of the state stores, the most significant result: massive out-of-stock issues. When products were on sale, the system wouldn't order enough product to make the sale effective. And since most stores received their deliveries only once a week, then out of stocks lasted several days or even weeks in some instances. The system also didn't consider holidays, weather, events, or products that sold at a faster pace. Purchase orders took weeks to be generated. The out-of-stock issues became severe, suppliers became irritated. Though sales declined on many popular brands, overall sales didn't because the public was forced to buy outside their comfort zone or whatever they could get their hands on. Their choices became even more limited than they already had been.

Monopolies Modify Rules at Any Time and Only for Their Benefit

Prior to Don and Ted's reign, the DABC employed a somewhat open-door policy. The DABC partly relies on the brokers and suppliers for their knowledge of current market and industry trends to help with their decisions when listing, delisting or issuing product trades. However, with them, it became a closed-door policy at the DABC offices, and literally, the doors were locked. They did not want any information on market and industry trends or new product information, at least for the time being, until they finished slashing inventory and reducing the total amount of products on the shelf.

The DABC instituted a "20k policy" and changed the rules with brokers and suppliers. If a general listed product didn't generate at least $20,000 profit each year, the product would be automatically delisted. There would be no more delisting meetings in which the brokers pleaded their case for retaining a product. There would also be no six-month delist review period. If the DABC decided to delist a product it would be done immediately, no questions asked. To track this, they created a Profit Loss Analysis Report that showed the performance of every product by category on a rolling 12-month basis. They furnished the report to the brokers upon request, which helped plan sale months to maximize revenue in hopes of maintaining profitability over the threshold. If a product was too close to the threshold, a request for a "trade out" could be made before something was delisted for not selling.

Trade-outs were granted upon review of all the information by Don and his staff and had to be within the same category and general price point area. If a trade-out option was not available within those limitations, then it was possible to request a trade for a new product in another category. Nonetheless, the DABC would have the final decision.

After the 20k policy came out, brokers began scrambling to submit trades for underperforming products. Overburdened with an excess of trade requests, the DABC again came out with a new policy: "No trades granted, ever." It would be their decision only; they would decide what they would carry, period.

Time Has No Bearing to Monopolies

For almost two years, I couldn't get a new state listing to save my life – general or limited. Before 2011, an even flow of old products phased out to support a wave of new products existed. Now there was nothing. It was beyond comprehension. Everything I submitted for review was either rejected or ignored. When the DABC rejected a new product, they simply put a piece of paper in the broker's file at the front desk with a check by a box explaining why the product was not chosen. 95% of the time the box that was checked read: "No need for additional items in this category." Stifled for two whole years, my only thought was that I had to outlast the current regime at the DABC.

Suppliers began to get anxious and annoyed. To appease them, I began submitting everything just to get them off my back, even though I knew they'd be rejected. I grew tired of telling the same old story about how they simply were not listing anything new, that the state was in delisting restructuring mode. I started to keep a log of all the wines I presented, so when asked by my supervisors and suppliers, I could easily show what had been done up to that point. Sales began to suffer with some suppliers due to a combination of the state actively delisting products and not replacing or listing any of their innovation products. The DABC, already slow to react to industry trends, was now almost two years behind the curve in regard to the innovation happening around the country.

As a result of stagnation, the demand for special orders increased as restaurateurs desperately wanted products to differentiate themselves from their competition. With the growth of the special orders, the one person in charge of issuing the PO's became inundated. Other people within the purchasing department helped with the workload from time to time, but special orders that took 4-5 weeks were now often taking over eight weeks. Restaurants that were big enough to carry inventory began to order in quantity, buying several cases or even a pallet. The restaurants that could not inventory a high amount of cases began to stealthily work with the state liquor store managers to hide their inventory in the back rooms of the state stores. This would allow them to buy a case at a time at their convenience rather than all at once. The DABC caught on, however, issuing an ultimatum that all the licensees responsible for the excessive product build-up immediately buy all the product stashed in back rooms at various stores around Utah.

The damage to the state wine stores and liquor stores was significant. Hundreds of highly rated but somewhat expensive products were delisted; grand Cru Burgundies dwindled; except for a few top wines, first through fifth-growth Bordeaux disappeared; several top sparkling wines, liqueurs, Barolos, Brunellos, and even California cult wines were cut from the state store shelves. After the massacre had lulled, a few changes finally happened within the DABC purchasing department: David Wadsworth was promoted to oversee General Listed products and Danny Mann was promoted to oversee the Limited Listed products. Everything though, would still have to be reviewed by Don Tomovich to ensure his direction was maintained.

With Monopolies, the Fish Rots from the Head

A pervasive non-caring laissez-faire attitude exists within a monopoly, one that starts at the top filtering all the way down through the lower ranks. Since there's no competition, employees exert the least amount of energy possible to get the job done. The path of least resistance. They know there are no alternatives so why should they give a shit about the quality or efficiency of their work? Plus, more likely than not, lower-rank employees are paid less and offered little to no benefits because the monopoly doesn't care about growing its business or its customer base; they know they have a necessity that people want so there is no need to overpay for help or overdeliver sales.

Well into 2014, there was yet another new audit, this time focusing on the state store employees and high turnover rate. Due to budgetary constraints handed to the DABC by the legislature, the result was a turnover rate within the state store system hovering around 55%. A survey within the state stores was conducted. Overwhelmingly approximately 42% of the anonymous respondents that replied said higher pay and benefits would help retain good people. Two-thirds of the state store workers are part-time employees, many of whom work two to three jobs just to make ends meet. It's no wonder the state can't retain good employees when they're paying a wage that doesn't allow them to live above the poverty line.

In my judgment, such a high turnover rate has added to the overall dissatisfaction of the customer base. Employees do not have a vested interest in doing a good job – without incentives or programs in place to make an employee feel valued, the general attitude is one of doing the bare minimum. If an item is out of stock, it's met with a shrug of the shoulders or an excuse – there is no attempt to correct the problem – knowledge, merchandising, and customer service fall by the wayside.

So, the big question: Does the state make enough money to correct this? Fucking A right, they do! The state consistently brings in profits of around a hundred million dollars or more each year, so it appears to me that they have the money to reinvest in their state alcohol control system. However, due to the religious beliefs of most of the lawmakers, they feel it's their moral obligation to manipulate and abuse a system that profits from the so-called sins of the non-Mormons, which is a hypocritical crime on their part.

Monopolies are Miserly and Operate in the Least Expensive Way Possible

Even after record profits were recorded in 2015, the state legislature decided to cut yet another $500,000 from the DABC budget for the fiscal year July to June 2015-2016. This left the directors of the DABC scrambling yet again. Without closing stores and further trimming store operating hours, the cuts had to come from somewhere, so with their backs to the wall, the DABC decided to cut existing security services in favor of a single company.

The security services that the state liquor stores use are actually contracted off-duty police officers employed part-time. Some stores have officers on duty all the time, while others only employ them during peak hours. At any rate, the officers provide a huge deterrent to theft, public intoxication, and other nefarious activities. Plus, the side job allows them to make a little extra money on the side.

The officers make around $25 per hour, and they can provide a level of security that a contracted security company cannot. If something criminal happens a security officer can only call the police, which brings them into the loop anyway. When the public heard of this new cut-back, a new round of emails, calls, and outrage resulted in the DABC backing off. Ultimately, the DABC offered the off-duty officers their jobs back but now at $19 per hour instead. Most officers said they would not work for that wage, leaving everything in a stalemate. Finally, after the showdown, the DABC acquiesced, asking the officers to return to work with the same pay – crisis averted.

So, where are cuts made when it appears that everything is running bare-bones as it is? The answer: state store employees – once again left to bear the brunt, ultimately passing terrible customer service and poorly stocked stores on to the consumer. Part of the plan the DABC came up with was to offer $8,000 as an early retirement incentive for some qualified managers, then leave those positions vacant. Plus, the DABC wouldn't fill vacant clerk positions either unless absolutely necessary. This forced many current store managers (who were given a slight pay increase for their efforts) to oversee more than one state store – often as many as three. When a manager wasn't on duty an employee was left in charge; an employee often making $9-$13 per hour, who didn't want the responsibility but were told to toe the company line.

Even deeper cuts were needed, so the directors of the

DABC slashed jobs and hours within the main warehouse, further fueling out-of-stocks in the state stores. Even with several loading bays, the warehouse couldn't keep up due to insufficient manpower. Exasperated, somewhere along the line, the state warehouse manager and workers stopped giving a shit. The sense of urgency ceased to exist with expediting special orders out to the state stores for pick up, making sure inventories were logged correctly, and receiving regular shipments and dealing with mis-shipments in a timely manner.

Monopolies Don't Care About Inefficiencies and are Accountable to No One

What follows are some examples (a small selection among the hundreds that I've personally dealt with) illustrating the inefficiencies of the DABC.

On February 3rd, 2015, I placed an order for Jackson Family Wines consisting of four different wines for a total of 190 cases. All the wines were state-approved, listed and carried in the state stores. The PO was issued, and vintages were confirmed and approved by the buyer.

Approximately six weeks went by, but I had yet to receive a confirmation that the order had arrived in Utah, so I sent an email to Jackson Family Wines inquiring as to the whereabouts of the PO. I was told that it had been shipped and delivered. With that information, I thought everything was progressing, that it was just taking time to get processed and sent out to the stores. Besides, with the DABC, it was not unusual to not get the confirmation of received products. Two more weeks went by before my sales reps began inquiring about the whereabouts of the wines. I asked if they had checked the product locator online and they confirmed the wines appeared to still be on order. So again, I sent another email to customer service at Jackson Family Wines: "Could you tell me if PO 131546 has been shipped?"

"Yes, it shipped and was received on February 19th, 2015." Pressing further, I asked them if they could get a Bill of Lading from the trucking company showing confirmation. One week went by before I received a reply. "Attached is the confirmation and Bill of Lading showing delivery of said product with a signature stamp by the state warehouse manager."

Armed with the new information, I obtained a meeting with the DABC buyer hoping to solve the problem. I presented a copy of the PO and the Bill of Lading, laying the information out on his desk.

"Is there any way to find out if this order is sitting in the warehouse? Jackson Family Wines is telling me this order shipped weeks ago, the Bill of Lading stamped with the warehouse manager's name confirms that it was received on February 19th," I said.

With a sigh, the buyer said, "Let me pull the papers for this." He stood, walked to a filing cabinet outside the door and returned with a handful of purchase orders, all from Jackson Family Wines. Sitting back down at his desk, he began flipping through them one at a time, stopping at the original order. "This order was held up at the warehouse because a vintage had changed on one of the wines. But I can see my approval right here, so let me call the warehouse to find out if they still have it." He looked at his watch. "It's getting close to 2:30, they may be gone for the day."

After several rings, the phone was answered up by one of the warehouse workers. The buyer spouted off the order number, then was put on hold. Moments later the conversation resumed. After hanging up the phone, he said, "The order was on hold because of the vintage change, so that's why it hasn't been released."

"Yes, but you approved the vintage, so it shouldn't have been held up, correct?"

"Well, that's true, but there must have been a glitch, and the warehouse didn't receive the approval paperwork."

Undeterred, I prodded, "This order was received on February 19th. It's been sitting on the warehouse dock for almost two months. If I hadn't discovered this, it could've sat there indefinitely?"

"Well," he said, "yes, I suppose so, but we would've gotten around to it eventually."

"Well, that's ridiculous," I said, raising my voice, "All four wines sell extremely well; the state stores have been out of stock on two of the wines for over a month. My sales reps and many restauranteurs are asking for product and it's been sitting in the state warehouse for almost sixty days?"

"Well, the vintage thing tied it up. That's why it was held up in the warehouse," he reiterated.

Trying my best not to blow my top, I asked, "When will the product be shipped out to state stores? I'm losing spots on wine lists each week the stores are out of stock."

"The product will be shipped out next week to each store it was in before it was out of stock. The restaurants should be able to pick it up then. If that's all, I have another appointment."

"Okay, thanks, I guess," I said, standing from my chair. "Have a good weekend."

With the prior debacle still on my mind, it was about two weeks later that I decided to wade through the files from all my other suppliers to look for older outstanding purchase orders. As it would be, I discovered a very old PO from one of my other major suppliers, Palm Bay, for a small Chilean Cabernet order. I called the buyer once again to find out what was wrong with the order.

After exchanging pleasantries, I stated, "In March of 2014, I placed a reorder for 28 cases of *Santa Rita Medalla Real Cabernet.* A week later, a purchase order was issued and submitted to the supplier, Palm Bay International. Palm Bay International expedited the order two weeks later."

"Yes," he replied.

"At the end of April 2014, while scanning inventory reports, I noticed the 28 cases had been received, showing up as inventory in the warehouse, yet none had been sent out to any of the state stores. At that time, it didn't strike me as particularly odd because at the store level I could see they still had a little bit of inventory. After another month, again I noticed the same amount of *Santa Rita Medalla Real Cab* inventory in the warehouse but also two of the state stores had sold out. Again, this didn't strike me as odd because the stores could have just run out, and the product may be scheduled for delivery. Are you following me?"

"Yes."

I continued. "At the end of June, two months later, upon scanning store inventories again, I noticed four state stores were now out of the product, and the 28 cases that were received back in March, were still sitting in the warehouse untouched. I sent you a note to please ship the wines to the stores to replenish their stock."

"Yes, go on..."

"July came and went, yet again this wine showed the same inventory number in the warehouse, but now five state stores were out of stock. Again, I sent an email asking for the wines to be shipped to the state stores."

"Yes, go on..."

"I repeated this process again the following month and the following month, but nothing happened. This is obviously a problem, correct?"

"Yes, go on..."

"At the end of October, I decided I'd see how long this could continue before the problem was fixed - it became a game or even an experiment in a way. Month after month after month I would ask, 'Please have this wine force shipped out to the state stores ASAP.' Absolutely nothing has happened until today, April 30th – over a year since the product had been received then shuffled off to an unknown location in the DABC warehouse still showing up as inventory!"

"I see," he said. "Hold on, let me go pull the paperwork on this PO." After a few moments, he returned. "It says here on the received notes from the warehouse manager that this wine is not what we requested. We requested *Santa Rita Medalla Real Cabernet* on the PO, but we were sent *Santa Rita Casa Real Cabernet*. It will need to go back to the supplier at their cost."

"But," I said exasperated, "this wine is over a year old. And, since this issue is over a year old, I highly doubt that the supplier will even be able to locate their paperwork. This could take another year to iron out. Are there any other options? What about just selling it out in the three best stores? Can't we just blow it out? Palm Bay appears to already have been paid for the product and you have inventoried it for the past year. Why not just sell it?"

"Well, I guess. If you could tell me that this wine is something better than what we carry I'd consider it. Is this a nicer wine than what we currently carry? Can you find me any ratings?"

I fumbled to find a rating and price while logging into websites – I had to resolve this once and for all. "The actual retail price for this bottle would be over $80. The rating from Robert Parker says it's 93 points. The rating also says the retail should be between $65 and $85 dollars, so it's legit. The wine we usually carry is $19.99, so we should just blow out the wrong wine for that price. Hell, at that price I'll buy a case myself!"

The buyer laughed. "Well, I will too, but I need some more information to get this done. Send me the rating and a picture of the label with a UPC code."

Later that afternoon, after submitting the paperwork to get the problem resolved, I received an email from the buyer: "This is a dead deal, we sent the wine back and never paid the supplier for it. The warehouse manager is updating his inventory."

What a goddamn joke! For over a year I had faxed and emailed, then finally after my grand experiment, discussed the problem with the buyer to find a resolution. Here's the finality of the problem: the DABC warehouse manager signed off on the product, made notes about it being the wrong product, then either failed to inform the buyer and/or the buyer failed to expedite the process with me, the broker. The warehouse manager sent the product back with the trucking company, returning it to the supplier. He didn't notify anyone in the DABC Purchasing Department or update the inventory, so the cases I saw each month in the warehouse never existed while the state stores ran out of product, costing all involved. This also meant the DABC inventoried 28 cases of product that didn't exist when they conducted their yearly inventory at the end of June, the closing of their fiscal year, so the profitability factor was false.

Additionally, it's reasonable to say that all the other brokers were having problems and issues of a similar fashion. As for the 2014 fiscal year, it's anybody's guess as to the true profitability of the DABC.

The state's warehouse system is so poorly run, they simply overlook or lose products from time to time. To further explain the inadequacies of the state warehouse, I offer the following short examples as well.

Many years back, after walking into a downtown Salt Lake City wine store to purchase some "professional samples," I noticed a few cases of *Matrot Meursault* white Burgundy sitting on the floor with a giant sale tag. The price on the tag: $6.00 per bottle. Taking a bottle to the cash register, I asked the clerk if he knew the story behind the discount. He simply said, "Apparently, the main warehouse lost it somehow; it was found tucked back into one of the corners. It's an older vintage so that's why they're blowing it out."

I looked at the wine through the glass to discern if there were any irregularities. "Well, white Burgundy can age nicely if the temp is okay; it's only just over four years old. How much can I buy?"

The clerk looked quizzically at me. "Buy it all if you like, there's no limit. But beware, you can't return it."

At six dollars a bottle it was worth a gamble, so I bought it all – twenty-two bottles total. Giddily, I put a few bottles in the refrigerator and the rest in my wine cellar. That evening, I popped one; it was absolutely extraordinary. Probably one of the best deals I've ever come across. I conserved it, opening a bottle every so often, and each bottle turned out to be incredible.

On the flip side, one afternoon in 2015, in the same store, I came across ten cases of 2008 *Chateau St Jean Cinq Cepages* in half bottles. Once again, after conferring with the clerk, the same story was told: the warehouse missed it somehow, so it had been sitting in the backroom for several years. This time though, since it was a red wine and a very good offering from a very good winery, they elected to sell the wine at the regular price: about $35. I bought a bottle to see if it was still good. It was well past its prime, turning into a thick raisiny high-alcohol bomb; extremely disappointing. I'm sure some customers and restaurants that purchased some of this product tried to return it after they encountered the same findings, but it was another caveat emptor situation and this time it stung.

During June of 2015, one of my employees asked me to research a special order that had been placed with the DABC a few months prior by one of his restaurant accounts. The order was for six cases of low-end Pinot Grigio used as a glass pour. Through the web portal on the DABC website, I could discern that indeed the product had shown up in the warehouse. With this info, I emailed the person in charge of special orders, asking if the PO had been received. The reply: "It looks as if the order is here, but I don't know where it's at."

"Could you check the warehouse?"

A day later, I was told, "We still can't find it; a big load came in, it's just taking time."

A few days later, the account, now running out of Pinot Grigio, contacted us once again to inquire to its whereabouts, so I went through the process again only to receive the same runaround. Digging deeper, this time on a visit to one of the liquor stores chitchatting with an employee that had at one time worked in the main warehouse, I found out this tidy bit of information: Because June 30th is the end of the Utah fiscal year, the warehouse just lets the special orders that arrive during the last two weeks of the month sit on the warehouse floor without checking them in so they don't have to inventory them.

This type of business attitude is unconscionable. Since waving accusatory fingers and ranting and raving gets nothing accomplished with the DABC, we just had to wait for July 1st for the warehouse to check in the product. And since July 1st, 2015 was a Wednesday, and the warehouse moves at a snail's pace, by the time they logged the special order in, then sent it to a liquor store so the account could purchase the wine, it ended up being Monday, July 6th. The restaurant had been out of product for more than two weeks while it sat on the state warehouse dock less than eight miles away. Absolutely ridiculous!

When will this stop? When will the state legislature wake up to building a system up, offer excellent customer service, and actually embrace the money-making machine that is the DABC? The short answer: never.

Yet Even in a Monopoly Sometimes There's a Little Light

Don Tomovich decided to retire during the fall of 2015. I'm sure the never-ending budget constraints and pressure from the public had something to do with his decision. I think as a manager Don was trying to do the best he could with the budget he had to work with. It's a manager's job to look for and implement solutions to help business move forward while remaining profitable. While I don't necessarily condone his direction or the way he butchered the selection of products under his watch, I can empathize with the frustrations he had to deal with daily. The DABC has the unfortunate position of sitting on the front line, left alone to bear the ire of the outraged public (even their own employees) while the ass-hat LDS members of the state legislature camouflaged as unbiased politicians pass laws and judgments from their lofty thrones on Capitol Hill.

Two weeks after Don's retirement, I stopped into the DABC to pick up any loose papers from the file kept for me at the receptionist's desk. From time to time the DABC deposits miscellaneous documents, received purchase orders, and/or reports containing important information they need to convey to the brokers into a folder labeled by broker. While thumbing through the pages, the fine wine buyer happened to walk by on his way to his office. We exchanged pleasantries as he flashed his ID card across the electronic device on the door to his wing of offices. Just as the door was about to close, he leaned back. "Hey, Spartacus, do you have any wines with at least a 93-point rating that would cost around $50-$60 on our shelves?"

I thought for a moment. "Sure do, why?"

"Well, we're trying a new pilot program in several stores. The idea is to have one rack that holds around ten different wines, and once one sells out, we find a new one. The rack will have signage that says something like 'One Time Buy Specialty Wines' or something to that effect."

I paused briefly to consider the program while he patiently waited for me to gather my thoughts. "When do you need the information by?"

"Today by four-thirty, if possible."

"But it's Friday." I sighed while looking at my watch. "Okay, I'll see what I can do."

Back in my office with only a few hours to spare, I frantically checked through my files while scanning websites for ratings. Luckily, as it just so happened, two new suppliers producing stellar wines had just come on board. While figuring out the shelf prices, current vintages, and compiling the press, my thoughts ranged from: *I can't believe my luck,* to *This is just a goose chase, nothing will come of it.* When all the information was compiled, I emailed the buyer just before the four-thirty deadline.

Later that evening, while checking email from my phone, I came across two new purchase orders from the DABC; both containing an order for forty cases of each of the wines I had submitted just that afternoon. Shocked but elated, I smiled as I opened a bottle of wine to celebrate the new orders and contemplate my good fortune.

For four years, a new fine wine listing had been virtually impossible to obtain under Don Tomovich. Oh sure, a few new listings were granted, but only for inexpensive and unimpressive boardroom brands to fill in low-end gaps. New fine wine listings were few and very far between. Now, just after Don had departed, I had been granted two new state listings in just under a three-hour time span with nothing more than a rating and a price – no fact sheets, no formalities, no samples.

The following few months produced another dozen new state listings for wines ranging from $12 to $300 – It was almost unfathomable. I had outlasted the old regime. Time proved fruitful for most brokers until mid-2016, when the DABC changed yet again – another turn for the worse.

TREND

MOSCATO

"STEP RIGHT UP!" the ringmaster bellows, another noble grape arrives for the gallows. The covetous capitalists must have their way, they manipulate and connive, another glorious payday.

Dry to sweet, even some are complex, a style, a form, that often perplex.

However... its true form is not what they're after, hooking sugar-crazed Americans, sitting back, belly full of laughter.

A simple rendition with notes of apricot and peach, it's fresh, even vivacious, but cloyingly sweet.

Moscato consumers mostly are young, it titillates the nose and beguiles the tongue.

I have one!

No, wait, look over here!

I do too – not to fear!

Wait, look at ours, we have a red one and one that is pink!

Ours was the first!

Ours is unique – yet, so easy to drink!

Ours is on fire – for sure you can't miss, but alas, just a fad, so easy to dismiss.

One by one, they all proclaim, groping and grabbing to

steal the grape's fame.

We have ten-thousand cases, the goal's a must-make, they are non-negotiable, for all our own sake.

The trackers are ready, now get to work, we want our wine placements, no one will shirk.

None want to miss the newly found trend before the pendulum swings, signaling the end.

More than 200 different grapes share a version of the name Muscat - Moscato d'Asti, Moscato di Canelli, Muscat de Saumur, Moscatello, Muskat, etc. Dating back to the Roman era, Muscat is one of the oldest species of grapes made into wine. Ranging from light and dry and low in alcohol to slightly frizzante, golden, rich and even raisiny and higher in alcohol - Muscat possesses diverse qualities, all the while never losing its integrity.

Enter the American version of Moscato, simple and inexpensive, most made overly sweet, designed to seduce and entice fledgling tastes. However, there are a few offering dry to off-dry versions, differentiating themselves enough to tempt even stern wine experts. Nevertheless, they're a tough sell to serious restaurant buyers unless spicy food is on the menu to foil its sweetness. A craze or a fad? Only time will tell if the American version of Moscato will stand the test.

The Moscato trend helped shift the mindset of many wine drinkers, stealing market share from other categories – namely, White Zinfandel and sweet Riesling. And the trend may have just served a secondary purpose: getting people to expand their horizons and try new products. Consumer eyes wide open, jammy red and white fruit bombs loomed around the next corner.

SOJOURNER TAKES OVER

AFTER SEVERAL YEARS, the partnership with the Oaks Corporation came to an end and it was time for Sojourner to take over full ownership. Aside from all the new logoed forms, email addresses, and general ways of doing back-of-the-house business such as expense reports and other particulars, the transition was mostly seamless.

Enter my fourth new boss. However, this guy was different – a self-prescribed liquor salesman, he knew very little about wine, and he wasn't shy about telling me so. Sure, there was a short round of analysis regarding pay for myself and my team, our contributions (and how we all could contribute even more), but instead of dictating business, the new boss simply relied on me to run my small division and supply all pertinent information, so he knew what to tell the suppliers when sitting in Top to Top meetings, which was refreshing.

With Sojourner now 100% all in, it was time to grow again, this time dramatically. Major suppliers immediately fired their old broker to align themselves across almost all the states in which SSW conducted business. Other smaller suppliers came on board as well, but the behemoths contributed almost 85,000 new cases annually, providing a significant bump to our annual sales revenue in just Utah alone. New cash flow meant another round of hiring; this time, three new sales reps in Utah and two in Wyoming, reporting to my state manager, then ultimately to me. I was now managing a small division of nine, bringing the totals to six in Utah and three in Wyoming. Administrative positions apparently did not exist in Sojourner's mind, so all daily paperwork, supplier communications, dealings with the state government, plus sales management rested on my lap while my pay stayed the same.

I was fairly lucky with my new hires. However, I did have a few who failed miserably; one employee even failed a random drug test for not turning in human pee (turns out he was fine, but his goat was pregnant). And one young millennial that just seemed unable to grasp what needed to be accomplished each month; she was more concerned with her social status and her dogs than working. I tried, I did, but it just didn't click with her, which was odd because she hounded me for over a year for a job. I figured anyone who had the resolve to continually pursue a job, had to be a good sales rep. Oh, but woefully I was wrong. And so, after a period of training, a considerable amount of time on the job, retraining, and coaching, I decided it was time to set her free; she just couldn't produce. However, I knew that the Human Resources Department must be consulted first before swinging the ax, and therein lies the problem.

Except for small independents, which may have some minor issues if randomly firing a person for the wrong reason, most major companies these days are terrified of firing people without proper documentation, for they may have to cough up large amounts of money to settle cases. As it turns out, if a lazy employee isn't pulling their weight and/or is always tardy, and/or sales continually flounder, it doesn't matter, because it is the manager's fault for not doing enough to help said employee thrive; to realize their potential; to become a vital part of the organization. The employee's non-performing actions must be documented three times, then the manager must consult with them three times before going to human resources. If problems still persist the employee must be put through personal improvement performance training by the manager, involving many more hours of consulting, training, and coaching. And finally, if problems still continue, the employee must be given three more written warnings.

The whole process could take months or even years. After all the bullshit is done, the employee can then be fired – but only with final approval from Human Resources! Argh! (A crock of bullshit, if you ask me.) Do people get fired unjustly? Yes, it happens. But in this modern-day, the injustices many individuals inflict against companies by suing them for wrongful termination, all the while knowing full well, they're simply lazy, uneducated, non-performing twat waffles scamming a system wrought with legal bullshit, is mind-numbing.

So, I did my due diligence with said lazy millennial (the whole time maintaining my composure, I might add). And it literally took years to finally have her terminated. I learned a valuable lesson from the whole ordeal: Hire effectively or don't hire at all. From that point on, it would require several interviews, a pre-test involving wine knowledge, and background checks before a person could work on my team.

With Sojourner's continual march toward market domination, it came time to court The Wine Group, Gallo's rival in box and value wines. Hundreds of thousands of cases (along with dollars) in each state were on the line. Obtaining them as a supplier in Wyoming seemed to not be a problem. However, in Utah, the Wine Group was represented by Pelican Wine & Spirits for decades, a local independent stalwart broker privately owned and operated, and they were doing a fine job, for that matter. The Wine Group valued their relationship with the Pelican owners almost as much as they valued their relationship with Sojourner Spirits & Wine, so a deal was struck between the two brokers on the supplier's behalf. Sojourner agreed to purchase Pelican, bringing The Wine Group and several other suppliers along, spawning a whole new division. Included in the sale: all employees and the owner for a prescribed period, after which he had the option to stay or go at his discretion.

However, after everything was finalized, somehow the responsibilities of overseeing the Pelican Wine Division fell into my lap. At first, I welcomed the idea, even helping interview the current employees so they could be "onboarded" under the Sojourner umbrella. However, as time went by, everyday tasks increased while my pay remained the same. And so, I protested, asking for more money due to substantially increased responsibilities, to which I was told there would be no more money. Noting my displeasure, my boss shifted all the responsibilities of overseeing the Pelican Wine Division away from me (which was fine because the old owner knew what the hell he was doing anyway). Asking me to oversee a veteran broker was like asking a major-league coach to oversee a major-league coach from another team – It just didn't work.

In just under ten years, I had gone from a one-man show to supervising a team of nine while the portfolio grew from just five suppliers with less than 4% market share to more than twenty-two suppliers with an approximate 20% market share of the products carried in both states. For me, it all meant substantially more in the way of responsibilities, stress, and paperwork, with less time – and, with the exception of cost of living raises – the same pay.

THE NUMBERS GAME

SUPPLIERS ARE, IN ESSENCE, THE WOLVES OF THE WINE WORLD; not so much the actual wineries, as they are just trying to gain a foothold or stay afloat, but those in the larger packs – the alphas that often own, import, manage or market wineries on their behalf; the giants or behemoths with a considerable market share. With these suppliers, it's never enough and they don't like to take no for an answer. They look for any angle (legal or not) to sell as many cases as possible even if only for a buck.

When it comes to goals, the numbers dance takes place in ritualistic fashion around the close or beginning of almost every supplier's fiscal year. I've sat through so many goal planning meetings over the years that I've become something I never thought I would – a guarded, often standoffish, benumbed cynic. I realize companies need to grow, but the wine market has become so saturated that some numbers are physically impossible to obtain. That is unless they've put enough sugar in their juice or given huge discounts on their products to promote sales. Nowadays, suppliers want to grow exponentially instead of a modest and organic growth rate. And dammit, it's taken all the fun out of selling wine!

Sometime during late summer of 2015, it became necessary to cover and sign off on the goals for the upcoming fiscal year of one of my major suppliers, Werner Family Wine & Imports. This supplier, like many others, had risen in both fame and monetary power during the Australian wine invasion of the late 1990s. Millions of cases were sold each year of their popular imported brand, Little Joey, pushing them into mega-corp status. The realized profits allowed them to import more products, develop their own boardroom brands, and buy wineries.

During the previous fiscal year, the Werner portfolio of wines was trailing down, mostly due to the continuing decline of the Little Joey brand, and the current DABC administration's idiotic ways of working. My new sales rep Burt Davies and his district manager Philip Smalls flew into Salt Lake City for a planning meeting to map out the goals and objectives for the new fiscal year. Their main objective – Stop Little Joey sales from declining and turn the brand around. My main objective – To not over-commit but offer limited solutions due to the reality of the current DABC anti-business atmosphere, which definitely needed to be understood.

We met around noon in a conference room just south of Salt Lake City. The room was nothing special, but it was easy and quiet and a good place to meet because they had Wi-Fi and a huge flat-screen TV on the wall for presentations. I had never met either of the men but after several low-key conference calls over the previous months, I gathered that they weren't all that bad.

I was early, they were a bit late. At about half-past noon I could hear the main door open. Burt, my official new Werner representative for Utah and Wyoming, arrived first. A bit younger than I (in his early forties, I guessed), he was tall and broad-shouldered and built like a middle linebacker. He had a wry humor and a sense of urgency when it came to driving business.

Philip, on the other hand, was quite a bit older than both of us and was also tall, but leaner with a full head of wavy gray hair, wired-rimmed glasses and a well-earned tan due to a recent move to Phoenix. Philip had been around the block more than a few times in the wine business; I gathered from his recent move this would be his last stint before retiring to the warmth of Arizona. Philip knew the ins and outs of the wholesale liquor and wine business, but the intricacies of a control state like Utah slipped his mind often. (Along with my name – he kept calling me Scott. Maybe I reminded him of someone else. It was humorous, to say the least.)

We shook hands then exchanged business cards, which for some reason, is still considered necessary in this day of ultrafast information and smartphones? While they went about setting up their workspace on the conference table, mindless jib-jab about the local sports teams and local weather ensued until a slightly uncomfortable gap in the conversation signaled it was time to launch into the discussion.

Philip started off. "Spartacus, thank you for joining us here today to set up solid plans and deliver the case goals for the upcoming Werner fiscal year. We hope that after we finish today, we can all walk away with a clear understanding of our objectives and how we can achieve the goals this year together." (Which really means, "We need you to work your ass off to make the numbers so that we can enjoy a fat bonus at the end of the year.")

"Sounds good," I replied. "Hopefully, the DABC will start bringing in new products again – it's been very difficult for quite some time now." (Each time a new sales rep from a supplier showed up it was necessary to make an initial statement about the current situation regarding working with the DABC, so they understood the difficulties of the present business climate.)

Burt then launched into the conversation. "Understood. Maybe you could take just a few minutes before we start to talk about what the current policies of the DABC, and maybe your overall business in general?"

"Sure, no problem," I said before taking a deep breath and gathering my thoughts. "The DABC is currently in a non-buying mode. In fact, their policy for some time now has been – NO NEW ITEMS. Reason being, the current administration believes that they have too many products in the state, so they've actually started to delist and get rid of many items. They've also launched a new store inventory management system because they decided that each state store had too much money tied up in inventory in the back rooms. Basically, they've created an algorithm that analyzes the store inventory each day then generates an order for the following week based on what's needed if a product is on sale or not. This has resulted in consistent out-of-stock problems at the store level and created a lot of havoc and pissed-off consumers."

It became very quiet in the room. Burt and Philip looked at me, arms folded on their laps, trying to comprehend all I was saying and formulate questions.

Before they could speak, I continued. "The DABC also cut back the number of times products can be put on sale each year, from five times to four. And they've instituted a twenty-thousand-dollar profitability standard. If a product falls under the twenty-k profitably mark for a few months, it's automatically delisted. No ifs, ands, or buts. In a nutshell, the current administration has taken the entire Utah alcohol business back twenty years. Most of my suppliers have had products delisted. And with the reduction of sale months, along with not bringing new products in, business has suffered across the board."

Philip rubbed his chin while Burt blankly stared out the window, then said, "Well, we have to do something, Scott. We have goals to obtain and people to answer to. We have to do something."

"Did you just call him Scott?" Burt asked.

"Err, Spartacus, I mean – apologies," Philip replied.

"No problem," I said, looking up at the flat screen to study some of their numbers while they thought about what I'd just said.

"Okay, maybe we can solve some problems while we work through the goals for the upcoming year. Burt, let's start with Utah goals, then move onto Wyoming."

Burt sat back in his chair, then launched into his spiel while looking at the screen. "Okay, jumping right into the numbers, on this first slide are the case goals." He rose from his chair as he spoke and walked to the side of the TV on the wall pointing at the top row of numbers. "As you can see, we've projected the upcoming year to come in flat. The last two to three years have shown a significant downward trend, so we just want to solve the problems and come in flat this year."

"Well," I said, "with the current regime and way of doing business I'd say flat would be a perfect goal for this coming year."

"Okay, great. Let's start with the biggest number at the

top - Little Joey. This brand, as you know, is our biggest moneymaker, but sales have slid in Utah. We really need to come up with solutions to correct the problem and grow sales."

Philip jumped back in. "We flew in early this morning to survey a few of the state stores before our meeting so we could get an idea of how the state goes to market. From what I've seen, the stores are clean and generally well-merchandised. However, we've found a major problem that could be the reason the Little Joey numbers have declined."

"Oh yeah? What's that?" I asked.

"Well," Philip said, looking at me while he leaned further back in his chair. "All the Little Joey wines are located in the Australian section."

I sat quietly for just a moment, reflecting and absorbing what he just said. After several moments of thought, I asked, "Okay, where should they be located?"

Philip leaned forward in his chair, placed his elbows on the table, and clasped both hands together. "Well, Scott, err... I mean Spartacus." Burt snickered under his breath as Philip started again, obviously mad about his continuous name stumbling. "You see..." he paused. "We like to think of Little Joey as a California brand."

They both looked at me while I tried to fathom what was just said. The room was quiet aside from the noise of the fan from Burt's laptop.

Disbelieving, I asked, "Okay, so you want the Little Joey wines moved from the Australian section to the domestic section in the state stores?"

"Yes, Scott. Goddammit, I mean Spartacus!" Philip said

firmly. Burt rolled his eyes and turned away, laughing into his shirt sleeve. "We believe that our true competitors are Mondavi and Barefoot wines, so we need to be placed right next to them on the shelf."

"Well, that's not going to happen," I stated firmly.

"Why not?"

"The state will never allow it. The state stores are set up a specific way – imports broken out by country of origin to one side of the stores, the domestic section on the other side. All the stores are set up the same."

"Well..." He paused. "What if Burt, and few others on our Werner team, along with some of your local team, went into the state stores one week and reset them all, moving all the 750mls Little Joey wines into the domestic section? Do you think we could get that done? Would they be okay with that?"

"You're joking, right?"

"Uh... no, I'm not."

"They'd never allow it. You'd be stopped on the first day, kicked out of the state, and who knows, they may even delist a few products just to show you who's boss. One of the things you don't want to do is mess with state liquor stores. They're set up a certain way and that's their way."

"Well, we have to do something," Philip stated firmly with a sigh, throwing his hands in the air while looking off as if he'd find the answer somewhere in the heavens.

Exasperated, I took a deep breath. "Let me get a few things clear just to prove a point."

"Okay," Philip replied.

"Do the labels on the bottles of Little Joey say Australia, or Product of Australia?"

"Yes," he replied.

I paused for a moment before adding, "And, is there a picture of a giant kangaroo on the label?"

"Yes."

"Well," I said calmly as my voice gained volume for emphasis, "then the products will stay in the Australian section next to all the other Australian wines!"

Out of breath, I leaned forward in my chair, then stood, throwing up my hands. "I need a break to hit the restroom." As I walked downstairs reflecting on the conversation, I shook my head in disbelief. Abso-fucking-lutely ridiculous!

After calming myself, I reluctantly walked back upstairs laughing, trying to regain my composure. Sitting back down, I said, "I can understand that you want sales to go back up on this brand, however, each of the Little Joey wines that are on the racks for sale in Utah are in the maximum amount of state stores and they all go on sale the maximum number of times per year. We just don't have much else that can be done within reason and within the state laws. Trying to get on more wine lists is a chore because the brand has been around for so long. It's seen its day." Both men watched me, listening while I continued. "I'm hoping that the DABC will review and bring in one or two more of the new wines from the Little Joey line-up. I think the best thing to do is just present the innovation wines one more time to see if they'll take one; it's really the only way to increase sales on this brand."

Burt broke the silence first. "Philip, I guess we'll just have to deal with it for now, as long as we don't lose any more sales or get anything delisted. I'd be fine with presenting the innovation wines one more time."

Philip shrugged and drew in an audible breath. "Okay," he sighed, "we just can't lose any more sales."

But before we could move on to another brand, I decided to get under their skin just a bit. "How is Little Joey trending in other states? In fact, Burt, how are Little Joey sales in your home state of Colorado right now?"

They both paused while looking at each other. "Uh, it's down in Colorado too."

"Hmm, really?" I asked, "How much?"

"That's not the point!" Philip huffed emphatically.

"Uh, we're down around 18,000 cases in Colorado."

"Whoa! What? That's crazy," I said, leaning back. "Holy shit. And you're mad about a few thousand cases over the past three years due to a state-controlled run system limiting what can be done?"

Not wanting to be beaten, Philip added emphatically, "We're doing well in a few states!"

"Okay, I'll bite. How many states in the country are in plus sales figures currently?"

Philip leaned forward onto his elbows, resting them on the table as he cupped his face with both hands. His tanned forehead furrowed deeply, "You know, in the majority of states Little Joey sales have declined, but we do have a few states that still produce, and even over-produce the sales numbers year in, year out." Pausing again, Burt and I waited for him to formulate the rest of his answer. After what seemed like several minutes, Philip raised his arms high then laid them down back on the table firmly. "Oh, hell, the brand is in decline, but Australian sales have struggled in recent years due to Malbec from Argentina and others stealing market share." Philip clasped his hands, banging his elbows down on the table. "Little Joey is still a viable brand and still bringing sales of over several million cases per year in the United States. We just need to stop the decline in our neck of the woods and get the brand to trend up again."

Burt and I glanced at each other briefly before I spoke. "Okay, I have a great deal for you concerning the Little Joey goal in Utah. If you get sales flat in Colorado, I'll definitely come in flat in Utah – Deal?"

They both looked at each other like I had just smoked a joint from one of Colorado's new pot dispensaries before both broke into fake laughter.

"That's funny. Really funny, Spartacus," Burt said. "Okay, moving on here, are you okay with coming in flat on the Little Joey goals for the coming year?"

"Yes," I said. "Let's keep moving."

With Little Joey as the driver brand delivering the most case sales, the rest of the Werner goals, except for Jib Jab and their new darling brand Splash, were fairly challenging but attainable. However, I still had to voice my concern, especially on brands that did not have anything listed and carried by the DABC. I learned long ago that when taking a goal on a non-listed product and delivering even a few cases meant the next year's numbers would be bigger, then, you're really screwed.

We finished the next Werner fiscal year just slightly down on Little Joey, which was acceptable, however, the small declines continued for years before leveling off around ten thousand cases in Utah and just under in Wyoming. And when the old administration at the DABC finally changed, I managed to obtain six new listings for Werner, which showed promise with immediate sales and ultimately got them off my back.

ILLOGICALITIES:
Utah Liquor Laws – Part 4

It is now legal to have more than one cocktail in front of a person.

A short time ago? "No way, Jose," but at the time of this writing, it's now perfectly fine to have a beer, or a gin and tonic, and/or a glass of wine in front of oneself. The reasoning here is that the wine is "breathing" while the others are being consumed. Prior to the present law, patrons were required to consume every last drop or give up anything left in the glass before a new drink could be delivered. Often servers and or bartenders stood and hovered patiently while patrons hurriedly downed their cocktails, beers, or glasses of wine, pissing them off in the process.

It is illegal to view full frontal nudity while consuming alcohol.

Strip bars serving alcohol require women who are dancing wear g-strings and pasties. I guess this law is to somewhat inhibit suggestiveness and protect them against the unwanted advances of drunken, horned-up men and lewd behavior. However, all-nude strip bars – of which there are a few in Utah, are not allowed to serve alcohol. Since most guys show up hammered anyway to the all nudie-clubs, it seems to me that making a dollar off beer or booze would be okay rather than have them drinking, drugging and driving, but whatever.

And apparently, it's also illegal to view a movie that shows electronic reproductions depicting sex acts, simulated sex acts, and genitalia while drinking booze. In fact, during the spring of 2016, the DABC compliance division sent an undercover officer from the Bureau of Investigation into a mainstream theater in Salt Lake City called Brewvies. The officer cited the establishment for allowing alcohol to be consumed during a showing of the movie "Deadpool." If convicted, the penalty imposed could be a 10-day suspension of their liquor license along with a hefty fine of up to $25k. As the story goes, the combination of some nudity along with the cartoon at the end of the movie showing a person simulating orgasm by stroking a unicorn's horn put him into a lather. This ridiculousness briefly gained nationwide attention, and apparently, it caught the attention of celebrity Ryan Reynolds, where it was rumored that he helped their cause by donating $5k for the establishment's legal defense and sent out a few tweets regarding the matter. As it turned out, the legal team for the movie theater filed a federal lawsuit against the state for violation of their First Amendment rights to free speech, and they won. Take that, LDS legislative bitches!

Soon after, Brewvies decided to sue the state for their attorney's fees of more than half a million dollars. And guess what? They won. That's right, because an overzealous (probably Mormon) undercover officer decided "Deadpool" violated old antiquated Utah statutes, statutes that are unconstitutional, by writing a ticket (which cost the state dearly) for around $478k I'm told. The message this conveyed to all licensees and everyone in the state is that they shouldn't cower to the LDS powermongers.

It is illegal for alcoholic beverage companies to sponsor an event or promotion.

Promotion is an ugly word with the DABC and state legislature because it means overconsumption. Products cannot be given away free of charge for sampling and or any part of promotional activity, even in a private setting.

 Coupons are illegal in Utah.

Discounting of alcohol is strictly prohibited. Again, it encourages overconsumption, so no mail-in rebates or coupon discounts given at the cash register - ever!

 The DABC is required by law to return all net profit to the state "general fund."

(Sounds, like commingling to me, which I'm pretty sure is illegal?) In return, the DABC requests an operating budget each year from the state legislature. The legislature then grants what they think the DABC needs to operate the whole system for a fiscal year. From 2003 through 2014, the DABC contributed approximately $1.168 billion to the state general fund.

TREND

KEG WINES

MY OLD FRIEND THE KEG and I share many fond memories, mostly from my high school days. However, sometime after my junior year, the state legislature banned the sale of kegs to the general public in the name of health and safety (Or, for a far better-known reason: to combat the infamous parties known as keggers.) And what do people do when "the man" outlaws something? They find a way to get it, so that's exactly what we did! On many a Friday afternoon, I would load several friends into my faded green van, resembling an old Sears repair vehicle, to make the seventy-minute drive to Evanston, Wyoming to purchase a keg (sometimes two or three) for a good old fashion kegger at Lark Sand Dunes on the outskirts of the Salt Lake Valley. With no one around for several miles, the sand dunes were the perfect place to hold a party complete with earsplitting rock music, four-wheel drives, bonfires, babes, beer – and a few other proclivities.

Fast forward a few decades: Even though I hadn't been to a kegger in years, I still had an affinity for kegs, so I jumped at the chance to own my very own Kegerator when my neighbor decided to go gluten-free. And maybe I didn't try hard enough, but I soon found out after tapping a few kegs that it's very difficult for a single guy to drink a keg of beer before a good portion unavoidably goes bad; even with several seasoned beer-drinking friends helping, quite a bit goes to waste. So, my Kegerator days were short-lived and it found a new home soon thereafter.

Kegged wine business started popping up sometime around 2013. As with any new concept, keg wines experienced a few pitfalls along the way, such as using proper gasses to push the product through the lines, line cleanliness and temperature, disposable kegs leaking, off-tasting wine, etc. Nonetheless, after trial and error and learning from their mistakes, producers quickly corrected the problems.

Keg wines are an interesting concept. Since most wines under a certain price point are meant to be consumed within a few months of their young life, they are perfect for by-the-glass programs. Kegs eliminate the possibility of cork taint and oxidized product and save money the producer normally spends on glass and closures, which in turn increases profitability for all involved. The use of kegs also eliminates thousands of tons of waste produced each year and takes pressure off our landfills. So, with all the cost savings, kegged wine by the glass should cost less for the end consumer, right? Guess again. Traditionally, wine by the glass has always been a bad deal for the end consumer; value-wise it's almost always better to buy wine by the bottle. However, undeterred, consumers still buy wines by the glass in record numbers while accounts, suppliers, and wineries reap the monetary rewards. So, as it turns out, I still have an affinity for kegs – wine kegs, that is.

Does anyone have a spare Kegerator?

CERTIFIED

MY GRANDFATHER HAD A SMALL PLAQUE THAT READ: *"Quality is like buying oats – if you want good clean oats, you must pay a fair price. However, if you're satisfied with oats that have already been through the horse – well, those oats are a little cheaper."* (Author unknown.)

As America unabashedly marched toward becoming the number one wine-consuming country in the world, I noticed quite a few different accreditation programs starting to appear, encouraging people to pay up, study up, drink up, and take a random test to become a "certified" wine professional of some kind. All the programs made similar claims about being the best, most prestigious, or highly recommended - but the biggest claim – after graduation, of course, was an illustrious career in the wine and liquor business.

But becoming a "certified wine professional" had become something of a paradox, mainly because this field of study is largely unregulated. Many programs offer different levels of certification but sadly miss the mark on delivering the information, thus ensuring their graduates have what it takes to be a sommelier. In America, capitalism rules, and as sure as the movie "Sideways" elevated Pinot Noir and its prices overnight - becoming "certified" elevated sommeliers and other wine professionals into the upper echelon of legitimate and illegitimate ways to capitalize.

You see, soon after "Sideways" became a hit, you had to pay a fair price, and you had to do a bit of homework if you wanted to sip a legitimately well-made American Pinot Noir. Becoming "certified" is similar in a way: you must do some research and discovery to find out which course offers the goods and is worth your time, money, and effort. The best and only true courses for oenophiles, in my opinion, are the *Masters of Wine* and the *Court of Master Sommeliers*. You must pay to play, and you will do a mountain of homework and tasting, or you won't obtain the highly desired MW or MS moniker or the notoriety and money that can accompany the title.

As Pinot Noir sales sky-rocketed, obtaining a decent drinking one around $10 to $15 became extremely difficult. "Sideways" made it fashionably chic to drink Pinot Noir, but sadly, due to supply and demand, an entry-level bottle became diluted and often fell short of truly expressing the varietal.

Getting "certified" is somewhat like the Pinot Noir story. "Sommeliers" or "wine professionals" have always been around but due to America's increasing appetite for wine and the knowledge thereof, sommeliers became something just short of rock star status soon after the start of the new century. With the right certification, you could write your ticket to a rewarding career in a field that lets you drink for a living and get paid very well. Whether on-line, private, large, small, at the college-level, or in a trade school, there are programs for just about everyone; some programs even included study abroad curricula. There is a multitude of "certifications"

or "accreditations" one can achieve – just Google "wine certification programs," and you'll find enough to keep you busy for years, and after paying all the fees, possibly the poor house too. But if you want one of the best accreditations behind your name, the MW and MS degrees are considered the Holy Grails.

The Institute of the Masters of Wine was established in 1953, and The Court of Master Sommeliers was established in 1977. They are two of the highest distinctions one can earn in the beverage industry. To obtain either accreditation, after lengthy study one must pass rigorous examinations, and of course pay fees, often upward of thousands of dollars. Both programs are very difficult for a reason – they want the best and only the best to achieve their certifications, thus keeping the pool of graduates small while guaranteeing their elite status. Thousands of people each year take their courses but only the top performers pass.

An MW or MS certification will almost guarantee a six-figure income working for a restaurant group, airline, cruise ship line, distributorship, winery, or a large conglomerate of wineries as their education specialist. The reason why this is almost guaranteed is that (as of this writing) there are less than 400 MW and 300 MS certified professionals in the world, making it an exclusive club.

If the MW or MS degree is unattainable for you for some reason, there are many other wine certification programs out there; some are very good and many even cost just as much. However, buyer beware, for there are many inferior programs lacking the in-depth study needed to certify that an individual has enough background knowledge and experience to compete in an industry of their peers. Some courses, although less expensive, are quite diluted, just like the $10-$15 Pinot. If you decide to go the cheap route for a wine certification, be prepared to make far less money than the MW or MS certified professional. Chances are, if your new "certification" comes from Johan von Gimmels School of Grapes, Charm, and Cheese, you may only be qualified to work at Hector's Wine Bar, Maternity and Baby Shop.

Obtaining a wine certification had always intrigued me, however, I had one small problem – make that two – time and money. Working days, and sometimes nights and weekends, left little time to study. And as the years went by, I became less than enthusiastic about cramming more wine information into my tiny skull during my off time from selling wine day in and day out. I mean, hey, there's a little more to life other than wine geekery.

Then, one fine spring day I received an email from my boss asking if I, and any of my team, would like to obtain the 2nd Level WSAS certification given by the Wine & Spirit Accreditation Society. He said he thought it was a "good idea," and anyone within the company who was eligible could take the course and they would even pay for it. "Sure, why not? Sign us up since it's paid for – but what about Level 1?" I inquired.

"The folks at WSAS are giving us all a pass on Level 1 since we work for Sojourner – they figure we must know the basics about wine to have such a job." Which, I guess, made sense in a way.

At the time, I had five people on my team who wanted to obtain the certification. After we officially signed up, about a week later I received a box of study material from the Wine & Spirit Accreditation Society. As a team, we were required to get together each week to taste wines, develop our palates, and work through the study materials. We would also, on our own time, be required to take weekly online quizzes to ensure we were staying up to pace with the rest of our coworkers in other states. After completing the study guide and quizzes, we would then have to take an online multiple-choice test and achieve an 80% or better grade to move onto the final exam.

Now, my team of sales reps were advanced in their knowledge of wine and spirits, so I knew they would most likely pass the tests, otherwise, I wouldn't have hired them. However, as I made it through the study guide, I found there were many tidbits of information even I didn't know at the time, and I was the leader of my division! While I felt confident about passing Level 2, I also knew that if I didn't, it wouldn't look very good. So, I actually had to make a bit of an effort.

With the exception of one person on my team, we all passed the initial online test to move onto the final exam. However, one caveat that neither my boss nor I were informed of, was that the final exam was to be proctored, meaning - we would have to take the test in either Denver or Las Vegas.

My boss was beyond a little upset, because even though the company was paying for the test – which was not cheap – all the travel costs came directly out of our division budget. After searching high and low, it was decided that flights were too pricy for the four of us, so we would have to drive. And the closest place for us on a direct shot of U.S. Interstate was, Vegas, baby.

With approval to take two days off to drive to and from Las Vegas (about a 6.5-hour drive from Salt Lake City), we loaded up a rental car full of food, music, and stories, and off we went – next stop Mandalay Bay Resort and Casino. We even studied a little along the way, each taking turns asking questions to the group using the course study guide.

Now, one might think a team of wine professionals from the Utah wine division arriving in Las Vegas to take a test the next morning at 9 am, proctored at company headquarters, would check-in, eat dinner, study, then go to bed for a full night's rest. Au contraire... With only one night in Vegas and staying at Mandalay Bay, it could only mean one thing – Have as much fun as possible and deal with the test hungover. And that is exactly what we did. After a nice Italian dinner, complete with numerous bottles of Soave and *Gaja*, we made our way to the casino floor where we proceeded to gamble until the wee hours of the morning; hitting the sheets around 4 am.

The next morning, tired and hungover, we frantically bought coffee, muffins, and fruit for anyone who could hold it down, then loaded our belongings into the rental for the drive to the main offices. Once there, we checked in then waited in a massive theater-style conference room for the test to start. There were many people from other divisions around the country taking the test as well.

Since it was now early summer and quite hot in Las Vegas, I began to overheat in my shirt and tie. Severely hungover, dehydrated, and shaky with a pounding head, I was quite sure that I would pass out at some point. Hell, even if I could answer all the questions, finishing the test would be doubtful. One of my employees sitting next to me was in the same boat – sweating profusely and green in the gills, he fidgeted uncomfortably waiting for the test to start.

Finally, a gentleman appeared to lecture us as to how the test would be administered. It would be fifty questions, multiple-choice, and the kicker: a passing score would be 55% or better. The questions, although not hard, were challenging enough, and I could tell that some people in the room were having trouble about fifteen minutes into the exam. I, on the other hand, had already knocked down about 24 questions, my strategy learned long ago: complete the test quickly then go back to review and confirm answers ensuring that I at least finished all the questions. Besides, at 55% or better, even a donkey could guess its way through.

Then, at about the twenty-two-minute mark, the sick employee sitting next to me inked in his last question, stood and handed his test to the proctor, quietly exiting the room to get some air and a much-needed drink of water. I laughed discreetly.

In the end, we all passed the test and received our Level 2 WSAS accreditation certificates via snail mail a few weeks later. To this day, I'm still completely baffled why they make you pass the initial quiz at 80%, then only 55% on the final. Whatever.

Now, I have nothing against the courses or the entity (which I renamed for this story), and I did learn some new information. While I'm sure the Wine & Spirit Accreditation Society courses may be difficult for many people and rewarding for some, and Level 3 is likely more difficult, I'm quite certain that I'll never know. And as impressive as the "Level 2 Certification" is, I don't think that putting the accreditation on my resume is going to land me a dream job as a well-respected sommelier at a prominent fine-dining destination or as the education sommelier for a major wine company. But, I guess I can always work at Hector's Wine Bar, Maternity and Baby Shop.

And that, my friends, is the $10 to $15 Pinot Noir.

TREND

PROSECCO

AND AT GAME TIME..., the cheering began!

PRO—SEC—CO! PRO—SEC—CO! PRO—SEC—CO!
PRO, PRO, PRO, PROSECCO!

PRO—SEC—CO! PRO—SEC—CO! PRO—SEC—CO!
PRO, PRO, PRO, PROSECCO!

One by one they emerge from the tunnel showcasing their talents. Each promise, even brag unabashedly of the unique qualities and heritage setting them apart from the other players. For even the most discerning oenophile, it is hard to ignore the gorgeous bottles adorned in new shiny eye-catching "uniforms." Competitive on any court, whether special events, weddings, races, or birthdays - in a pinch, they spring from the bench, often substituted into the game to replace their dominant cousins, that of Champagne and California sparkling wine. The fair prices of the flashy young Proseccos offer extreme value and alternatives to the higher price tags of the veterans and free agents and even value-conscious Spanish Cava. Once the game began, several key players emerged to lead the pack, sales skyrocketing in what appeared to be a lopsided battle. You snooze, you lose, the Johnny-come-latelys missed the tip-off.

Prosecco, made primarily from the Glera grape in northeastern Italy, has been around for centuries. However, until improvements in winemaking started during the 1960s, progressing through the modern-day, most Proseccos were sweet, unappealing and indistinguishable. Inexpensive bubbles are hard to pass up, especially on a budget. However, all bubbles are not created equal. Prosecco's light, fresh, aromatic qualities with notes of pear, apricot, and spring blossom should never be confused with the rich complex qualities of Methode Champenoise. Champagne has no equal as many age beautifully for years, while Prosecco, on the other hand, meant to be consumed young, should never show age unless from a high-quality producer or established single vineyard – even then, consume within three years is a good rule of thumb.

THE SUPPLIER NEXT DOOR

IT'S ONE THING WHEN A SUPPLIER VISITS YOUR MARKET OR TERRITORY, but an entirely different animal when they live within your territory. I've heard horror stories from peers in other markets of suppliers riding the local sales teams so hard for results and placements that many have actually quit from duress. Due to case volume factors, supplier sales reps are often based in larger metropolitan areas, so I have been lucky in that regard. Since Utah and Wyoming are small markets, few supplier reps have resided within my territory. And, of the reps that did reside within the state of Utah, they actually helped more than hurt when promoting their products, driving business, and working with the local teams to achieve goals.

But then there is another scenario; an even worse animal than a supplier sales rep residing in your territory: When the owner, partner, or relative of a supplier, lives within or has a second or third home, or even vacations within your territory on a regular basis. Often, they are taken aback that all their products are not state listed or in every account that they like to frequent. They take it personally when they dine at an account and find out that not one product from their line-up is available. And, if they are entertaining guests and the account does not have any of their products, then look the fuck out, because the following day of business, you will be electronically violated by their market DVP (Division Vice President), your boss, your bosses' boss, and even possibly the owners of your company. A good old-fashioned ass-whooping, demanding results, leaving you mentally wrecked while scrambling defensively until the problem is fixed.

Not all are bad. In fact, many winemakers, importers, or owners realize it's impossible to have all of their wines on every list in the world, let alone every account where they reside; there are just too many products out there. And, I do get it. If I was an importer, owner, or winemaker with a substantial investment in my livelihood and passion, I would want to drink my own products at the restaurants within my geographical location or buy my products at local retail shops or liquor stores.

Over the years, I have met many from this select special demographic that feel their products should be on every wine list in a particular area, all of the time. This leads me to my next story. I will refer to her as Francesca Pavoni (a pseudonym to save the real Francesca from any undue embarrassment and possibly save me from any undue retribution). You see, I'm not sure whether true or not, but the low-down on the streets is: Francesca Pavoni and her family are possibly in cahoots with some shady characters from the seedy underbelly of this fine country. That said, I will refrain from pointing any direct fingers because literally, I have grown quite fond of them – my fingers that is, and I wish to retain them along with my limbs, body parts, and life as well. If the real Francesca Pavoni's massive ego is somehow shattered upon reading this true story and thus feels she must seek retribution, I have all the facts, figures, and info saved in many safe places. I mean, really... C'mon, it's only booze.

In July of 2013, I was notified that our company would be representing part of Pavoni Fine Wines. Known for their fine wine import portfolio, including a few family-owned domestic properties, they decided to split their massive portfolio into two divisions, putting half under my division and half under my main competitor. This accomplished two things: a.) it ensured that all, or most, of their brands received attention, and b.) it pitted the two companies against each other to try and outperform the other, which had a potential downside – One company doing something the other wouldn't, resulting in a "they do this, how come you don't?" type of situation.

When I found out that we would be representing Pavoni Fine Wines, I was slightly apprehensive as my wine brokerage division was getting quite big, very fast. I did, however, view it as a challenge and knew it would reinforce the luxury brands we already represented. Shortly after the news broke, I ran into one of the senior wine representatives from our competitor. After exchanging pleasantries, she said quite matter-of-factly, "You're going to hate selling Pavoni Fine Wines. It's a giant pain in the ass and Francesca Pavoni is a complete bitch." Oh great, I thought: *Another terrible supplier to appease... I can hardly wait.*

In Utah, their volume was about 600 cases per year, and in Wyoming about 200 cases. Though the volume was small, and we did make decent commissions, it paled in comparison to the volume we sold with our other companies. In any territory, priority is usually given to larger suppliers. Nonetheless, the small sales volume didn't matter to Francesca Pavoni, for she demanded results, so I received a constant beat-down by her, her team, and my superiors, who were copied on every email and call, resulting in what I refer to as the Pavoni Effect.

Essentially, the Pavoni Effect is this: It is vital to threaten, browbeat, and intimidate the broker or distributor as much as possible to get desired results. If there is any push-back or the results are not acceptable, be absolutely sure to call and/ or copy the bosses on every email – It doesn't matter what the market constraints are – If it means someone's job, so be it!

Francesca Pavoni, daughter of the founder and now co-owner of the company, loved Park City, Utah, and Jackson, Wyoming, in part, due to the well-off population that lived, vacationed, and played in the ultra-chic resort settings. As she continued to visit these areas, she demanded that more of her wines be present within the accounts in these areas. However, due to the constraints of both control states, obtaining all the wines she wanted carried by each state liquor board, restaurant, and resort area was very, very difficult, if not impossible.

It started quite innocent enough, just like most new supplier/broker introductions. The western sales director for Pavoni Fine Wines sent an email introducing himself and his Utah territory sales rep Harriet Chisholm, including all the pertinent information about their backgrounds, the brands we would represent, pricing, and much more. I had met the gentleman some years prior in Jackson, Wyoming at one of the wine events. He struck me as extremely knowledgeable, driven, and capable in his position, but I also knew him to be very direct, opinionated, and quite frankly - cocky. I knew of Harriet also, from seeing her in the market with my competitors's sales rep. Harriet was based out of Portland and she was a very pretty, petite brunette; somewhat soft-spoken but very knowledgeable. She dressed impeccably, and although not needed, her looks helped sell her products. We agreed on a date for them both to fly to Utah to meet the local team personally for dinner, see a few accounts, and talk about goals, priorities and market strategy.

After they arrived, I met them at their hotel in the conference room, where we discussed the portfolio, ways of working, my Utah and Wyoming teams, current business in both states, opportunities, and goals. One of the biggest factors to our relationship, as I would be told over and over and over again was, "Francesca Pavoni, one of the company owners, visits Park City and Jackson regularly. In fact, she's considering buying a house in Park City, so we need to make sure that the brands represented under your supervision are on wine lists in restaurants and on the shelves in the liquor stores." After the meeting, we visited a couple of state liquor stores, purchasing a few bottles from their portfolio for the staff to taste at dinner. Since the first trip was just a meet and greet, all went well, and I came away with a better understanding of their company.

A short time later, Harriet sent me a sales analysis for both Park City and Jackson. Listed down one side were the restaurants that Francesca Pavoni frequented, and across the top were the wines we represented in our division. The list would be updated monthly based on depletions or full cases bought by the accounts. The spreadsheet would tell if an account was buying a wine, how much, and how often they were going through it. It was their gauge to see if we were doing our job.

Often, when Harriet sent me the spreadsheet, she'd copy her boss in the process. In her notes, she would add that they needed to, "See more movement in the accounts," or my favorite, "Our wines are not seeing the recognition on wine lists in the resort areas they deserve." Her boss would then send a note to our VP in the Pacific Northwest, telling him he was concerned that we were not making enough headway, each time reminding us that Francesca Pavoni visited Park City and Jackson and was now considering buying a house in Utah. Shortly thereafter, I would then receive an email from said vice president copying my direct boss, stating that, "the Pavoni portfolio of wines is important to us so we need to execute better in Park City and Jackson." This email chain must have been sent a few dozen times over the winter of 2013/14 – absolutely ridiculous. Pavoni Fine Wines acted like they were the only supplier on the face of the earth. At the time we were doing over 400,000 cases annually with our other suppliers, but I had to babysit a portfolio and satisfy a prima donna owner doing just under 600 cases per year. Fucking crazy.

Now, I'm very good at picking apart any program or set of goals that are skewed unfavorably. And the biggest problem with the wines from the Pavoni portfolio under our brokerage was that most were over-priced, in some cases, excessively. Herein lay the problems: Due to the state's 88% tax mark-up on wine, most of their wines we were tasked with selling were expensive to very expensive, and only a small selection of wines was listed and carried in the state liquor stores. Of the 150+ Pavoni wines available for us to sell in my division, only 28 wines were carried in Utah at that time. And, within those 28 wines, only 12 were priced under $50 cost to restaurant accounts. All of the other wines not for sale in Utah had to be special ordered specifically by an account. Because restaurants have to buy special order wines in full cases, the high cost of many Pavoni wines made an account think twice, especially if the wine was going to cost more than $75 per bottle. Since wines of that caliber sell more slowly, wine costing over $500 per case could feasibly be on a restaurant wine list and inventoried for years before they would need to buy it again. And excessive inventory means a lot of cash could be tied up in perishable goods.

As I relayed earlier, the only legal way to sell wine in Utah is by telling the account about the wine, showing product notes, reviews and ratings, along with pricing. The other way, or rather "illegal" way, is to have samples with you so accounts can taste the wine, thus convincing them it was worth the investment and worthy of a spot on the wine list. Though sampling is illegal, nonetheless, it happens some of the time. The penalties if caught sampling wine in an account could be stiff fines and/or possibly loss of our State Manufacturer Representative License, which could put us out of business altogether. That said, since we shared the Pavoni Fine Wine portfolio with our biggest competitor, I had a feeling that sampling would come up at some point. While splitting a large portfolio between brokers is a great way to maximize selling potential, it is also, as I later found out, a good way to catch an adversary doing something wrong.

One morning, a string of emails sent by Harriet Chisholm arrived, sealing my feelings about conducting any illegal activities on behalf of Pavoni Fine Wines. Basically, she asked me to confirm if it was illegal to send wine samples via UPS, FedEx, or any other way, and if indeed illegal to sample accounts in Utah. As I read down the email chain, I became quite surprised that Harriet would actually forward the body of the email to me in the first place, in its entirety, and not a separate message to confirm the information. The email was basically a Pavoni Fine Wines internal communication between her boss, two Pavoni vice presidents, and Francesca Pavoni herself. It indicated that another Pavoni rep, the rep calling on our competitor, had been in Park City showing and tasting wines with various accounts illegally. The email pointed out that they specifically met and tasted with the buyer for a large restaurant group in Park City, even going as far as to name him and my rival's sales rep with them during the tasting. It also stated that they would be sending several mixed cases of Pavoni Fine Wines not available for sale in Utah via UPS, with special lower pricing, so the account could sample them in hopes of bringing them in via special order for the wine lists of their various restaurants. Not only is this very illegal, but the corroboration with our enemy and the Park City buyer undermined my position on the playing field.

Within that simple thread, I now possessed hard evidence demonstrating the unlawful activities of Pavoni sales management, including Francesca Pavoni herself, the sales rep from my rival, and a state-licensed account. I made my mind up at that point that no matter what, I would not do anything illegal for Pavoni Fine Wines, as it could get into the hands of my competitor. A competitor, that if the shoe was on the other foot, would not hesitate to turn me into the DABC Compliance Department to be reprimanded or have my license suspended or revoked.

Sometime later that same summer, there was news that Francesca Pavoni had indeed found and purchased a second home in Park City; the onslaught over Park City placements would not let up, but in fact, get worse.

Every so often, I would get emails from my market rep, handed down from Pavoni management, that went something like this:

"Francesca Pavoni will be in Park City for the Christmas holiday and she wants to make sure that her wines are in accounts, so she can buy them. Please review the spreadsheet and come up with a plan of attack. I will need an outline ASAP so I can relay the information. You do not want to upset Francesca."

or

"Francesca Pavoni was in Talking Tree Café for lunch in Park City yesterday. Not one Pavoni wine was on the wine list. She is very angry with your company. What can we do to change this?"

or

"Francesca Pavoni wants to conduct a winemaker dinner at an account in Park City so that all her friends can attend. Please provide a venue and the wines that you will be able to obtain in that account."

or

"Francesca Pavoni was in the state liquor store in Park City yesterday and she could not find any of her family wines on the shelves. To avoid pissing her off, we need to change this ASAP. When can you present them to the Utah buyer and what is the timeline for getting the wines on the shelves?"

Maybe I was reading too much into it, but it appeared Francesca was quite a bitch. I wondered why anyone would want to work for her. Back against the wall, I had to try and get more wines listed and carried with the DABC. Since the Pavoni family-owned and operated Pavoni Family Vineyards based in Edna Valley, it had been mentioned several times that she wanted to see her family's wines in the Park City accounts. Upon reviewing the offerings, I found the lower-end wines to be marginal at best, so I concentrated on five of the higher-end lower production wines. The 2009 vintages had just rolled out with some decent press, so I gathered the information and pricing and made an appointment with the buyer in charge of limited listings.

In the meeting with the buyer, I made it clear that Francesca

Pavoni had bought a house in Park City, so to have a couple of her family-owned wines on the state liquor store shelves would be a good idea - not only for the restaurant accounts - but it would hopefully get her off my back. I explained that she would probably spend a few months a year in Utah, so she would actually help promote the wines along with my sales team. The wines were sure to sell. To my amazement, the buyer agreed. After reviewing shelf price points and where the wines would fit in the state stores, he told me to complete the final paperwork on two Pavoni Family Wines along with their new trendy New Zealand Sauvignon Blanc. Relieved, I completed the paperwork and turned it in within the week. After that, all I could do was wait, and wait, and wait... Until he finally pulled the trigger and issued a Purchase Order for the products. As time began to slip by and the next ski season began to get underway, it would turn out the wait would be longer than I had anticipated. In fact, Pavoni Family Wines never got ordered, even after I prodded the buyer several times.

Undeterred, just before the ski season started, my team made significant progress in the accounts Francesca Pavoni had pinpointed with 41 points of distribution, even adding 18 new placements on wine lists in restaurants that she had never stepped foot in, but it was not enough.

Toward the end of January 2014, the Pavoni Division VP Mike Hart sent an email asking me to procure a meeting in early March between the fine wine buyer at the DABC and Francesca Pavoni herself. Francesca apparently had decided enough was enough; it was time to personally meet the buyer face to face.

Now, I usually don't judge a person too harshly without meeting them directly, however, even without meeting

Francesca Pavoni in person, I already loathed her.

I set the meeting in early March with fine wine buyer Danny Mann and the general listing wine buyer David Wadsworth. With the date fast approaching, I decided we should at least present a line of wines, or otherwise the meeting would be a complete waste of time for all parties involved. With the assistance of the Pavoni Division Manager, we managed to put all the necessary paperwork together accompanied by samples just in time for the meeting. The line of wines we were presenting was a spin-off from the Pavoni Family Wines in California, in essence a second label. With a complete listing packet and samples, and the owner there to talk about the wines, we should be able to have a shot at getting them listed by one of the buyers. Because of the pricing, I knew it was a long shot, but Francesca Pavoni herself would see the process and how long it took for the DABC to review the wines once the meeting was over.

The week before the meeting I received a phone call from Mike Hart. Unbeknownst to me, he had asked the brokers for the other half of the portfolio to meet with the buyers at 10 am, then I would come in and meet with them at 11 am for my side of the portfolio. He explained that Francesca Pavoni only had so much time, so they wanted to maximize the morning by having her meet and discuss both sides of the portfolio under each respective brokerage. He also said he would be in attendance as well, and oh, one other thing – both he and Francesca wanted to meet with me afterward to discuss business.

With just over ten years in the business, I knew one thing for sure: Francesca Pavoni and Mike Hart were going to railroad me over both the Park City and Jackson Hole markets, so I prepared an arsenal of facts and figures and sales history from both markets showing progress and anything else that would bolster what we had been doing for them up to that time. I absolutely did not want the conversation to be one-sided. Stored away in my back pocket, that I would produce only if backed into a corner, the emails documenting illegal proceedings conducted by Pavoni Fine Wines and my competitor. And if necessary, I would use them.

For some reason, I slept like a rock the Monday night before the meeting. Though I had never met Francesca Pavoni or Mike Hart, and come to dislike them, I felt refreshed and relaxed. I arrived at 11 am, only to be told that the meeting with my rival was taking more time than they had thought, so I was to wait just outside. No problem, it would only be a few minutes longer, I thought, but after thirty minutes had gone by, I was becoming quite agitated. Finally, Mike Hart appeared, looking more like an older wannabe hipster than a gangster; lean and middle-aged, about six feet tall with blond hair and a pasty white complexion, wearing extremely tight striped suit slacks cropped high, more like capris or shants – not shorts but not quite pants either – an expensive dress shirt, although it did not remotely compliment his pants, a sports jacket two sizes too small, and brown Brogue shoes without socks. After introductions and a handshake, we exchanged pleasantries and went into the meeting.

The meeting was in David Wadsworth's office around a small round table; far too small for five people, so we all sat arm's length away with legs crossed. Portfolio books and Francesca's laptop were placed on the table. And finally, after years, there I was face to face with Francesca Pavoni herself. Francesca stood to shake my hand, completing the introductions. Also middle-aged, Francesca was medium in stature with a wide-body and roundish face, puffy from years of excess, and a full head of curly hair accented her deeply lined skin. Though this gal was wealthy, she had on an old worn pencil skirt, so worn it frayed at the bottom. She did, however, wear what appeared to be a pricey *Versace* jacket, a French-cuffed shirt, *Rolex* watch, and what I am sure were very expensive handmade Italian pumps.

Francesca told me they had already covered the brands from the other side of the portfolio, so now it was time to cover my side. All was quiet for a moment, until she began to go brand by brand, talking about the owners, how she and her family personally knew them and their families, and how outstanding the wines were. She waxed on and on about staying at each other's luxury homes, driving expensive cars, private planes, yachts, riding thoroughbred horses through their estates and drinking expensive wines. The buyers, however, were unimpressed. Over and over, she stated, "These are excellent products, and the DABC should carry all their wines for sale in their state stores." Estate after estate, family after family, it went on and on, until finally, after about 60 minutes of the ongoing musings of a tiresome egotistical owner, she was finished. Finally, I was able to show the presentation and paperwork on the wines we wanted them to actually review for listing.

I asked Francesca politely to tell the buyers about the wines, hoping she would add something of value. However, after literally a few sentences of meaningless minutiae, she was done. I thought to myself: *Here's her big chance to wow them with her impressions and knowledge of the wines, and she mutters out two or three short sentences? Absolutely fucking ridiculous!* Well, that was that, the state buyers sat in stunned silence. They had just listened through almost three hours of worthless blather when they originally had allocated two hours. I knew they were pissed off. These guys are overworked as it is, barely getting to all they have to complete each day, and they had to listen to the constant droll of a self-absorbed owner.

As we were leaving, Francesca stopped to ask Danny Mann one more question. "I just bought a house in Park City, and I'm wondering what the laws are regarding shipping wine to my new house?"

"Congratulations. What do you mean?" the buyer replied.

"Well... I'd like to ship in a small truckload of wine from my personal wine cellar from another state to stock the new wine cellar in my Park City house. Wine that has already been paid for, that I personally own."

"I see," said the buyer. "It's actually against the law unless you notify us of the shipment and provide us with a list of the bottles you're sending in. After we value the wine, we'll levy a tax that you must pay before shipping them. As a new resident, you're allowed to ship in wine one time to your personal residence, however, you must pay a tax. Anything you want to purchase for your Park City cellar in the future must be bought through the DABC, paying the full taxes."

"Uh... okay," said Francesca shaking her head disbelievingly. "If I decide to do so, I'll let you know."

As we quietly walked to the parking lot, I felt relieved the meeting was finally over, however, I was also angry, as I had missed a conference call with another supplier due to Francesca Pavoni. And just as I had thought, once we had arrived at the back of Francesca's SUV, they ambushed me, but I was ready. Francesca opened the back hatch and laid out across the floor was a printout: "Sales Analysis" for Park City. With her finger, she began to trace down the right-side showing depletions. She asked point-blank, not pulling any punches, "Look at these depletions. What are you and your damn team doing in the market? Is this a goddamn joke? Whatever it is, it's not getting done and I'm not happy. I may have to contact your boss and company owners to get to the bottom of this."

Shocked by her profanity, I paused briefly. I barely knew this bitch; I never had a supplier speak to me in that manner. My voice shook slightly as I countered with positive numbers and depletions over last year and that we had indeed made progress.

Francesca interrupted me angrily, looking at the wine brands listed down the side of the list. "Some of these wines do not have any sales at all. What is the goddamn problem? I'm beginning to think we made a bad decision to bring these fine wines over to your incompetent team! What do you want me to tell those poor winemakers?"

I wanted to say: *Maybe you should tell the poor winemakers that you and your family are so goddamn greedy that you over-priced their wines so you can fly on a fucking private jet and drive expensive sports cars.* But I held back replying, "I only have so many wines to work with that are listed and carried in the state, so in that regard, we look very good."

She then shook her head while pointing to one of her imported wineries. "This line of wines is some of the greatest ever produced in the world and you do not have any depletions. Surely accounts in Park City want this wine?"

The level of the conversation escalated as I explained that due to the state tax, the cost was well over $400 per bottle.

To which she asked angrily. "Then why had no one bought the introductory wines from the line that is less expensive?"

"Even the least expensive bottle costs $250 in Utah after taxes, and since it was a special order, the accounts had to purchase in full cases!" I replied.

Francesca did not want to listen. Now face to face, inches away, I felt as though I had just crossed a line, that my days were numbered. Just before starting in on me again, Mike Hart suddenly stepped in pushing Francesca back, face red with rage jamming one finger into my chest while waving the other fist in my face yelling, "We're not satisfied with what your team is doing in the Park City accounts! You need to make more progress goddamn it!"

I winced at his candor, backpedaling slightly to get away, completely caught off guard at his sudden outburst. He had crossed the line and they both knew it. Then Francesca stepped to our side, placing a hand on Mike's arm before calmly asking, "What do we have to do to make more impact? We'll do whatever it takes to get it done."

I could tell that they wanted me to lead the conversation at that point and tell them to send in samples illegally to taste the key buyers, so we could get orders. I knew what they were getting at, and I had already made up my mind – I would do nothing illegal for these assholes, no matter what. I told them that due to the nature of the split portfolio, I wouldn't do anything to jeopardize my license; that there were too many variables working with a split book between two major brokers. I would just work with what I had and within the constraints of the state laws.

Taken aback, Mike Hart asked me what variables I was talking about. So, I began to explain how I came across their email exchange and the illegal samples sent in directly for a major account, incriminating them in the process. I told them that if the shoe were on the other foot and the tables were turned, my competitor would have no issue turning me into the DABC; that they wouldn't even bat an eye. I pointed out that over the years they had turned in other brokers for infractions in the market so they could gain more foothold, and I was not about to let it happen with me. Then I told them that if need be, I would have no trouble turning the email over to the DABC, incriminating the whole bunch.

Both stood in silence, staring as if sizing me up for a pair of cement galoshes. Francesca shook her head in disbelief while throwing her hands up in the air. Done talking, she got into her car. Mike wasn't finished. He stood glaring at me skeptically, his eyes filled with rage as his fists balled ready for a fight.

Then realizing others in the parking lot were looking on, he calmed slightly, asking if he should talk to my competitor to make sure we could work together. I told him that under no circumstance would he talk with my rival and that everything we did for them would have to be done the legal way. We may not get as many placements or cases sold, but at least I wouldn't have to worry about losing my license. I turned to walk to my car, every so often glancing back to find Mike still standing there, staring at me, absolutely furious. I couldn't believe what had just happened. Over wine, of all things?

The following week I received an email from the Pacific NW Division VP, again copying my boss, telling me he received a follow-up email from Mike Hart stating that we had met, made presentations, and that he under no circumstance wanted me to do anything illegal for the division of Pavoni Family Wines under our direction in Utah.

And that is the worst confrontation I have ever had with a supplier during my entire career. For years to come, I would have to endure many more, though minor, Pavoni episodes.

TREND

RED AND WHITE BLENDS

Often, in casual conversation at events or in mixed company, I'm asked various questions about wine. This question seemed to pop up frequently during 2016: "I was in the wine store the other day and I noticed a section with a bunch of new wines called blends... Ever hear of them?"

An innocuous enough question, I guess. However, unbeknownst to them, their ignorance waving violently in the wind disguised as exuberance. I know I'm not perfect. I shouldn't judge, but I do. I'm old school. Sometimes haughtiness gets the best of me. *But they just want to learn*, I tell myself. Oh, but I haven't got time. Oh, wait, yes I do. I must edify to clear my conscience or inflict disservice upon the classics.

Meritage, Super Tuscans, Bordeaux, Chateauneuf du Pape, and other Rhone wines - among many others - are the original blends. A wine where each varietal contributes its own distinct qualities swirled seamlessly into a harmonious mélange offering an extraordinary curious expression. Multi-layered, multifaceted, sometimes earthy, ominous, complex, brooding – wines with unique character exhibiting not only their varietal correctness but the terroir from which they came.

Sure, the newcomer blends are enticing, what with their provocative labels and shameless jammy juice laden with residual sugar. All are not bad; a select few are made very well, even evoking subtle nuances of their ancestor's highly regarded qualities. The boardroom brands, however, are posers, even imposters, relentlessly seizing palates with lush mouthfuls of grippy, syrupy juice, and mugging the novice consumers with one-dimensional delusions.

BECAUSE, IT'S WHAT
MONOPLIES DO
Part 2

ON JULY 1, 2016, THE DABC rolled out a new purchase order and inventory management system complete with new software. It's not that the old system didn't work, it just didn't work as well as it should; the old software was severely outdated. Tremendous strides with inventory management had been made during the past decade while using their old software. The new system promised to be state-of-the-art, easier to use and highly automated. The auditors wanted to streamline the inventory system from ordering to warehouse to the state stores. Since the new system was automated, it would also take the task of ordering Limited Listed products out of the broker's hands; something that had been a required duty for as long as I had been a broker. Several companies submitted bids along with mountains of supportive information. And, as one would expect with a state-run monopoly, working with a small budget granted by the legislature – the DABC chose the cheapest, lowest-rated product, and committed to a ten-year contract to use the software.

Monopolies do what they want, when they want, beholden to no one, often acting without thinking.

As was customary with the DABC, information about the new system, its processes, and what to expect was given to the brokers only by word of mouth rather than a detailed memorandum or email, because in truth, they really had no idea how the new system would work. Also, they failed to notify the hundreds of suppliers, restaurant licensees, store employees and their customers - the imbibing public. They were confident the new software would work without too many problems. Without first testing the product, the old program was uninstalled, and the new software went live July 1, 2016 - the start of the state's fiscal year.

Proactively, the DABC did bring in a team of technicians from the company that sold them the software. However, even with several technicians helping, the roll-out was very rough, to say the least, and problems started immediately. Weekly inventory reports for the central warehouse in Salt Lake City did not exist for the first few months, then when they were available, they provided false data. With false data, purchase orders could not be generated. Without purchase orders, products ran short or out of stock. There were so many problems in the beginning, the support technicians, in over their heads, purportedly walked away from the job after two weeks, leaving the DABC staff and their own IT technicians to fend for themselves.

Monopolies do not care about the inconveniences to their customers.

Similar to the older system that had been modified during the last DABC regime, one of the functions of the new software was to analyze the inventory within a particular store then generate an order to resupply products from the main warehouse. However, due to glitches with the system, store inventories were skewed by the new system, often registering inventory for a product only to find that the product was truly out of stock, and vice versa, a product that was listed as out of stock was actually in stock. On delivery days to their satellite state liquor stores, a product that wasn't ordered would arrive, and consequently, an out-of-stock product a store badly needed failed to arrive. Severe out-of-stock problems mounted, resulting in empty wine racks and shelves at the state stores. Retail customers became furious.

The owners and managers of the restaurants and bars were also angered because they had to make several trips to many different state stores, often driving over 10 to 20 miles or more, but still couldn't find the products they so badly needed. Special orders that restaurants had placed for distinct products were entirely erased from the new system, while some special orders arrived but sat in the central warehouse without registering as inventory. Many accounts had to reprint their wine lists and menus or just tell patrons they were out of a product. Brokers and sales representatives fielded calls and emails daily from restaurant accounts trying to locate products, but we were in the same boat because the DABC offered no information or solutions to the problem; they were in over their heads.

A monopoly will fix problems, or attempt to fix problems, on their own time.

Along with the inventory problems, new purchase orders for products, even if completely out of stock in the state warehouse, were issued infrequently, sometimes taking weeks to be generated. A key "feature" of the automated system for ordering products was to analyze the sales volume from the previous two months in the state liquor stores against the present inventory in the central warehouse, then recommended a new purchase order be cut for enough product for the coming two months.

There are a couple of problems with this equation: Not all state liquor stores are equal in regard to alcohol or wine sales. Half of the state stores that sell the most product will run out of popular products faster than the other state stores. When the program analyzed current inventory on hand, the liquor stores that still had the products in stock skewed the information used to generate a PO to replenish the stores that sell wine and liquor at a higher volume; many shelves and racks sat empty in the high-volume stores while stores in rural areas had plenty of product. Plus, the fancy algorithms could not consider the 2-4-week lead time necessary for a supplier to deliver the products. Coupled with insufficient analyzation, the system did not generate purchase orders for enough product to adequately replenish store shelves or the main warehouse.

Example: A popular product costing $10.99 on the shelf that sells very well, particularly in the five biggest stores, is usually ordered in 56-case increments, and most of the time, the state orders 112 to 224 cases, or even more at a time, to ensure they do not run out. Though the product may be low or out of stock in the central warehouse in Salt Lake City, the system recognizes several state liquor stores in the outlying rural areas still had inventory, so after the system analyzed the store data purchase orders would be generated for only 7-14 cases.

Additionally, the new system could not differentiate between products that had been discontinued and no longer available but still had a code. Purchase orders were generated for products that had not been sold in Utah in years, maybe even decades.

Also, purchase orders were simply lost. They were issued, but either the system or the person issuing the purchase order within the purchasing department failed to send the order to suppliers. The only way to find out if an order had been lost or not sent – the waiting game. After a significant amount of time, the DABC buyers would send out emails inquiring about outstanding purchase orders only to find out the suppliers never received them, resulting in considerable delays, meaning further out of stock issues.

Often when product(s) arrived, they would sit in the warehouse for months before a broker, a warehouse worker, or someone in the DABC purchasing department discovered the problem. For example, *Opus One*, a very expensive wine of which the state only gets a small allocation of less than 40 six-pack cases per year, arrived around the 1st of November, but the wine sat in the warehouse until almost Christmas, missing part of the most lucrative selling season.

A monopoly doesn't care if it runs out of popular products. Since they are the only game, a customer will just choose another product, even if they have to pay a higher price.

During the first holiday season, the new system failed to adequately stock up the state stores before or during the busiest days of the year. On the day before Thanksgiving, Christmas Eve and New Year's Eve of 2016, several stores ran out of the most popular products first, so customers were forced into buying alternative products or drive to other stores across town or part of the state. Angered customers took to social media, posting and tweeting pictures of the empty shelves. On New Year's Eve, several state liquor stores completely ran out of all Champagne and sparkling wines; after 5 pm, the state warehouse was closed, so thousands of cases of bubbles sat safely tucked away, while state liquor stores were empty. Even Senator Jim Dubakis took to Facebook, posting a picture chiding the new system.

(Dubakis 2016)

Monopolies only do what is necessary to get by for the time being.

Another major unforeseen problem with the system: All the stored information from the old software was too much data for the new software program to handle. The new program had to be rebooted several times per day. Purchase orders that needed to be fixed due to a new vintage, pricing, case spec problems, or codes, took days and weeks to fix because the program kept crashing. I recall many afternoons sitting with the state buyers, correcting problems. One afternoon it took three hours to fix five purchase orders. The new system had rendered the folks at the DABC powerless and inefficient; they couldn't do their jobs properly. In exasperation, they threw up their arms, doing the bare minimum (as always) to get by.

Monopolies do not apologize – ever.

The DABC reports all their sales data to an entity referred to as NABCA. NABCA compiles all the sales data by item for each month and year, right down to account sales data, such as hotels, bars, restaurants. This sales data is extremely important to the state, the suppliers, and the brokers. The new system was so screwed up and such a problem to deal with that the DABC reported false sales for the month of July 2016. The DABC even acknowledged the sales were wrong for July but had no way of correcting the data. Sales from the following month of August reportedly were not entirely correct either.

Suppliers were in an uproar as many depend on that data to report back to their investors, owners, and wineries on how they are doing. If one or two months of sales data are false, then their fiscal year numbers are completely off, affecting profit and loss statements, bonuses, and how to build goals for the following years. The account data showing sales to restaurants and hotels, by item, was not downloaded to NABCA from July through October until mid-November (even then, the data was incorrect), so incentives could not be paid out to the local sales reps. When all was said and done, the DABC was not able to accurately and efficiently report sales data for the period of July through December 2016. By the end of January, they did finally catch up, but they would still suffer multiple problems for the next year. The DABC never apologized for the "inconvenience."

A monopoly doesn't have to relay information or commit to anything, and may change its mind at any time.

With the purchasing department up to its elbows dealing with the new inventory and management system shit storm, delisting, reviewing, and ordering new items fell by the wayside. The state of Utah, already a year behind liquor and wine trends taking place in the larger markets, fell further behind.

In April of 2016, I presented four wines from a company named Accolade. Three months later, the DABC still had not tasted or reviewed the wines. However, the DABC is notorious for failing to notify the brokers when they review wines, so thinking that they reviewed the wines from Accolade and did not choose any, I decided to present five Italian wines from the same supplier. However, nothing was reviewed for the rest of 2016. When I asked the DABC if the products had been reviewed, they just said, "No, we're too busy with other problems right now."

In February of 2017, I received notice that the DABC had chosen two of the four items from the wines I presented in April of 2016 from Accolade. A full ten months later. I notified an elated supplier of the new listings, but the DABC did not issue a purchase order for the new wines until five months later. By the time the new wines were actually received in Utah and on the shelves for sale, it was August 2017, a full sixteen months after the presentation had been made. Of the five Italian wines presented in July 2016, they chose one, but they never ordered it, simply telling me they had changed their minds.

In November of 2016, I presented twelve wines from two different companies, 4 Front Imports and The Stoli Group. The DABC reviewed and tasted the wines in May 2017 – almost seven months later? Though they chose one wine from each company, the wines were never ordered even after I badgered the buyers at the DABC several times. Finally, after more than a year, I gave up because the vintages and pricing had changed. This same problem happened with several of my other suppliers – several wines were chosen, months and months went by, but none were ever ordered.

A monopoly changes the rules whenever they want to.

In the spring of 2017, the DABC, feeling the pressure from hundreds of suppliers submitting innovative product information and samples, came up with a new policy with a time-frame approach. They set up a calendar, a tasting schedule if you will; beer, liquor, and wine would be tasted on a three-month revolving schedule. For instance, in July 2017, wine submission paperwork and samples were due, and during August the DABC was supposed to review them. Finally, if a product was chosen, a purchase order would then be generated in September.

Due to the size of my portfolio, I submitted 25 wines for review in July of 2017. The DABC supposedly reviewed the wines in August but didn't notify me – nothing new here. September came and went, the month they were supposed to issue purchase orders for new products, but I didn't receive any new orders. As the middle of October approached, I still had heard nothing, so I asked, and I was told that they were still working on purchase orders. So, I waited. Just before Thanksgiving, completely frustrated, I sent the purchasing department an email to inquire about the results, but this time, I copied the deputy director of the DABC. And, wouldn't you know it, because their boss was copied, they got back to me. I found out the purchasing department failed to review and taste the new products I submitted in July 2017. They said that too many wines had been submitted by other brokers, so none of the wines I presented were reviewed. The DABC failed to live up to its new protocol – once again!

Feeling pressure to taste and review my products, the buyers told me they would set up a tasting for my wines only during the first week of December 2017. Although frustrated with their lack of follow-through on their original time-frame, I told them that would be fine.

The month of January 2018 started a new period for brokers to present wines once again using their three-month review, tasting, and order plan. So, once again, I compiled wines and information to present to the DABC – 18 wines total – submitting all paperwork by the January 31st deadline. Keep in mind, I still had not heard or received purchase orders for all the new wines they were supposed to have tasted in December.

On February 8th, I had a supplier in town to meet with the DABC buyers regarding three new wines I had just presented the paperwork and samples for in January. The supplier wanted to make sure the buyers knew his products were some of the hottest brands selling in the rest of the country, so they would remember them during the process. When the meeting was over, I asked the supplier to wait for me in the lobby while I spoke to the buyers. I needed to ask them point-blank if they had reviewed and tasted the wines I had presented in December. Both buyers looked at me with blank faces before one of the buyers spoke. "Oh yeah... I think we did taste and review the wines during December. The results are in my notes somewhere in my office."

"Do you recall if any of them were approved?" I asked.

"Ugh, gosh, you know... it's been a while. I couldn't tell you right off hand," he replied.

"Well, can we go take a look? I mean, since I'm here, it would be nice to know."

"Ugh, I can't right now. I'll take a look and get back to you by next week."

"Uh, okay. No problem, thanks for your time today."

The following week came and went without an email or phone call from either buyer. I sent several emails to follow up and each one went unanswered. I didn't hear about the results for another six months. Ridiculous, right?

Do not point out inefficiencies or offend the buyers in a monopoly, or business will suffer.

During the spring of 2018, I noticed that purchase orders for Limited Listed fine wines began to take a very long time to get generated. This meant that either the new system was still not recognizing that products were out of stock or the buyer was holding up the orders for one reason or another. Each week I fielded complaints from my sales reps, restaurants, and suppliers that products seemed to be out of stock with nothing on order. Each week, several state liquor stores ran out of product, leaving empty racks with nothing to replenish. Proactively, using an online product locator on the DABC website, I began to print out screenshots of the inventory page. After verifying vintage and pricing, I hand-wrote the day's date and something to the effect of: "Please order ASAP, almost out of stock, nothing on order." I faxed the pages to the buyers in hopes that a PO would be generated. In fact, quite often I had to complete this process numerous times until a PO would be generated.

Then one morning, I received a message from one of my large suppliers informing me that the buyers at the DABC had sent him an email containing a spreadsheet showing at least 25 wines they planned on delisting due to low sales. After opening up the attachment, I found that of the 25 wines they planned on axing, 20 of them were Limited Listed fine wines that had not been ordered in several months – some hadn't been ordered in six months or more. Without inventory, surely sales would suffer. Exasperated and incensed, I took updated screenshots of the inventory page of each wine and attached them in an email. In direct bullet points, I laid out the facts and accused the state buyers of not doing their job. Lastly, just to make sure my supplier knew I was angry, I copied the state buyers and the upper-ups at the DABC before hitting send.

Here in reference are the bullet points:

- The new system is supposed to examine inventory then issue purchase orders for Limited Listed wines for the brokers – this process was supposed to be automated!

- However, I have had to fax orders to the DABC begging to order Limited Listed items on a steady basis! Often several weeks go by before orders are cut?

- I have numerous wines that are low or out of stock from several suppliers!

- The new system is not working, and actually, it has never worked, therefore sales have suffered!

- With low sales, the DABC buyers now want to delist wines. This is complete shit!

- Attached are numerous screenshots showing inventory as of today - many products are almost completely out of stock with nothing on order!

- The wines in question are viable products that sell very well – when in stock!

- We cannot do our job successfully if the state buyers aren't doing their jobs!

- How can brokers possibly present and sell wines to restaurants and bars that are out of stock and not on order? Several wines have been out of stock for so long numerous restaurants have discontinued use.

- We work very hard to obtain restaurant wine list placements only to be undermined by the incompetence of the DABC!

To get the buyers off their asses, I also added that maybe I should tell the local newspapers as well, figuring at least it would make a good story. I didn't feel any remorse after hitting send. I had finally had enough bullshit; my blood was boiling. I'd broken the cardinal rule: Never bad-mouth, discredit, anger, or threaten the DABC. Someone had to say it, and that someone was me. Though very nice and congenial, the people who run the DABC are inefficient, ineffective, and sometimes vengeful.

I didn't hear from anyone at the DABC regarding my email and didn't get any wines ordered during the following three weeks. Since I obviously upset them, I guess they decided not to order any of my products as a sort of retribution for my outburst, punishing me and my suppliers for calling them to the carpet. Since the state buyers work for a monopoly, they know they have the final say with the ability to manipulate a broker's business at will. This sort of business practice is unacceptable on any level.

Almost a month had gone by with no new purchase orders. And even though I was right, I knew I had to swallow my pride, so I personally made appointments to apologize to the buyers and the upper-ups. I met with each person individually, apologizing for my accusatory and threatening outburst, but also explaining the facts from my side of the equation, noting the numerous phone calls from restaurants, my sales reps, and suppliers regarding out of stock products. To which, they explained their side: that the new system was still a work in progress and they still needed patience, even after implementation eighteen months earlier. One of the directors added that they (meaning the DABC) "did not appreciate being threatened." In the end, they all accepted my apology, and the following week, new purchase orders for my out-of-stock wines began to arrive via email once again.

When a buyer at a monopoly has a tantrum, everyone suffers.

The buyers at the DABC give out very little information, often forgetting or even purposely failing to send out a red flag if a problem needs to be fixed. During May of 2018, I submitted the necessary paperwork to place both *Riunite Lambrusco* 750mls and 1500mls and *Bolla Valpolicella* on sale for the month of August. I immediately received an email back from the DABC stating they had discontinued all three items without notifying me or my supplier.

Normally in this situation, I would research the problem so I could accurately describe to the supplier why their product would no longer be available in Utah, and that would be that. However, this problem was exponentially bigger. Riunite Lambrusco is one of the most well-known Italian brands in the United States. Banfi began importing this product during the late 1960s, quickly turning it into one of the largest import wine brands in U.S. history. Not to be outdone, Bolla in its own right is an extremely well-known brand as a go-to everyday, inexpensive Italian quaffing wine.

I immediately reviewed the sales history of all three items to find out if there had been a decline during the previous twelve months. However, all three items showed positive growth. I was stumped. Next, I checked the profitability factors of all three in their respective categories. The DABC publishes a report on its website that analyzes the sales history of each brand in case and dollar volume against its competitors. Both Riunite sizes were #1 in their category, and Bolla Valpolicella was # 2 in its category. Now I was really baffled.

Armed with facts and figures, I emailed the buyer at the DABC an extensive list of my research illustrating sales and profitability over the prior year. I copied their boss, the deputy director, and my direct reports to ensure a reply would follow. Since it was just before Memorial Day weekend, I didn't hear from him until the following week. Basically, in three short sentences, the buyer overseeing these particular products stated that the reason the products had been discontinued was because of shipping anomalies. Banfi had failed to deliver the products by the time frame the DABC requested on their purchase orders several times. And because the products showed up late, the warehouse sometimes ran out of product, so they discounted the products to recognize the seriousness of the problem and their power.

So, just like that, a buyer at the DABC discontinued three products selling over 3,400 cases and delivering over $267,000 in sales per year. No inquiries as to why the products were taking so long, no email or phone call warnings – he just quietly discontinued three extremely popular products without telling me, their broker, Banfi – the supplier, the many restaurants that use the products, and the consumers who shop in their stores. The DABC took products away from their customers just to prove a point. Utah was now the only state in the union where Riunite Lambrusco was not available for the masses who loved the product.

It would take several months of apologizing via emails, phone calls, and face-to-face meetings to convince the DABC to re-list the products. Finally, after the supplier and I formulated a plan to ensure the products would be delivered on time and that they would be a priority, the buyer acquiesced issuing a purchase order for all three items. In the end, the damage was done: Utah consumers were unable to buy the products for almost six months. Many either bootlegged the products or simply reached for other brands on the state store shelves. The negative impact would take several months, if not years, to overcome.

When a buyer at a monopoly goes on vacation, nothing else matters, and nothing will be addressed.

In the fall of 2018, I sent an email to one of the buyers at the DABC, who, unbeknownst to me, was on vacation. As per usual, his autoreply shot back an instant message. However, his terse message informed everyone not only that he was on vacation but that any email sent to him prior and or during would not be reviewed or replied to. It went something like this:

"Because I am currently on PTO, I am not accepting messages regarding anything, and any emails sent to me during this time will be automatically deleted because it would negate any benefits from my personal time off from work. If you need any assistance, please contact…"

Monopolies do not operate in reality.

Toward the end of August 2018, I received a purchase order for a wine the DABC decided to list as a new item. Normally this would be cause for celebration. However, on this occasion, I would have to find out if the wine was even available as I had presented it to them for consideration in November of 2016 – almost two full years prior?

A buyer working for a monopoly doesn't "have to do" anything.

For several years I'd been selling a very good Pinot Noir to a number of restaurants via special order as the state wouldn't carry it in their state liquor stores. This particular wine costing just over sixteen dollars represented a very good value because it was 100% pure Pinot Noir that had been aged for four months in French oak and had received a high rating from a venerable publication. In other states, the same wine was selling for twenty dollars. The reason it cost less in Utah was that it qualified for a small winery discount. This meant the state taxed it less because they made less than 8,500 cases per year.

The winery notified me during early spring of 2019 that they had an excess of wine from 2014 they wanted to sell at a discount so they could move to the next vintage – about 1,500 cases.

With rating and discount in hand, I met with one of the buyers at the DABC. I told him I could get him the wine for a price that would equal $12.99 on the shelf if he could buy a significant amount, around 500 cases. He asked that I have a sample of the wine sent overnight so he could taste it with the others in the purchasing department.

A few days later (after the sample had been sent and tasted), the buyer called to discuss the offer. He said he really liked the wine and wanted a thousand cases, but only if I could get it to him for $10.99. After confirming with my supplier that the price could be met, a purchase order was issued for the product.

After the wine arrived, the buyer sent a dozen cases to each state store, telling them to floor stack it with a large discount sign. The wine became an immediate hit with consumers. In fact, the first order for a thousand cases sold out in almost three months, so I was able to sell him the balance of the 2014 vintage.

A few months later, I decided to ask the buyer if he would consider listing the wine as an everyday offering on their shelves but for $12.99 rather than $10.99. I explained the winery barely made money by selling the wine at the lower price, but they had to so they could move to the next vintage. The buyer replied, "I'll consider buying this as a regular item, but I still want it at $10.99 on the shelf."

"But a two-dollar price increase for a wine of this quality will not hurt the demand that's already been created," I stated.

The buyer scoffed. "I'll buy it, but I want it at $10.99."

"But the winery has to make some money or it's not a good investment."

"Well, that's the deal."

"Oh, come on, several restaurants are now selling it on their wine lists and the consumers are hooked – You've got to bring this in as a regular item."

The buyer stepped back, looked me squarely in the eye, and replied, "No... I don't gotta do anything."

The state of Utah should abandon alcohol beverage control.

Since a monopoly does not have competition, it can use the cheapest solutions to get by. It doesn't have to furnish information to anyone. Problems are addressed and fixed on their own time, often without explanation. There is zero need for accountability; if they are out of stock on a product, they shrug their shoulders. If threatened, they can cause segments of business to suffer. If customers are pissed off, oh well, it doesn't matter, for they are the only game in town – IT'S WHAT MONOPOLIES DO!

Because of certain exclusivity over a product, service, or commodity, monopolies are unjust, unfair, unethical, and illegal. Without competition, prices, selection, and availability can be unfairly manipulated by the controlling interest. These are the simple reasons that monopolies are antitrust and, in most cases within the United States, against the law.

The Department of Alcoholic Beverage Control is a system that pays for itself while contributing a significant profit to a state that could care less about the rights of their citizens – unless they are a Latter-day Saint. Each time a person pays for alcohol at a state liquor store, part of the taxes collected pay for the infrastructure and the employees that run this department. Essentially, as tax-paying citizens, the imbibing public are the bosses in charge – yet they are continually abused by a system that's broken.

Though this is a free country with guaranteed rights, the imbibing citizens of Utah are considerably less free because of a system that has no competition. Their laissez-faire attitude, antiquated systems, and monopolistic outdated business model directly correlates to public animosity and hostility regarding the state's authority to effectively run the distribution and sale of a legal product. The LDS religious biased state legislature, including the Department of Alcoholic Beverage Control, has demonstrated they should not in any way be involved in the distribution and sale of alcoholic beverages.

These stories are my own, but there are more from other brokers, state employees, suppliers, and even consumers – countless stories of the extremely inept, unprofessional, unfair business habits of the DABC; each a continuation of absurdity and idiocrasy from the last. However, I think dear reader, you get the point, so I must stop... for now.

TRUTH IN MARKETING?
Super Bowl

WHEN SALES DECLINE, STAGNATE OR NEED A boost on a big brand, a supplier will do just about anything to increase sales – heavy discounting, coupons, giveaway trips, free cases when an account buys a large amount, and even spending obscene amounts of money on promotions.

To their credit, Deutsch had been running *Yellow Tail* commercials for numerous years to stay at the forefront and stimulate business. Many of the commercials were even somewhat clever; a meteor racing across the sky producing a "Yellow Tail," a man and a woman singing opera about a spilled bottle, and even a commercial with Godzilla sporting a yellow tail. And who could forget all the seasonal and holiday commercials about Yellow Tail being the "go-to" wine complete with chaotic flashing neon colors, kitschy tag lines, funky people and music? These commercials always seemed to run during late-night; I guess maybe to capitalize on the younger crowd or maybe because they had a limited budget – I'm not sure.

At the beginning of 2017, email after email began to appear about a new direction for the Yellow Tail promotional commercials. The new campaign would be completely different than what they had been doing in the past, and apparently, the big wigs made the decision to go in the direction of a life-size kangaroo using CGI effects or some kind of puppet.

The first email that arrived explained the new direction. Scrolling down through the text there was a link at the bottom that when clicked, showed a video of the CEO with a very real-looking life-size kangaroo, explaining the new direction of the commercials, and that they would kick-off the new campaign during the Super Bowl. Subsequent emails followed each week, outlining details around the promo that would tie the commercial into executing case stack drives and promotions at wine and grocery stores around the country, building up to the big debut in February during the big game! The emails were relentless, reminding all the minions across the country responsible for executing the case stacks about the commercial and how important it would be to have floor displays in all retail stores to promote the product before the big game. Small fake football fields made of Astroturf and goalposts and barbecues were sent out to enhance displays and catch the eye of the bumbling consumer. To pound it even further into our heads, they decided to have country-wide display contests complete with trackers that had to be filled out weekly and submitted with pictures. (Luckily, they didn't apply in my states.)

As the weeks progressed, links within the emails showed tidbits of what the final commercial would look like, and needless to say, each week they were a little more involved and... bizarre. One link showed the CEO talking to an Australian super-model on the beach in Barcelona – during winter? The next week showed the model running around the same beach wearing a skimpy white bikini while music played in the background. Then finally, a link with the actual commercial they would run during the Super Bowl, and I dare say it completely threw me for a loop.

Most Super Bowl commercials try to be cutting-edge, to sway the consumer; few are memorable, while many are downright stupid, and this one... This one surely tried to be cutting edge. The commercial opened with a gentleman in a yellow suit, at a beach barbecue, talking about parties and fun and how Yellow Tail wine fits the bill. Then, the Yellow Tail CGI kangaroo is shown flipping hamburgers dressed in an apron that says, *"KISS THE ROO."* Suddenly, the super-model in the white bikini walks along the beach when she is spotted by Mr. Yellow and the Kangaroo, who by the way, is now sporting a pair of yellow sunglasses. Mr. Yellow asks her, *"Do you want to pet my roo?"*

To which she shrugs, then replies, *"Sure,"* and starts to pet the kangaroo.

Finally, the commercial ends with Mr. Yellow dancing at a rooftop club while the kangaroo spins records. Whew, mind-blowing, huh?

Now... (deep breath, please) I understand that it's the job of marketing professionals everywhere to come up with ideas to sell a product and pitch it to the big wigs at various companies. However, I'm completely in the dark as to how in the hell the decision was made to produce a commercial with a CGI kangaroo and a man dressed in a neon yellow suit selling Australian wine on the frigid winter beaches of Barcelona, Spain, with an Australian super-model airing during the American Super Bowl. I don't know about you, dear reader, but when I think of American football I think beer, shots, burgers, brats and nachos and, why, yes... even super-models may creep into my mind, but never would I give a flying rat's ass about Australian wine!

The big game came and went, and Monday morning arrived with a hangover for many. The results, after being analyzed by the Deutsch upper-ups, indicated the Yellow Tail commercial was a huge success, placing it in the top ten all-time commercials during the game. Sales were up considerably – the upper-ups were pleased – more commercials surely would follow. I don't know, it could have been the CGI kangaroo or the dude in the yellow suit, but it was most likely the T and A flashed by the Australian model that did the trick. And that's why I'm not a marketing wizard. Decent value wine. Crazy campaign.

ILLOGICALITIES:
Current Utah Liquor Laws – Part 5

FROM AN EARLIER PART OF THIS BOOK, if you recall, new restaurants seeking a liquor license before 2009 and after 2013 were required to install a barrier of some sort on top of their bar or pour alcohol in a backroom or service bar so minors could not view the process. Dubbed "Zion Curtains" by everyone, including LDS lawmakers, these barriers had been around for a very long time except for the brief period when Governor Jon Huntsman was in office. The act of bartenders mixing cocktails, pouring wine and beer is considered promoting alcohol consumption to minors by the LDS teetotaling lawmakers.

During the January 2017 legislative session, representatives from the hospitality industry and their lobbyist worked with Representative Brad Wilson (R-Kaysville), to formulate a bill that would remove the "Zions Curtains" from restaurants once and for all – but there would most definitely be compromise. Compromise that came at a cost.

 Compromise 2017 – Zions Curtain Law Abolished.

Instead of a shield or barrier on the bar or walled-off area, the requirement is to have at least ten feet of spacing between the actual bar and minors, with options that moderate its effect.

- *A pony wall or railing, five feet from the dispensing area delineating an area where minors are not allowed.*

- *Grandfathered restaurants, however, those that had a bar without a shield during the Huntsman years, can seat minors at tables within ten feet with adult consent.*

- *Or, restaurants may choose to keep their "Zion's Curtain" or employ back bar service, if they so desire.*

Restaurants are able to subtract bottles of wine costing over $175 and glasses of wine over $30 from the calculation of percentages used to analyze food to alcohol ratio requirements – *Utah law requires licensees to have a dominant ratio of food to alcohol sales in order to retain their liquor license.* (The prior law stipulated $250 for bottles of wine with no allowance for by-the-glass.)

Checking IDs is only necessary if minors are at the table, adults are ordering alcohol, and the guests look under 35 years of age.

Unless grandfathered in, new restaurants in proximity to community spaces and church buildings may not be closer than 300 feet walking distance or 200 feet as the crow flies – no variances granted. This new part of the law put a few new restaurants out of business, even sending some searching for a new location, and required the local major league soccer stadium to move its entrance to the other side of its building at a cost of nearly $250k.

An overall tax increase on alcohol from 86% to 88% generating millions more in revenue, part of which was to be used for battling underage drinking – Oh, and also steer more people across state lines to bootleg.

And finally, a few of the many different liquor licenses were simplified. Prior to this new law, since several restauranteurs wanted bars on their premises but did not want to have unsightly "Zion's Curtains" marring their theme, many obtained a "Dining Club License" or simply had two liquor licenses – one for their restaurant, where minors could be served – and one for the bar area. This meant spending inordinate amounts of money to ensure bar areas were separated from dining areas in some sort of way so as to keep minors from viewing alcohol. The 2017 compromise did away with the Dining Club License and the need for multiple licenses – restauranteurs now just had to decide if they were a full-service restaurant or a bar.

Therein lies a new problem: Many restauranteurs with a Dining Club License didn't want to change because they would have to spend thousands upon thousands of dollars to modify their premises. If they decided to go full bar, then minors were not allowed. If they decided to go full restaurant, then they must modify their bars. If they decided to keep both licenses, then the bar must be walled off entirely from the restaurant without any ingress directly from the dining room as they must operate independently. Either way, restauranteurs must spend a pile of money to conform to the idiosyncrasies of the LDS nincompoops that are the state legislature.

While I am grateful to all the people, including forward-thinking LDS Representative Wilson, that were able to "tear down the wall," I am appalled that "tit for tat" negotiating took place rather than just allowing the barriers to come down for what they actually were – an expensive eyesore and a ridiculous inconvenience. When the state legislature enacted the "Zion's Curtain" laws, they didn't negotiate or consult the hospitality industry – they just did it. Having to negotiate with LDS lawmakers over what simply is the right thing to do is humiliating. The state legislature is not unbiased; they act as if Utah is their own independent country, serving only their own religion, rather than the whole. By enacting stupid laws and controlling alcohol ineffectively, they do a disservice to tourists and residents that are not of the LDS religion. Now, prices go up, bootlegging increases, customers go away and… Utah still looks ridiculous.

Licensees must post a sign in a conspicuous place that reads: "This Premise is Licensed as a RESTAURANT NOT A BAR" or "This Premise is Licensed as a BAR NOT A RESTAURANT." A sign of the times or just BS?

NORMAL THINKING

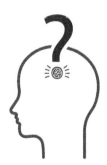

UTAH STATE LDS LAWMAKER'S THINKING

One of the juicy little tidbits hidden away from the limelight of the new "Zion's Curtain" law bullshit was a new law so simpleminded, I am quite certain an LDS politician inserted the idea without any input from the Utah hospitality industry, then hid behind the pulpit before anyone caught wind. Just as the state's imbibing population was coming to grips with the new liquor law changes, the news appeared in April of 2017: Licensees now must display signage declaring their type of license so as not to confuse the public – Or more so, the dull-witted LDS public that may inadvertently walk into the wrong establishment alone or with their family without being properly warned that the demon alcohol may be within sight.

Signs no smaller than a standard sheet of paper must be conspicuously posted on their premises that clearly states the following: "This Premise is Licensed as a RESTAURANT NOT A BAR" or "This Premises is Licensed as a BAR NOT A RESTAURANT." And at the bottom of each sign, a disclaimer: "This sign was approved by the Alcoholic Beverage Control Commission."

But there was some good news: the DABC allowed

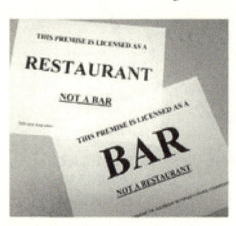

accounts to "sexy up" their signs so as not to deter from the natural surroundings of said account. However, they must be approved before being displayed. Whew – Hallelujah, we are saved, thank you, LDS legislature... Thank you for looking out for all of us!

Not to be outdone, one of the local fly-fishing shops, Western Rivers Flyfishers, posted this sign in their window mocking the new law.

And even this one from our great neighbors to the northeast – Wyoming.

One year later, the legislature allowed restaurants to take down the signs, but bars are still required to post them in conspicuous places.

New Blood Alcohol Content Law - 0.05 BAC. (What?)

Also, during the 2017 legislative session, HB155 was introduced by Representative Norman Thurston (R – Mormon, Provo). HB155 effectively would lower the BAC (blood alcohol content) from 0.08 to 0.05. His arguments: It is simply about public safety, and 84.5% of the world live with laws of 0.05 or even lower, so we should too. Special interest groups such as the NTSB and the LDS church backed the bill. If Utah were to enact the law, it would make it the first state in the union to make the move.

The bill passed without so much as a hiccup. Against the consternation and opposition of the local hospitality industry and national beverage associations and a large segment of the population, apprehensively, the Governor signed the bill into law shortly thereafter. When Governor Herbert signed the bill, he cited public safety and other reasons for his decisions, but then he added that he "hoped it would be tweaked" and that he would call a special session to address "unintended consequences" of the law, including delaying the implementation after 2019. He also "thought" that tiered penalties could be implemented for people who are between 0.05 and 0.08 BAC and higher.

The mere fact that Governor Herbert said he "hoped" that the law would be "tweaked" and that the "unintended consequences" be studied and addressed should have been enough for him to veto such a bill, sending it back to the legislature for revision or failure before officially signing. A law cannot be changed or "tweaked" unless the whole formal process is subjected through the legislative voting body in the future. By signing the bill into law, Governor

Herbert demonstrated an egregious disservice to the state and illustrated that he is unfit for office by guessing and "hoping."

Furthermore, the governor did not call the state legislature to a special session at any time during the remainder of 2017 to discuss or "tweak" the 0.05 BAC law. It was purely talk to appease public discontent; he had no intention of calling a special session to tweak anything. We were, however, assured by our esteemed Mormon governor that tourism would not go down, hospitality businesses would not be affected, and that DUIs and false arrests would not go up. Only time will tell.

Once again Utah, makes national news for its repressive liquor laws. Several groups and companies, including restauranteurs and the public, protested the bill citing irrational data and adverse impact on tourism and business. Newspaper ads were taken out with slogans such as: "Come for Vacation, Leave on Probation" and "The New Mighty Five – Not the National Parks – But the 0.05 BAC Limit." Many religions, including non-active and somewhat active Mormons, opposed the bill. On the flip side, the people most in favor of the bill were very active non-drinking Mormons. Hmmm.

The state of Utah is already stigmatized for having the most archaic and authoritarian liquor laws in the nation. By enacting a .05 BAC limit, lawmakers confirmed that stigma. If it were any state in the union other than Utah that enacted the law first, people would think twice when labeling or lampooning an otherwise fine state. The new 0.05 BAC law is not really about public safety but rather the LDS Church's attempt to limit alcohol consumption. The unmistakable coincidence of a Mormon lawmaker drafting the bill, an overwhelming Mormon majority legislature passing the bill, and finally, a Mormon governor signing the bill into law reeks of the LDS Church's continued attempts to stifle something that is against their value system. With stigma firmly in place, it's entirely possible that people will think twice about vacationing or relocating themselves or businesses to Utah. Will other states follow? Maybe at some point, but it's anyone's guess.

Now, I'm completely in favor of smart laws, and without a doubt squarely against drinking and driving, but 0.05 BAC is not reasonable. Why? Because a slew of products will put a person at or above 0.05 BAC – Mouthwash such as Listerine and sprays such as Binaca, medicines, and even some maladies will register above the limit on a breathalyzer. Yes, a person could get a DUI for using mouthwash. These and a few other reasons are the "unintended circumstances" Governor Herbert referred to. Threats such as texting and talking on a phone while driving pose a much higher and credible hazard than the previous 0.08 BAC law. People will still drive impaired whether the BAC is .05 or .08. This ultimately should be about fairness – the entire country should have the same BAC threshold, not variances state by state.

Flashforward to the legislative session of January/February 2018. With the new law set to take effect in December of 2018, Governor Herbert stated in a Salt Lake Tribune article, "delay of implementation or repeal of the 0.05 BAC law will not pass through the legislature." Well, duh, no kidding. He then goes on to say that he "heard from the legislature this morning that they've done some testing" with the DABC, "to see how people will react when they get their alcohol level to 0.05 BAC and the consensus is that a person is impaired at 0.05 BAC." Further, in the article, he states, "I think this has been studied for the last year," and that discussions regarding "minor changes" in the law are "expected." (Davidson, Low DUI Threshold will Stand, Guv Says 2018)

How can the figurehead and leader of the state just dole out guessing and speculation willy-nilly? The governor knows that LDS lawmakers are going to do as little as possible (or nothing at all) to "tweak" the bill, and since he is LDS, the governor once again proves that LDS influence in Utah is supreme. The only reason he made such speculative comments was to get out of the spotlight. A "real" governor stands his ground realizing that the entire population needs to be served and addressed and that certain bills should be vetoed or amended before implementation. It's called "checks and balances." Maybe one day soon, Utah will elect an impartial, unbiased governor and, for that matter, legislative body. Until then, citizens are relegated to live with the whims and decisions of the inadequate idiots that are the Utah government.

 3.2% Beer in Grocery Stores

To end this series on illogicalities, I give you 3.2% beer. Well, I mean figuratively. Prior to the fall general election of 2016, only five states required beer sold in convenience stores and grocery stores to contain no more than 3.2% alcohol – Colorado, Utah, Kansas, Oklahoma, and Minnesota. The amount of 3.2% beer sold in these states accounted for under 2% of the total beer volume sold in the United States. After the fall election, the voters in Colorado, Kansas, and Oklahoma decided to drop 3.2% beer in favor of higher alcohol offerings to be more reflective of the craft brewing movement. With only two states left in the country to brew 3.2% for, the mega-brewers decided to limit their offerings and scale back how much 3.2% beer they make for only two states. This meant that some pack sizes and even many brands would disappear from the grocery store shelves leaving big gaps and holes in the dedicated beer aisle. It would also substantially reduce sales in grocery stores and piss off consumers that may not be able to get the beer they love.

Enter the 2019 legislative session. Senator Jerry Stevenson crafted a bill to raise the alcohol content to 4.8%. In fact, Mr. Stevenson had been studying and working on the bill since three of the other states abandoned 3.2% beer. Not only would the new bill address the limited selection, lower sales, and consumer consternation, many beers carried in the state liquor stores could be moved to the grocery stores providing more shelf space for wines and spirits. As per usual, The Church of Jesus Christ of Latter-day Saints vocally opposed the bill and sent their lobbyists in to enforce their message. The bill passed the Senate but failed to pass the Health and Human Services special committee in the House of Representatives. The reasons they cited were: They were worried about the impact high-volume beer would have on DUIs, even after they lowered the BAC limited to .05 just one-year prior; increased alcoholism, and increased access to teenagers. Their reasons, though somewhat plausible, were just an excuse in order to appease their church and reduce access to alcohol, thus tightening their grip on the feeble minds of the masses. Mormon Senator Lyle Hilliard from Logan, Utah stated, "I'm voting no on this bill. I think the next step will be to put wine in grocery stores. You say, 'Oh no, it's not going to happen.' Mark my words: It's going to happen." (Winslow 2019)

However, just a few days after the 4.8% beer bill was defeated, news broke that the legislature came to an understanding between the Senate and the House, with a blessing from The Church of Jesus Christ of Latter-day Saints, of course, that a modest increase in alcohol to 4% would be sufficient for now, once again proving that separation of church and state doesn't exist in Utah and LDS over-reach is in fact real.

TREND

ROSÉ

"A rose is a rose is a rose," they say. That is unless it's a wine – then… it's called **rosé**. The phrase, by Gertrude Stein, translates loosely as: by merely using the name of something, whatever it may be, simply infers certain images, thoughts, sounds, smells and feelings by association alone. However, this cannot be completely true, for not all **rosés** are created equal – wine that is!

Rosé is one of the world's oldest known wines ranging from cloyingly sweet to very dry, effervescent to still, pale salmon or strawberry to an intense reddish-purple hue. Grape skin-to-juice contact is the primary method, although skimming or bleeding pink wine from red grapes or blending small amounts of red wine into white imparts similar results. Blush wines, such as sweet even slightly effervescent inexpensive White Zinfandels, were the rage in America during the early 1980s, but tastes have given way to a drier style, often trying to imitate the timeless Provençal **classic**. During 2017, pink wildfire spread as each supplier jumped on the bandwagon.

Rosés from all corners of the earth, almost every varietal and blend; come one, come all – rosé of Pinot Noir, Merlot, Zinfandel, and even Syrah – for sure there is no limit, so buy more than one, the cash cow has arrived, hurry before it's done!

UTAH – SEPARATION OF
CHURCH AND STATE?

SOMETHING EXISTS DOWN DEEP WITHIN A HUMAN'S GENETIC CODE compelling us to dominate and dictate the fate of others; to tell them how to live, how to think, and how to act. Surely, certain individuals or groups know what is best for the rest of the population.

With the creation of currency, its origins beginning with the trade of precious cloth, metals, or stones in exchange of goods and services, mankind quickly learned that through sheer accumulation and hoarding, one's power and status was elevated, thus tipping societal scales. Similarly, religion has developed domination tactics through its fear and guilt-laden doctrine. And finally, the government, allowing some humans the right to enforce law and order upon a society, even if unjust, exploitive, and immoral.

The main component of domination is fear; fear that's derived from many sources – mental dominance, monetary control over necessary goods and services, or an eternity in hell or a hellish place if specific religious doctrine isn't followed. Or, if societal laws are broken, it could mean being ostracized, jail time, or death. Whether psychological or physical, or any combination thereof, the usual outcome is dominance over another simply because of fear.

While we need government, laws, and rules to keep society from becoming utter chaotic anarchy, at the very least, they need to be fair. And as man has progressed (in most civilized areas of the world anyway), we strive to improve the laws and rules so they are non-discriminatory, impartial, non-exclusive, and just. However, even in this day, unfair and unjust laws and regulations still exist favoring one group or person over another.

The enactment of the first amendment to the U.S. Constitution illustrates the core reasons the colonists rebelled, then ultimately left England to inhabit North America. They wanted to escape the established uniformity of faith, the corrupt Anglican Church headed by a king. As the dominant religious governing body, it stifled its citizens through suppression of free speech, non-recognition of the establishment of other religions, and quashing assembly and the ability to protest or establish a voice against the government.

The First Amendment to the U.S. Constitution reads:
Congress shall make no law respecting an establishment of religion, or prohibiting the free exercise thereof; or abridging the freedom of speech, or of the press; or the right of the people peaceably to assemble, and to petition the Government for a redress of grievances.
(Congress 1788)

Church/state separation topics have been discussed, debated, disputed, and litigated since their inception.

Countless attempts to dissect and define the true meaning has led to its use as an excuse or to enforce, reinforce, denounce, and protest, and will continue as sure as time progresses. Instead of listing every legal excerpt and try to define its true meeting, I offer one out of thousands that I believe offers a sound interpretation to the religious aspect of the First Amendment.

The "establishment of religion" clause of the First Amendment means at least this:
Neither a state nor the Federal Government can set up a Church. Neither can pass laws which aid one religion, aid all religions, or prefer one religion over another [...] No tax in any amount, large or small, can be levied to support any religious activities or institutions, whatever they may be called, or whatever form they may adopt to teach or practice religion [...] In the words of Jefferson, the clause against establishment of religion by law was intended to erect "a wall of separation between Church and State."
(*Everson v. Board of Education 1949*)

Though fundamentally America was founded on Christian values (references are emblazoned on our money, monuments, and in our songs and pledge of allegiance, etc.), it welcomes all religions and guarantees through the First Amendment that the government will not discriminate or favor any one religion over another. Because religious beliefs can govern, dictate, and dominate the minds and actions of people, it is one of the most personal and powerful endeavors in which a human can invest their time. And because America is a melting pot with diverse cultures and beliefs, it is with utmost importance that religion should be held entirely separate from any government or political associations for fear that any one dominant religion could enact and enforce laws aiding their own flock while alienating, infringing, and undermining the rights of their fellow countrymen and women.

When the Mormon pioneers came to Utah in 1847, they did so to escape their own religious persecution in the midwest. Upon arriving in the barren territory, the settlers, after establishing living arrangements, most likely tended to their spiritual needs first by building churches and reestablishing The Church of Jesus Christ of Latter-day Saints followed by setting up a local government. Since the majority of the settlers were practicing Latter-day Saints, it's feasible to say that the provincial government at that time was comprised mostly of, if not all, Mormons. Thus, it is also reasonable to assume that LDS influence over government affairs was absolute. And, aside from the state becoming more secular since its founding, not a lot has changed. In the year 2017, 62% of the state's total population was listed as LDS, and 88% of the members of the state legislature were practicing Latter-day Saints.

The Utah State Constitution has its own section on religious liberty modeled after the First Amendment of the U.S. Constitution adding, "There shall be no union of Church and State, nor shall any Church dominate the State or interfere with its functions."

Article I, Section 4. [Religious liberty.]
The rights of conscience shall never be infringed. ***The State shall make no law respecting an establishment of religion*** *or prohibiting the free exercise thereof; no religious test shall be required as a qualification for any office of public trust or for any vote at any election; nor*

*shall any person be incompetent as a witness or juror on account of religious belief or the absence thereof. **There shall be no union of Church and State, nor shall any Church dominate the State or interfere with its functions.** No public money or property shall be appropriated for or applied to any religious worship, exercise or instruction, or for the support of any ecclesiastical establishment.* **(Legislature, Utah State Legislature 1895)**

Unfortunately, over the years, Latter-day Saint lawmakers have neglected and even overlooked this section, for they are regularly swayed by their church's stance on political matters. It's common knowledge that lawmakers consult with LDS Church authorities when crafting specific laws affecting the state. No other special interest group in Utah receives the same amount of regard and attention from the local government than that of The Church of Jesus Christ of Latter-day Saints.

Tiptoeing around the legalities of their actions, The Church of Jesus Christ of Latter-day Saints contends and maintains a stance of political neutrality. To avoid legal problems, the Church issues several statements regarding their policies on political neutrality, but hypocritically violate them on a regular basis by pushing buttons and pulling strings like a wizard behind the drapes. From a link within their website dated September 14, 2017, their official position reads:

Political Neutrality

TOPIC

The Church's mission is to preach the gospel of Jesus Christ, not to elect politicians. The Church of Jesus Christ of Latter-day Saints is neutral in matters of party politics. This applies in all of the many nations in which it is established.

THE CHURCH DOES NOT:

- Endorse, promote or oppose political parties, candidates or platforms.

- Allow its Church buildings, membership lists or other resources to be used for partisan political purposes.

- Attempt to direct its members as to which candidate or party they should give their votes to. This policy applies whether or not a candidate for office is a member of The Church of Jesus Christ of Latter-day Saints.

- Attempt to direct or dictate to a government leader.

THE CHURCH DOES:

- Encourage its members to play a role as responsible citizens in their communities, including becoming informed about issues and voting in elections.

- Expect its members to engage in the political process

in an informed and civil manner, respecting the fact that members of the Church come from a variety of backgrounds and experiences and may have differences of opinion in partisan political matters.

- Request candidates for office not to imply that their candidacy or platforms are endorsed by the Church.

- Reserve the right as an institution to address, in a nonpartisan way, issues that it believes have significant community or moral consequences or that directly affect the interests of the Church.

In the United States, where nearly half of the world's Latter-day Saints live, it is customary for the Church at each national election to issue a letter to be read to all congregations encouraging its members to vote, but emphasizing the Church's neutrality in partisan political matters.

RELATIONSHIPS WITH GOVERNMENT

Elected officials who are Latter-day Saints make their own decisions and may not necessarily be in agreement with one another or even with a publicly stated Church position. While the Church may communicate its views to them, as it may to any other elected official, it recognizes that these officials still must make their own choices based on their best judgment and with consideration of the constituencies whom they were elected to represent.
(newsroom.churchofjesuschrist.org January)

So, does the LDS Church really have influence over the state legislature, thus directly dictating and swaying the outcome of specific laws? The answer: Only a fool would think otherwise. The "wall of separation" between The Church of Jesus Christ of Latter-day Saints and politics simply doesn't exist. It is obscenely and embarrassingly obvious at times with various LDS public statements and stances over the years coinciding with the outcome of certain laws passed, revised, looked over, or shut down.

During my fifty-plus years of living in Utah, I have witnessed the hierarchy of the LDS Church issue "revelations" and public statements on a myriad of political issues. The statements illustrate their position, which ultimately directs the lives of their members. Since Salt Lake City and immediate surrounding areas are the equivalent of Mecca for the Mormons, LDS Utahans zealously practice, adhere, and defend their Church, its admonitions, values, and its beliefs. If they didn't, The Church of Jesus Christ of Latter-day Saints would fail to exist. A religion without a flock of followers to sustain and support their values and beliefs is not a religion, but rather a jumbled bunch of philosophies. When the Church issues a public statement as to their stance on a sensitive issue regarding the laws and societal issues in the state, the LDS members of the state legislature, pay heed through their actions as lawmakers so as not to oppose or upset their LDS peers.

The Church often follows up such public statements by directing their lobbyists to bombard their Mormon brethren in the legislature, thus reinforcing their stance. Even if the Church doesn't feel compelled to make a public statement on a topic, if the issues are of a high degree of sensitivity, or conflict with how they view the state should be run, they will send in their lobbyists, so their voice is heard. And even though some LDS lawmakers may feel torn with how they should vote, it's usually by an overwhelming margin that they are compelled to cast their votes reflecting the stance of the Church, which is viewed as revelation.

A strong argument can be made that if the religious affiliation of the members of the state legislature consisted of less than 50% practicing Latter-day Saints, the outcome of specific bills and laws would most certainly be different. Quite frankly, the state liquor laws would undoubtedly be more liberal.

Aside from the domineering LDS Church, their gospel Nazi members, and archaic liquor laws, Utah has been a very enjoyable place to grow up and simply, live. I've traveled to many places around the world but realize that Utah will always be home. Four distinct seasons, diverse topography, five national parks, several national recreation areas and monuments, numerous ski resorts, lakes, rivers, endless trails, inexpensive golf, an international airport minutes from downtown, Major League soccer, the Utah Jazz – What's not to like? I've watched Salt Lake City, Park City, and surrounding areas evolve from sleepy farming and mining communities to major tourist destinations. With those changes, the dining and bar scene has dramatically changed too. Just prior to and specifically after the year 2000, an influx of newcomers made Utah their home, establishing new concepts that have literally changed the dining and nightlife landscape. Utah has grown up. Sure, some of the old staples are still around, but times have changed.

A palpable level of dissension and animosity toward state

liquor laws has existed for a very long time, mostly by non-Mormon drinking residents, but also with those who visit for business and pleasure. Due to changing times and forward-thinking, many have challenged Utah's Liquor Laws with hopes that someday, a normal way of doing business will arrive. Dissent hit an all-time high after the 2012 legislative session, with the Department of Alcoholic Beverage Control making several mistakes and wrong steps, even making national news in some cases. The governor and some members in the state legislature also took notice through their public statements, admitting that maybe it was time to look at changing the liquor laws. But talk is talk, and theirs was only nonsense to appease and pacify, so nothing ever transpired.

For years, discord continued along with numerous attempts to alter various liquor laws. Just before the 2014 state legislative session, a newspaper article appeared in the January 23, 2014 edition of *The Salt Lake Tribune* titled: LDS Church: Don't Change Utah's Liquor Laws, written by Robert Gehrke. It reflected statements made by an LDS authority in a Church-produced video, including commentary from a few notable lawmakers. I personally didn't see the video, but I didn't have to; I know their views, so why waste my time.

In the video, D. Todd Christofferson, a member of the Church's Quorum of the Twelve Apostles said: "How could *we* suppose that changing *our* system to reflect that of [other states] is not going to yield the same results that they're seeing?" furthermore, adding, "*We* need to stay where *we* are because *we've* established something that has struck the right balance." (Gehrke, LDS Church: Don't Change Utah's Liquor Laws 2014)

By his use of *our* and *we* and *we've*, he infers that the LDS Church is tied to the government process. And, as a "general officer" of the Church, moreover, he violates policy by using his moniker, thus influencing LDS lawmakers through his statements. If Mr. Christofferson simply had changed ownership within his remarks, he would have been in the clear. But he didn't, so the Church must own his statements. His position violated LDS policies by attempting to "direct" and "dictate to government leaders," by voicing ownership through a political platform. And by allowing the production of such a video along with the statements of one of its officers, the Church directly violated the U.S. Constitution, Utah Constitution, and their so-called position of political neutrality.

The article continues to note that alcohol policy is tied to the "moral climate" of the state. The "moral climate" they refer to is that of the 62% LDS population. If their members are in any way influenced to consume alcohol, thus liberating their minds, it could disrupt that climate and hurt their business. And by merely making the statement in the video, "legislation should not enable, promote or contribute to an alcohol culture," the Church influenced and dictated to LDS lawmakers. By limiting access to alcohol, it gives the Church a better chance to convert the non-Mormons within Utah.

Though meant to sound as if pleading, Christofferson's comments intended to drive fear into the minds of his LDS brethren. Fear that (without using actual data) other cities experienced higher levels of alcohol-related problems. However, his comments also illustrated a certain level of obtusity. Sure, there are other states with higher alcohol-related problems, but they are also a lot larger. Utah's low incidents of alcohol-related problems correlate to the high ratio of Mormons residing in the state and the low overall population. It's entirely possible that if the LDS population is taken out of the equation, the number of incidents compare to that of larger cities.

The state of Utah is not immune to problems. In fact, it's the number one pornography-viewing state in the union. And the LDS population significantly contributes to the high rates of obesity and opioid abuse.

It's well-known that if government limits or outlaws something, people will find a way to obtain it and hoard it. The experiment of Prohibition from 1920 to 1933 is proof. Crime and corruption skyrocketed during those years birthing the black market.

Later in the piece, LDS Lawmaker Ryan Wilcox (R-Ogden) illustrates that though "uncomfortable," his position is influenced by the statements of apostle D. Todd Christofferson, which he viewed as slightly less than coming from God through the LDS hierarchy. He goes on to admit that it would basically be a waste to spend much time on alcohol legislation because the "make-up" (LDS make-up) of the Senate is the same as in prior years which derailed previous attempts to liberalize Utah liquor laws. This shows that efforts to normalize liquor legislation in the past were thwarted by his LDS brethren. Representative Wilcox's public statements demonstrated that LDS influence regarding state alcohol law is absolute, and he was unfit to hold public office because of his biased views.

Lastly, LDS Senator John Valentine (R-Orem) publicly admits that his church's views align with his own. He then goes on to literally cheer the fact that since one of the leaders within the Church made statements not to amend current liquor laws, it meant they would not have to listen, review, or consider any changes during that legislative session.

Valentine's statements show that because the Church simply opposed liberalization by voicing their stance, it directly manipulated the outcome of the 2014 legislative session by influencing LDS politicians to basically do nothing; even if any bills were presented in regard to changing the liquor laws.

As with Wilcox, Senator John Valentine was un-fit to hold public office due to his Mormon-biased views of alcohol control within Utah, and his statements prove he was and is influenced by his church leaders.

When it comes to all things Utah, many Latter-day Saint members exude a certain level of ownership, or cockiness, or entitlement. They feel that since the state was established by Mormon pioneers, then it's only right that their religion has the final say, in everything. And when it comes to the Book of Mormon-thumping masses, they are Latter-day Saints first and U.S. citizens second.

Following the legislative session in the spring of 2014, the LDS Church, feeling as if it needed an affirmation that its poop didn't stink, conducted an internal poll among its members. The poll had been kept private for many years before the results were posted in a *May 10, 2017* article titled: Mormons Don't View Church as Political Heavyweight, written for *The Salt Lake Tribune* by Jennifer Dobner. However, the opening statements contradict the title right off the bat with the poll showing the Church should "wield considerable influence." (Dobner, Mormons Don't View Church as Political Heavy Weight 2017) Still, since many LDS folks live with their heads in the sand, they do not think that Church influence plays out.

The story lays out facts and figures regarding the makeup of the poll respondents. The majority being local religious leaders (bishops and stake presidents) of the many satellite LDS Churches that dot the Utah landscape. Since the leaders of the local wards and districts fervently sustain and support the leaders of the Church and their direction, it is only natural to say they believe their church should have a strong influence in local politics.

The vast majority of LDS residents believe they are the chosen people, and since their church is the predominant religion (and there are almost more churches and temples than convenience stores in Utah), it should dictate Utah law. It is their view that everyone not of LDS faith living in Utah should yield to the Mormon majority.

In sections of LDS Church Opposes Cannabis Proposal dated February 6th, 2016 by Robert Gehrke, medical marijuana is shut down by the Church, once again demonstrating their overreach and influence in government affairs.

Sen. Mark Madsen (L-Lehi), an active and forward-thinking member of the Church, used sound judgment to draft a bill to legalize medical marijuana, something that's proven effective in treating debilitating maladies. However, he is completely snubbed by his faith because they did not want to back anything they feel would liberate the minds of their flock. Liberated minds equal less tithing, and less tithing means less power for the LDS Church. So, the Church employed lobbyists, thus violating their stance of neutrality, to murmur direction into the ears of their Mormon comrades.

Direction that LDS lawmakers dare not ignore. Because of the direct influence over their members, the state legislature would not put their stamp on the bill.

In the article, Sen. Madsen states that he, "loves and sustains and supports the ordained brethren," and "would never contradict them." (Gehrke, LDS Church Opposes Cannabis Proposal 2016) This declaration is indicative of the mindset of the LDS masses. It demonstrates that he's not able to make an unbiased decision, therefore he is unfit to serve the population as a whole and should never have been a Utah state senator.

As a lawmaker, Senator Madsen cannot (nor should he ever) say anything that shows state lawmakers are influenced by LDS Church direction. Yet, publicly and candidly, he admitted their impact in directing the outcome of a significant bill. Many laws of the state of Utah are enacted first and foremost by ensuring that the LDS population will not be affected, but will ultimately benefit, which is wrong. A large segment of the community should not have to capitulate to the beliefs of religious zealots.

In a piece titled: "Lawmakers Discuss Crossing of Mormon Faith, Politics," October 4th, 2016, by Michelle L. Price from the *Associated Press*, several Utah politicians admit that due to the mere fact lawmakers of LDS faith dominate the legislature, and the majority of the population of the state is LDS – Mormon influence with political and government affairs is in fact, real. I will say, to put themselves out front on a panel and openly make references, assertions, and candidly admit that the Church continually influences their stance on state laws that support, contradict, or coincide with their principles, takes massive cojones!

While the Church notes that it reserves its right to "express its views" and lobby elected officials directly, they plead their stance by also stating that lawmakers must make up their own mind. But even though the Church issues the statement that "politicians must make their own choices," they know full well that the LDS religion and its teachings are the first or second most important part of life to any active practicing Latter-day Saint. And, since members of the Church love, sustain, and support their brethren and never contradict them, the Church holds significant sway over an LDS individual – politician or not.

Some valid points are also made within the article about Church influence by LDS Senator Todd Weiler. He admits that lobbyists contacted him regarding alcohol legislation, which by definition is influencing political outcome. Weiler then said, "since the Church employs a lot of people and owns a large sum of land," they should get their say as to the laws of the state of Utah. What a load of shit that statement is – just because someone owns more land than someone else does not dictate the outcome of federal or state laws! This is not a feudal system! This statement illustrates the pervasive attitude that exists within the Church and LDS lawmakers: that they and their Church are above the laws of this state and country.

The question: Is the Utah Legislature Representative of the People, is posed in an article written by Lee Davidson of *The Salt Lake Tribune*, December 11, 2016. At the beginning of the article, a point is made that most lawmakers contend that the LDS Church is not influential. But c'mon, what else would they say? If they admit they are influenced, they violate Church political policy and state and federal constitutions. It's only natural that they would deny influence, which by the way, is a lie and a sin, and hypocritical. So, it is reasonable to say that LDS lawmakers would rather lie about political influence and interference, then repent on Sunday, rather than admit wrongdoing, so the Church can get its way.

The article points out that a member or members of the legislature directly met with the Church to craft legislation on LGBTQ issues. Why would the members of the state legislature feel compelled to consult with only the LDS Church and not any others when crafting legislation affecting the whole population? Reason: Since LDS lawmakers are first and foremost bound by the principles governing their religion, and they control the state legislature by an overwhelming margin, it's only natural for them to feel obligated to consult their religious leaders or risk being rebuked. Is it legal? No! Does it occur? Regularly! Is it unscrupulous? Without a doubt.

Past Sen. Jim Dabakis (D-Salt Lake), a former Mormon and outspoken voice in the Utah community, comments within the article that LDS members act in accordance with how their Church would act. Which bolsters the stance that LDS influence is absolute in regard to specific legislation that contradicts their values.

But, the most damning part of the article is that state lawmakers met with Elder L. Tom Perry before even taking the issue before the state legislative body. Because Elder L. Tom Perry, an officer and a leader within the Church, met with Senator Dabakis to craft a bill prior to anything formal with the whole legislature, the LDS Church violated its neutral policies by promoting their platform and dictating their stance and position to a government leader. To my knowledge, no other churches or special interest groups were involved. This is a violation of rights! The state of Utah is not just a territory or an interest, but part of the union of the United States of America. Therefore, "no religion or church can dominate the state or interfere with its functions." Because The Church of Jesus Christ of Latter-day Saints directs and dictates to government leaders, they are anything but a neutral special interest group.

The tragic end, in my opinion, is that of Former LDS GOP Rep. Carl Wimmer (R- Salt Lake). After becoming so disheartened and disillusioned when the LDS Church blatantly and egregiously directed and influenced him regarding a piece of legislation, felt compelled to quit the Church for another religion. There are many religions on the planet, all of which, may claim that they are the one true religion. But for someone to quit their faith, something they feel so deeply passionate and committed to, that they have invested time and money in, then denounce its actions, illustrates that national and local laws and his own civil liberties were likely violated.

If the LDS Church doesn't actively get involved with local politics, why do they need lobbyists? While I understand that religious organizations have the right to voice their opinion or stance on any issue, why not just issue a public statement? If their followers sustain and support them, there should not be a need to hire lobbyists.

Part of the definition of lobbying is: "the act of attempting to influence governmental decisions," something the LDS Church adamantly says it doesn't do. If the Church is indeed neutral, employing a lobbyist is unnecessary and is contradictory to their position. Because the Church is so powerful, all they really need to do is issue a public statement regarding their stance. They know LDS lawmakers are inclined to adhere to the direction of the Church because following their leaders is part of their social and religious make-up.

In the fall of 2017, the former LDS Church top lobbyist began working directly for the state legislature as the head of the Office of Legislative Research and General Counsel. Why would the state legislature hire a former top LDS lobbyist to work in their office of Research and General Council? Simple – he's one of their own (Mormon, that is) and the ideal candidate to push their agenda. In desperate need of another lobbyist, the LDS Church hired the former Speaker of the House of the Utah State Legislature, Marty Stephens. So, effectively the Church and the LDS lawmakers covered both bases. By the way – Mr. Stephens is Mormon also – imagine that.

For several years a segment of Utah residents has wanted access to medical marijuana. However, each time a bill was proposed during the legislative process, it was defeated. Part of the reason was due to The Church of Jesus Christ of Latter-day Saints merely voicing their opposition. Well, the Utah voters eventually became fed up with the religious bureaucratic bullshit, so they introduced a public initiative to bypass the state legislature. After gaining enough signatures to put the initiative on a ballot, it was finally put to vote in November of 2018.

However, leading up to the actual vote, Church officials issued ultimatums to their members stating that if any of them signed the initiative, they must make efforts to have their names removed and even help coerce other members to do the same. In excerpts from the article, Count My Vote Initiative is Dead, Opponents Say, dated May 16th, 2018, written by Lee Davidson of *The Salt Lake Tribune*, a Mormon local is in tears because of the request made by her immediate church leaders.

On November 6th, 2018, the people of Utah voted into law access to privatized medical marijuana effective December 1st, 2018, throwing the leaders of The Church of Jesus Christ of Latter-day Saints and lawmakers into crisis mode. As the day drew near, Governor Gary Herbert called a special session of the legislature to convene on Monday, December 3rd, to override the will of the people and introduce a compromise bill. In no time at all, the new law was repealed by the legislature and a new bill, one that was formulated with direct input from the LDS Church, was supplanted.

Basically, the LDS Church and its lawmakers were so freaked out about privatized medical marijuana that they put the distribution, sale, and profit of cannabis into state control. A pile of new provisions was included, such as limiting specific ailments, access, and the ability to grow one's own if too far from a dispensary. They must think they're so good at controlling alcohol, controlling medical marijuana should be a snap?

In the December 4th, 2018 *Salt Lake Tribune* article, "Utah's Cannabis Compromise Wins," by Bethany Rodgers, LDS governor Herbert praised his Mormon comrades in the state legislature. "This is a historic day," he said in a news release. "With the passage of the Utah Medical Cannabis Act, Utah now has the best-designed medical cannabis program in the country. Working with trained medical professionals, qualified patients in Utah will be able to receive quality-controlled cannabis products from a licensed pharmacist in medical dosage form. And this will be done in a way that prevents diversion of product into a black market." (Rodgers 2018)

Not to be outdone, medical cannabis advocates, the Epilepsy Association of Utah (EAU), and Together for Responsible Use and Cannabis Education (TRUCE), filed a lawsuit against that state for overriding the will of the people and LDS Church violation of separation of church and state. At the time of this book's writing, they are still in litigation. (I, for one hope they win!)

And to finish, on Thursday, January 31st, 2018, Governor Gary Herbert gave his annual State of the State Address to the legislature. The event was televised for every citizen that cared to listen. One of the key topics was a sales tax cut on certain services and products due to a surplus of $200 million in state coffers. Hmm, now is it just a coincidence that the state brought in about $175 million in profit from alcohol sales during the fiscal year ending 2019?

The way I see it, LDS lawmakers don't have a problem exorbitantly taxing the so-called sinners and operating an illegal monopoly. It's just fine with them that sinners' dollars pay the way for the so-called saints. But, who's really the sinner or saint in the end? The imbibing people of Utah whose rights and freedoms are violated every day, or the one-sided teetotaling government forcing their will upon the masses? It seems to me that the audit I cited earlier in The Town Hall Meeting chapter was wrong. The state of Utah has not grown dependent on the liquor revenue. In fact, if they left the sales tax rate alone (which all citizens pay, not just drinkers), the state could privatize and benefit from a levied excise tax on alcohol that pumps money to their general fund without the cost of infrastructure. Voila, problem solved – illegal monopoly disbanded, LDS influence over a product they disdain absolved and imbibing citizen's rights restored!

The LDS lawmakers, as pious as they think they are, are in fact no better than the shady politicians who work in the nation's capital (supposedly on our behalf) making laws in favor of a special interest group similar to big pharma, coal, gas, oil, and others in the name of money and power. Although the LDS Church probably doesn't bribe Utah lawmakers with money, they know that due to the mental control they exert over their members, by simply stating their stance, their followers will heed their direction. LDS politicians are first and foremost devout Latter-day Saints. By following the direction of The Church of Jesus Christ of Latter-day Saints, these lawmakers believe the word of their leaders as a revelation from God. Furthermore, LDS lawmakers must believe that since they have followed the direction of their Church, they are receiving blessings and will be exalted on Judgment Day.

And this is wrong. It is against the law for a body of people following one religion to pass laws respecting only their beliefs and not those of the whole population. It is against the law for a church or religion to dominate and interfere with state functions (which is habitual behavior for The Church of Jesus Christ of Latter-day Saints).

And it will go on, unfortunately, until the Feds step in, or the LDS make-up of the population comprises less than 50% of the popular vote. Even then, the Church will encourage their members to seek public office. And the decision-makers within the Church and the legislature will find a way to gerrymander the voting districts, so LDS candidates have a better than average shot at obtaining office.

But one day it will happen... the monopoly will crumble. Wine, liquor, and beer will be sold in grocery and convenience stores. Residents will be able to have wine direct shipped from their favorite wineries. And the unconstitutional overbearing and controlling entities that are the LDS Church and state legislature will yield their dominance. Non-LDS Utah voters will have their say to privatize alcohol, and who knows... maybe even recreational marijuana. Until then, we resist and wait patiently with bated breath.

TREND

CANNED WINE

OH, YEAH, IT REMINDS ME OF THE WORDS TO THE SONG

Sign, Sign, Everywhere a Sign, by *Five_Man_Electrical_Band.*

♫And the suppliers said to their fleet of salespeople,

"We have an endless supply."

So, I presented them cans to the DABC so, they could deny.

And they said to me, "Get them cans outta here,

whatcha you gonna do?"

And I shot back, "Well imagine that, huh,

these working for you?"

Can, can, everywhere a can, got to get them listed,

it's supply and demand.

Drink this, don't drink that, gotta sell those cans!

And the suppliers said, "Anybody not sellin,

would be fired on sight!"

So, I sent off an email that simply read,

"Hey, that ain't right!

To make them demands in a state like this

and expect them results?"

The DABC simply don't give a damn,

So, it's really not my fault!"

Can, can, everywhere a can, got to get them listed,

it's supply and demand.

Drink this, don't drink that, gotta sell those cans!

And the suppliers replied, "We've got to overcome

and get them to play!

Let's sweeten the deal, with a better price,

c'mon what do ya say?"

After shaking my head, I put pen to paper,

to get a final price.

But when they looked at the cost and smaller profits,

they said, "Well shit, that ain't nice!"

Can, can, everywhere a can, got to get them listed, it's
supply and demand.

Drink this, don't drink that, gotta sell those cans! ♫

After bottles, kegs, tetra packs, and bag in box, they've got to be just about out of ways to get that magical, euphoria inducing grape juice into our bodies. Who knows, maybe one day Constellation, Treasury, Gallo, Diageo, and all the others will figure out a way to pipe it directly into our pie holes while we binge-watch millions of hours of TV or play video games. Why, we probably won't even need to leave the house – we'll just sit in a reclining bed with virtual reality goggles, a tube supplying liquid cheese and crackers, glazed donuts, and hamburgers, and another supplying water and booze, while even another couple of other tubes carry out the excrement.

And I guess for some people that may sound slightly appealing, but in all seriousness, I'm a fan of wine in cans. After being diagnosed with Celiac disease, beer has taken a back seat in my liquid regimen. While there are some fine gluten-free beers out there, and I do enjoy them from time to time, wine seems more relevant and vital to my everyday health and sanity. And since I'm an avid outdoors guy, a couple of cans of wine rather than a glass bottle while fly fishing, boating, or playing golf make them even more attractive. Whatever the future brings, whether it be a drone dropping off wine deliveries or me drinking wine through my ear, my mind is open. Bring it on.

JUST ANOTHER JOB

IN JANUARY OF 2016, THE COMPANY I WORKED for morphed with another family-owned company, making them the largest alcohol distributor/brokerage in North America. (This meant I'd need a new business card, making it my fourth while working the same market in the same position in just under 13 years.) Their immense power brought a plethora of new suppliers wanting to break into smaller markets.

About eight months later, after all the details had been tackled, another major announcement followed – a new division leader had been hired to take charge of all the control states, including Canada, which acts as its own sort of control state-run monopoly. Shortly thereafter, my boss of the previous few years was relieved of his duties.

As it turned out, I knew the new boss (quite well, in fact); he had been to my territory several times. Our new leader was once employed as a VP for one of the major suppliers I represented when I started my wine-schlepping career. During the fall of 2016, Mr. Control, as I will call him, hit every one of the control states under his supervision to tour the market, press the flesh and gain a better understanding of the infrastructure in each territory.

At the time, due to the size of the supplier base, the Utah team consisted of three divisions: two wine divisions and one liquor division. The leaders of each division, including myself, were told to prepare presentations for a meeting outlining our current suppliers, sales, and commission rates. (Which was fine, however, since day one, I never had to worry about commission rates. New suppliers and commission rates had always been negotiated at the top, while accounting took care of the rest, leaving me to simply focus on driving sales.) Undeterred, I submitted what limited information I had in a small PowerPoint presentation.

On the day of the big meeting, Mr. Control and a few other gentlemen introduced to us as our new territory division leaders reporting to Mr. Control toured the state liquor stores along with the local teams; it was me along with the other two division managers in tow. I had an edge. I was ready. I knew Mr. Control, or so I thought. At the first state store, Mr. Control began to question us about commission rates on some of the products we represented. Dumbfounded, we hemmed and hawed, searching for answers, finally lamenting that we had no idea. I began to see where this was going – overall profitability – so the rest of the morning, I distanced myself, dodging his questions the best I could. It was a long day.

That afternoon the entire contingent retreated to a boardroom at the local offices just south of Salt Lake City to review each team's presentations. Unimpressed with the simple details within each division, Mr. Control skipped to the profit and loss sheets of each division outlining commission rates and sales. As it turned out, my division was very profitable while my counterpart over at the other wine division, even though selling more cases, was too low; the liquor division seemed to be holding its own. After Mr. Control explained the profitability factors and how it related to our jobs and our divisions, we were told our responsibilities would change slightly.

In addition to our present enormous workload, we were now in charge of increasing the commission rates within our respective divisions, finding new suppliers to increase profitability, and oversee and help implement an app that, when loaded onto our rep's phones, could track and collect data in real-time – basically Big Brother for the sales teams. Emotions heated, head spinning, feeling skeptical, I held my breath the rest of the afternoon doing my best to digest the new direction along with the new tasks.

As time went by, it became apparent I was just too busy with regular day-to-day duties to help find new business. So, Mr. Control and management went on the offensive, adding numerous importers, wineries, and companies aligned across the country. Now, with over fifty suppliers and thousands of wines, workdays had evolved into a mad scramble. Each morning I played catch-up to the previous day dealing with the new DABC regime that cared nothing about sound business practices, let alone basic customer service, answering endless questions and fixing problems for my company, our demanding suppliers and the nine employees under my direction – it was now an endless grind of mind fucks. I felt like the classic clown act from the circus, spinning plates on top of tall wooden sticks – just as one was about to fall, I would catch it, correct its course, then react to another falling plate. I began to feel helpless, angry, constantly behind, forever trying to catch up.

With no end in sight, surely it would get worse, so it

was time to go. I had lost my soul. But, how could it be? I had a great job selling booze (I know, everyone told me). But something had changed. My first boss told me, "The job is supposed to be fun, so go out and sell some wine and have some fun along the way." And I did just that for a very long time. Exploring and tasting new wines from great wineries, sharing a client's epiphany in the taste along with the romantic and sometimes incredible stories behind them, rejoicing when I obtained new listings with the state, relishing the incentives from the sometimes-hard work, enjoying left-over samples, having a car allowance and expense account along with health insurance and trips to wine country. All of it was great.

Yet I had become an empty, frustrated (even bitter) curmudgeon. I dreaded each morning, as it took longer and longer to muster the strength to simply get up and log on. Each email, phone call, and text became an annoyance sending me into a raging torment. It was no longer a sales job repping one of the best products on the planet, but rather just another problem that needed fixing. Gone were the days of the unsupervised one-man show, working according to my time-frame, making my own rules, working with a manageable portfolio of five to seven decent-sized suppliers; even dealing with the DABC the first seven or so years of my career had been easier. Life was good back then but it had changed for the worse. Pissed off, tired, and frustrated by the "new direction," it was at that point in time that I made the decision to move on. It was almost unfathomable. The career that I had enjoyed so much had evolved into something I despised – Just another job.

I couldn't let another day pass without bringing attention to the unethical, shameless, and immoral Church of Jesus

Christ of Latter-day Saints and their overreach and collusion with the state legislature. Their ridiculously archaic, ludicrous state liquor laws and their illegal monopolistic gluttonous model of theocratic fascist capitalism. The DABC consistently a year or more behind national trends, constant products out of stock, little, if any, communication regarding their ways of doing business, and neglect for their employees and the Utah consumers. With the legislature and DABC, it always seems to be two steps forward, five steps back. Their incompetence had taken its toll on my psyche.

I grew tired of enduring hundreds of daily emails from voracious suppliers, often fleecing the public with overpriced boardroom brands, tripping over themselves while vying for wealth and domination – it's never enough. Chasing cases upon cases each year, always overpromising, sometimes even delivering the outlandish goals often set by people in a boardroom in another part of the country with little if any insight into the state of Utah or Wyoming control laws and their realities.

As I have watched, endured, and learned in the past, the U.S. economy suffers serious recessions from time to time, usually because of some unregulated segment within our system; capitalistic piggishness spinning out of control, leaving the taxpayers of this country footing a bill left by a group of voracious, ignorant, self-centered egomaniacs. A byproduct has arisen in the past ten years since the 2007 economic meltdown – endless, mindless greed – with people grabbing as much money as possible before the next downturn. These days it seems like companies have become so rapacious, any dip in net profit is unconscionable, so they heap as much work on one individual as humanly possible to ensure they do not have to hire more people. VPs in charge of a multitude of states, district managers in charge of ten or more territories, supplier sales reps so bogged down with their large markets within their territory that they have little time for smaller areas, resulting in neglected business that spirals downward rather than up. Even at my level, managing 50+ suppliers and providing adequate attention is not humanly possible within the time constraints and a multitude of other duties.

A magazine article many years ago proclaimed that the United States had become the number one wine-consuming nation on the planet – What a load of bullshit. America has become the number one CRAP-consuming nation on the planet due to the unregulated voracious behaviors of the mega-corporations that make the rules. Not because America has come a long way oenologically speaking, but rather because busy Americans are misled into "thinking" they are drinking decent, good quality wine made in a rural setting by hard-working farmers. However, the joke is on them because the mass-produced wines they ingest are made by self-serving marketing assholes creating brands in boardrooms and laboratories by embellishing and aggrandizing fake stories of fake wineries, then producing shit wines made of overly sugared, manipulated, inferior juice. Massive factories now exist to churn out wine to whatever taste profile that has been dreamt up, slapped with a kitschy label, then shipped out to the masses. The marketing platforms have become so refined that it is sometimes difficult to distinguish between a boardroom brand and that of a true winery. Even I'm fooled from time to time. No one really knows what years of exposure to wine additives such as *Mega Purple,* oak "essence," liquified wood and smoke, or the myriad of other fake flavors added to wine do to a consumer's body, but one day the results will be in and the guinea pig research will yield data we may not want to hear.

Many major wineries and conglomerates have done research on what the majority of consumers like in a wine. The result: sweet (or sweeter) wines. Several studies have found that eight out of ten Americans prefer wine that has a sweet or slightly sweeter profile. The large corporations and wineries know that sugar interacts with the brain, releasing dopamine and encouraging people to consume more sugar to "stay on that high." Do they care? Hell no, they want people to consume more sugar. They give zero fucks about adult-onset diabetes, heart disease, or cancer. It's all for the almighty dollar. The mega-corps are at the root of the problem. Instead of making balanced wines that change from season to season because of terroir and technique and teaching people the nuances of the different varietals and how they interact with food, they produce absolute plonk. Many wines, no matter the varietal, have become something they're not: riper, richer, fatter, flabbier, jammier versions of themselves – Just like many of the Americans that consume them.

Truly great wine, whether it's a village wine, table wine, mid-priced wine, or an iconic brand, is made in vineyards and wineries by passionate individuals and families that really care about what they put in the bottle, not in a boardroom full of marketing monkeys telling us what wine should be. We not only need to be worried about this, but we need to be downright pissed off that we're being lied to every GODDAMN day. I understand that massive wineries resembling petroleum plants need to exist to keep up with the demand of an over-populated planet, however, the deceptive practices of manipulating wine by adding coloring, sugars, or fake flavors such as oak, smoke, or leather (or a multitude of others) rather than the interpretation of the grower, vintner, grape pedigree, barrel, and terroir is an appalling, immoral, and terrible business practice. Real wineries and people are the backbone of the industry and small producers and small import brands are the lifeblood, for they are the wineries offering a true rendition of terroir-driven products differentiating themselves from the vast commercial wasteland.

Mammoth corporations and conglomerates steal from small producers and winemakers because they have the monetary power to overshadow and outplay them by saturating the land through a web of distributors and salespeople. Their vast resources give them the power to command greater shelf presence in retail accounts and on restaurant wine lists, even though their products are cheap and commercial. Their immense budgets allow them to drive sales through clever ads and marketing campaigns and issue deeper discounts, ultimately outspending the small wineries into submission. The industry has become soulless, and I was now one of its casualties.

Life is too short to drink boardroom wine. While I understand budgetary constraints can come into play when choosing a wine, I humbly implore wine buyers from every demographic take a small amount of extra time to research the wineries and brands they purchase so that they can make better choices in the future. Do not be taken with clever marketing or satisfied with the cheapest price. Learn, smell, taste, explore – Small producers depend on your choices.

After spending years adapting and adjusting to new company processes, industry trends, state laws, and DABC incompetence, I was finished. I had to reinvent myself, even if it meant less money. Making a major life-changing direction is daunting; I had no idea what I would do. I had already been working on this book when I had time, but something snapped deep within while sitting in a boardroom listening to the "latest" upcoming goals for an insatiable supplier, so I stepped up the efforts. Though just a novice writer, I had to get my stories out. If one person can do it, so can another. While writing this book has taken a tremendous amount of time and effort, this C-student has found it to be an almost therapeutic, mind-healing labor of conviction. I hope through all my ranting and raving, I have provided some insight into the wine industry and what it's like selling wine in an absolutely hopeless, ridiculous setting. And I hope the tax-paying citizens of Utah, imbibing or not, are enlightened and enraged with the despicable business practices and utter bullshit of the DABC and the state legislature and join with me to act and do something about it. I will be there to help lead the charge; it's time to take a stand and do what's right!

But one final thought.

In the bible, Jesus turned water into wine, and it was of the highest quality so that it could nourish the body and feed the mind. And Louis Pasteur wrote, "Wine is the most healthful and hygienic of beverages." Yet, The Church of Jesus Christ of Latter-day Saints continues to deny this blessing, its benefits, and Utah citizen's desire to live as God intended.

And that's the cuvée – À Votre Santé!

BE YOUR OWN SPARTACUS.

References

Congress, US. 1788. "The United States Constitution." U.S. Constitution. June 21 . Accessed July 4, 2019. https://usconstitution.net/const.html.

Control, Utah Department of Alcoholic Beverage. 2019. https://abc.utah.gov/about/index.html . July 2. Accessed July 2, 2019. https://abc.utah.gov/about/index.html.

Davidson, Lee. 2018. Count My Vote Initiative is Dead, Opponents Say. Newspaper Article , Salt Lake City : Salt Lake Tribune.

Davidson, Lee. 2016. Is the Utah Legislature Representative of the People. Newspaper Article, Salt Lake City : Salt Lake Tribune.

Davidson, Lee. 2017. LDS Church's 'Puppet String' Lobbying Irks Ex-lawmaker. Newspaper Article, Salt Lake City: Salt Lake Tribune.

Davidson, Lee. 2018. Low DUI Threshold will Stand, Guv Says. Newspaper Article, Salt Lake City : Salt Lake Tribune.

Dobner, Jennifer. 2017. Mormons Don't View Church as Political Heavy Weight. Newspaper Article , Salt Lake City: Salt Lake Tribune.

Dobner, Jennifer. 2016. State Senator Criticizes Mormon Church for Torpedoing Hate-Crimes Bill. Newspaper Article, Salt Lake City : Salt Lake Tribune.

Dubakis, Jim. 2016. "Empty Shelves Utah Liquor Stores." Facebook. Salt Lake City.

Everson v. Board of Education. 1949. 330 (United States Supreme Court).

Gehrke, Robert. 2016. LDS Church Opposes Cannabis Proposal. Newspaper Article , Salt Lake City: Salt Lake Tribune.

Gehrke, Robert. 2014. LDS Church: Don't Change Utah's Liquor Laws. Newspaper Article, Salt Lake City: Salt Lake Tribune.

Grant, Heber J. 1934. Conference Report. Conference, Salt Lake City : Church of Jesus Christ of Latter-day Saints.

Harris, Joel Chandler. 1881. Song of the South. New York.

House, Dawn. 2011. Cuts Would Force 13 Utah Liquor Stores to Close. Newspaper Article, Salt Lake City : SL Tribune. Accessed July 4, 2019. https://archive.sltrib.com/article.php?id=51379779&itype=CMSID.

References

House, Dawn. 2011. Hope Ends as First of State Liquor Stores Closes. Newspaper Article, Salt Lake City: SL Tribune. Accessed July 4, 2019. https://archive.sltrib.com/article.php?id=51533016&itype=CMSID.

House, Dawn. 2011. Liquor Store Outcry: Utah Lawmakers Having Second Thoughts. Newspaper Article, Salt Lake City: SL Tribune. Accessed July 4, 2019. https://archive.sltrib.com/article.php?id=51532458&itype=CMSID.

Legislature, Utah State. 1851. Utah Constitution - Utah Legislature. on-going. Accessed July 2, 2019. https://le.utah.gov/xcode/ArticleXII/Article_XII,_Section_20.html?v=UC_AXII_S20_1800010118000101.

—. 1895. "Utah State Legislature." www.le.Utah.gov. March 4. Accessed July 4, 2019. https://le.utah.gov/xcode/ArticleI/Article_I,_Section_4.html?v=UC_AI_S4_1800010118000101.

MacLeish, Archibald. n.d.

Price, Michelle L. 2016. Lawmakers Discuss Crossing of Mormon Faith, Politics. Newspaper Article , Associated Press.

Rodgers, Bethany. 2018. Utah's Cannabis Compromise Wins. Newpaper Article, Salt Lake City : Salt Lake Tribune.

Romboy, Dennis. 2013. 'Zion Curtain' will continue to stand in Utah restaurants for now. March 12. Accessed July 3, 2019. https://www.deseretnews.com/article/865575564/Zion-wall-in-Utah-restaurants-will-stand-for-now.html.

Saints, The Church of Jesus Christ of Latter-day. January. newsroom.churchofjesuschrist.org. 22 2019. Accessed July 4, 2019. https://newsroom.churchofjesuschrist.org/official-statement/political-neutrality.

Shakespeare, William. 1596. Merchant of Venice.

Winder, Kristen Reese. 2015. OpEd. Newspaper OpEd, Salt Lake City : Salt Lake Tribune.

Young, Brigham. 1869. "Journal of Discourses." Volume 12 (Albert Carrington 42 Islington) 376.

WHAT'S IN A LABEL?

Thank you for buying this book and supporting
the movement to privatize alcohol in the state
of Utah. This label represents a satirical blend
of humor and cold hard reality. We live in the
United States of America, not the country of
Utah. A large segment of our local society and
the tourists that visit want change – Not next
year or in ten years – NOW.

Make a declaration for your rights by taking a
stand with Spartacus Falanghina.

Made in the USA
Monee, IL
09 May 2022

96113813R00267